INDEPENDENT FUTURE

Creating user-led disability services in a disabling society

Consultant Editor: Jo Campling

BASW
BRITISH ASSOCIATION
OF SOCIAL WORKERS

First published in Great Britain in April 2006 by

The Policy Press
University of Bristol
Fourth Floor
Beacon House
Queen's Road
Bristol BS8 1QU
UK

Tel +44 (0)117 331 4054
Fax +44 (0)117 331 4093
e-mail tpp-info@bristol.ac.uk
www.policypress.org.uk

British Library Cataloguing in Publication Data
A catalogue record for this book is available from the British Library.

Library of Congress Cataloging-in-Publication Data
A catalog record for this book has been requested.

ISBN-10 1 86134 718 9 paperback
ISBN-13 978 1 86134 718 3 paperback
ISBN-10 1 86134 719 7 hardcover
ISBN-13 978 1 86134 719 0 hardcover

Cover design by Qube Design Associates, Bristol.
Front cover: photograph supplied by kind permission of Tetra Images/Alamy
Printed and bound in Great Britain by MPG Books, Bodmin.

Contents

List of figures and tables   vi
Acknowledgements   vii
Notes on the authors   viii

one   **Examining user-led services**   1
        Introduction   1
        Re-thinking disability   2
            Citizens, consumers and users   3
            User-led organisations   4
        Doing disability research   5
            A note on terminology   5
        Overview of the book   6

two   **Traditional approaches: disability policy and the
        welfare state**   9
        Introduction   9
        Historical perspectives on disability policy   10
        Disability and the welfare state: 1940s to 1970s   13
            Moving to the community   17
        Disability as a personal tragedy   19
        Changing policy perspectives on disability since 1979   22
            New Right   23
            New Labour   25
        Review   27

three   **Disability activism and the struggle for
        independent living**   29
        Introduction   29
        Towards a new disability politics   30
            The Independent Living Movement   31
            Disability activism in Britain   33
        The social model of disability   35
        Critiques of traditional community services   38
        Building user-led services   43
        Review   48

four **Researching user-led organisations** 51
Introduction 51
Taking issue with 'conventional' disability research 51
Disability research from a social model perspective 54
    Research gains 55
    Accountability 56
    Social and material relations of research production 57
Methodology and methods 59
The *Creating Independent Futures* study 63
    Stage One 63
    Stage Two 64
    Stage Three 66
    Stage Four 67
Review 68

five **User-led organisations: building an alternative approach** 71
Introduction 71
From user consultation to user-led services 72
The growth of user-led services 76
Applying the social model of disability 82
Accountability and user control 86
Review 91

six **Service design and delivery: opportunities and
constraints** 93
Introduction 93
Delivering services in support of independent living 94
Service patterns 97
Service monitoring or control? 102
Resources: economic, physical and human 106
    Funding 106
    Location and premises 110
    Paid staff and volunteers 111
Review 113

seven   **Service users' views and experiences**   115

Introduction   115

Views on mainstream services   116

Promoting user-led services   120

   Accessing user-led services   122

Use of services   123

Wants and aspirations   130

Review   135

eight   **Politics and campaigning**   137

Introduction   137

Politics: the local viewpoint   137

Campaigning issues and activities   141

   Direct action   143

Empowerment and consciousness raising   147

Don't upset the applecart   152

Review   156

nine   **Policy change or retrenchment?**   159

Introduction   159

Dependence, independence or inclusion?   159

Professional dominance and new styles of working   166

   Partnerships   169

Same old services: SOS or something else?   172

Review   179

ten   **Future directions**   181

Introduction   181

Key themes and issues   182

Independent living: beyond 'social care'   184

   Equal worth: right to life and childhood disability   184

   Work and employment   186

   Physical environment   187

   Implementation   188

Independent living in an inclusive society   190

Review   192

References   193

Index   217

List of figures and tables

Figures

5.1	Establishment of user-led initiatives	76
5.2	Disabled people as a minimum percentage of the management committee	88
5.3	Formal accountability of user-led organisations	89

Tables

6.1	Services offered by user-led organisations (%)	97
6.2	Services offered by case study organisations	99
6.3	Perceived under-representation of selected groups within user-led service organisations (%)	104
6.4	Major sources of funding over the last three years for the case study organisations	107
6.5	Number of paid staff members in case study organisations	112
7.1	How users accessed user-led services	122
7.2	Pattern of service use	124
8.1	Campaigning activity – at different levels (%)	139

Acknowledgements

This book could not have been written without the cooperation and continued support from Britain's disabled people's movement and in particular those disabled people and their allies involved in the development of Britain's network of user-led disability services who contributed, willingly and without payment, to this book. We are also indebted to the British Council of Disabled People's (BCODP) Research Committee, chaired by Mike Oliver, for their encouragement when developing the *Creating Independent Futures* project, upon which much of the field study discussed in this book is based, and members of the research project Steering Committee: Peter Beresford, Jane Campbell, John Evans and Frances Hasler, for their help and advice. Special thanks must also go to Hannah Morgan, the principal researcher throughout this project, for her research and organisational skills, the National Lottery for providing the funding for this project, and last, but not least, Jo Campling and The Policy Press for their patience and support while writing this book.

Notes on the authors

Colin Barnes is Professor of Disability Studies in the Centre for Disability Studies, School of Sociology and Social Policy, University of Leeds, UK.

Geof Mercer is Reader in Disability Studies in the Centre for Disability Studies, School of Sociology and Social Policy, University of Leeds, UK.

ONE

Examining user-led services

Introduction

An extraordinary politicisation of disabled people began to gather momentum in Britain during the 1960s. It ranged from demonstrations and protest campaigns to the growth of self-help groups and disabled people's own organisations. The driving force was a deep sense of injustice fuelled by poverty, discrimination and social exclusion. Despite the expectations of improvement associated with the welfare state reforms of the 1940s, the 'reality' of living with an accredited impairment, long-term health condition or 'disability' was very different.

How was this wide gulf between the life chances of disabled and non-disabled people explained or justified? The dominant account equated 'disability' with disease and impairment as defined by an established medical profession. This constituted a 'personal tragedy' in that an individual's 'disability', and particularly any ensuing inability to function 'normally', determined their social exclusion and dependence on family and friends, charity, and the statutory and voluntary sector health and social 'care' services (UPIAS, 1976; Oliver, 1983).

Disabled activists began to challenge this exclusive preoccupation with individual, medicalised 'deficiencies', and explored instead an alternative 'social barriers' or 'social model' approach to disability. This shifted attention to the 'disabling' impact of social and environmental barriers experienced by people with designated impairments and viewed as 'disabled'. Mainstream statutory and voluntary social and welfare services were criticised for their failure to provide appropriate support services to enable disabled people to lead 'ordinary' everyday lives. Rather, they reinforced the dependence of people with impairments and perpetuated their separation from the rest of society.

One radical option for disabled people was to develop organisations that they ran and controlled. This book explores the experiences of user-led (that is, user-controlled) service organisations in Britain. It offers a revealing picture of disabled people's attempts to change the direction of welfare services and facilitate moves towards 'independent living'. In this introductory chapter, we outline, first, the clash of theoretical perspectives that underpin the analysis of disability, welfare policy and practice, and second, our approach to undertaking research with user-led organisations. The final section outlines the major issues raised in subsequent chapters.

Re-thinking disability

At least since the 17th century, those individuals regarded as unable to look after themselves, including the broad category of the 'sick and infirm', had access to a mixed economy of welfare support. This comprised state-administered Poor Law relief, the activities of a significant charity and voluntary sector, and a very considerable amount of 'informal care' provided by family and friends. Historically, the level and balance varied considerably across these sources although, in general, individuals deemed incapable of work because of their impairment or age were more likely to be recognised as 'deserving' of charity or public assistance.

Into the 19th century, there was a notable growth of institutional 'solutions' as a way of regulating the sick and infirm poor. The forms of segregation included workhouses, hospitals and 'madhouses', with a growing number of institutions targeted at specific disease groups and impairments. By the start of the 20th century, there was a selective but expanding system of state compensation payments for injuries received at work or on war service. With the arrival of the welfare state in the 1940s, legislative measures were aimed at disabled people promising a broad 'safety net' of benefits and improved opportunities to lead more 'normal' lives (Oliver, 1990; Drake, 1999).

However, most disabled people did not experience a decisive advance in their life chances. Across the life course, there remained a comprehensive set of exclusionary barriers, ranging from education, employment, housing and the built environment, to leisure and social relationships (Barnes et al, 1999). This provoked a growing number of disabled people to contest their marginalisation. In the 1960s, Paul Hunt, one of the most influential of the early disabled activists in Britain, argued that disabled people were perceived as a direct challenge to commonly held societal values and 'set apart from the ordinary' as 'unfortunate, useless, different, oppressed and sick' (Hunt, 1966, p 146). In the following decades, others described the public perception of disabled people as spanning 'imaginative concern, mawkish sentimentality, indifference, rejection and hostility' (Thomas, 1982, p 4). To have an impairment was a 'personal tragedy' (Oliver, 1983).

In Britain, as elsewhere, a specific stimulus to protest action was the enforced institutionalisation of disabled people and the resulting 'warehousing' of inmates, because of the lack of appropriate support to live in the community. The development of a social interpretation or model of disability gave a critical impetus to a new form of disability politics. This focused on confronting the pervasive social and environmental barriers and attitudes to the inclusion of people with designated impairments in mainstream society (Abberley, 1987). Disabled people's activism also challenged their stereotype as passive and grateful for whatever 'care' they received (Campbell and Oliver, 1996).

Disabled people's protest campaigns gained worldwide prominence with the emergence of the Independent Living Movement (ILM) in the United States (US) during the 1970s (Coleridge, 1993; Charlton, 1998). Further momentum was injected by high-profile international initiatives such as the United Nations' (UN) declarations on the rights of disabled persons (UN, 1985, 1993), the designation of 1981 as the 'International Year of Disabled People', and in the same year, the formation of Disabled Peoples' International (DPI), an umbrella body for national organisations directed by disabled people (Campbell and Oliver, 1996).

Citizens, consumers and users

Initially, disabled activists attracted little sympathy for their critique of social welfare services. However, there were a few crucial exceptions where local managers were persuaded to explore alternative support options to live 'independently' in the community. This was most notable in the progress, albeit slow, towards providing (direct and indirect) cash payments to enable disabled people to employ personal assistants (PAs) in lieu of receiving statutory services. Disabled activists regarded such support as central to their goal of exercising greater choice and control in their lives.

Then, during the 1970s, major shifts in the wider political and economic context and the election of a 'New Right' or 'neo-liberal' Conservative government paved the way for radical alterations in state policy and governance. In the field of health and social care, the 1990 National Health Service and Community Care Act enshrined the new philosophy of increased market competition between service providers and an enhanced role for 'consumers' (or service users). However, its implementation at the local level revealed the wide gulf between what policy makers and service providers were sponsoring and disabled people's demands for tangible advances towards 'independent living'.

A similar market orientation informed the policy focus of the New Labour government after its election in 1997. Its plan for *Modernising Social Services* (DH, 1998) promised fundamental reforms in the highly centralised welfare state apparatus established in the 1940s – with new policies, practices, organisational forms and relationships. It extended previous government moves towards greater choice for 'consumers' coupled with enhanced information on the performance of providers as the preferred option for enhancing the quality of services. At the same time, New Labour emphasised the importance of addressing the root causes of social exclusion (DSS, 1998) and assisting people to escape from welfare dependency.

Furthermore, New Labour support for independent living gained a heightened prominence in the government Green Paper *Independence, Well-being and Choice* (DH, 2005a) and the *Improving the Life Chances of Disabled People* report from the Prime Minister's Strategy Unit (PMSU, 2005). Although these documents are not always united in their analyses or proposals, they suggest a striking degree of overlap with the goal of independent living articulated by organisations of disabled people.

User-led organisations

Throughout most of the 20th century, organisations *for* disabled people (that is, run by non-disabled people) have monopolised the representation of 'what disabled people want' to policy makers. With the politicisation of disabled people, there has been an increase in self-help groups and organisations *of* (that is, controlled by) disabled people. Key examples at the national level included the formation in 1981 of the British Council of Organisations of Disabled People (BCODP) – since renamed the British Council of Disabled People. Equally, at the local level, organisations controlled and run by disabled people were a primary factor in advancing the new disability politics.

Particular significance has been attached to the emergence of Centres for Independent or Integrated (and more recently, Inclusive) Living (CILs) in the 1980s, although not all user-controlled service organisations adopted this label or their service orientation. Their general ethos has been to enable people with impairments, regardless of 'cause', to challenge their exclusion from mainstream society and to draw on support services for living in the community, including the option to employ PAs as part of a direct payments package in lieu of using 'mainstream' services (Hasler et al, 1999). Indeed, user-led organisations are now regarded as a vital component in the 'progress' and performance of the Disabled People's Movement around the world (Charlton, 1998).

Doing disability research

In 1998, the BCODP Research Committee initiated discussions about undertaking a research project on user-led organisations. Members felt that this should be developed in collaboration with the National Centre for Independent Living (NCIL), which was established in 1999 by BCODP to provide a coordinated approach to developing independent living-type services.

A BCODP/NCIL steering group was set up to identify preliminary aims and objectives, and to explore these with researchers in the BCODP Research Unit, now called the Centre for Disability Studies, at the University of Leeds. Three main aims were identified:

- to provide a critical evaluation of the development, organisation and services provided by CILs and similar user-led initiatives in the UK;
- to identify the principal forces – economic, political and social – hindering their further development;
- to produce and disseminate, in a variety of accessible formats, findings and recommendations to disabled people, their organisations and policy makers in both public and private sectors.

On these foundations, the BCODP/NCIL research project, otherwise referred to here as the *Creating Independent Futures* study (Barnes et al, 2000), was launched.

A note on terminology

Over recent decades there has been a gathering interest in the role of language and its influence on general attitudes towards contested social issues, and particularly discrimination towards minority groups. In most cases, there has been a positive response by policy makers and practitioners, although the same sensitivity has been slow to extend to people with impairments.

The debate over definitions and language has been central to the Disabled People's Movement's critique of academic approaches in the social sciences and humanities. In this volume, we shun words such as 'spastic' and 'mongol', which have become terms of abuse, or, like 'cripple' and 'handicap', which carry associations with deficit, begging and charity, or that depersonalise individuals as 'the disabled', 'the deaf' or 'the blind'.

The choice of an alternative terminology remains a highly contested issue, even among disabled people. We have followed the preferences of the British Disabled People's Movement as set out by BCODP in 1981 (Barnes, 1991). This is based on a distinction between 'impairment', which refers to a medically classified condition, and 'disability', which is a generic phrase used to denote the broad social disadvantages experienced by people with an accredited impairment. The phrase 'people with disabilities' is avoided (except in quotations from others) because it blurs the crucial conceptual distinction between impairment and disability and the sources of social exclusion. Similar concerns mean that terms such as 'care' and 'carer' are placed in inverted commas because they reinforce a personal tragedy view of disability. What is at issue is far more than a choice of words; rather it revolves around basic differences about the best way to understand and contest the wide-ranging barriers to social inclusion.

Overview of the book

The discussion commences in Chapter Two with a review of the historical trajectory of disability policy in Britain, from its Poor Law and charitable origins and the development of a welfare state in the 1940s through to recent 'neo-liberal' attempts to re-build a 'mixed economy of care' with an emphasis on market competition, consumerism, and enhanced service user involvement in the policy process. Despite these shifts, service provision for people with impairments has been dominated by an individual emphasis on 'personal care' and (medical) rehabilitation.

The spotlight turns in Chapter Three to attempts by disabled people to develop an alternative social interpretation or model of disability that highlights the social and environmental barriers confronting people with impairments. In Britain, this has provided the impetus for a new disability politics with organisations of disabled people in the vanguard challenging social exclusion. A vital contribution has been made by CILs and equivalent user-controlled organisations in promoting independent living by designing and delivering service support for disabled people.

Chapter Four begins with a review of the competing approaches to researching disability, with specific reference to the significance of studies located within a social model framework. This underpins discussion of the *Creating Independent Futures* research project with user-controlled organisations. The chief issues considered comprise: the emancipatory research strategy and design; specific research questions; choice of data sources; sampling; data collection; processing and analysis; and the dissemination of the project findings.

Attention turns to the origins and development of user-led organisations in Chapter Five, with specific reference to nine case study sites. Contrasting expectations of user involvement are examined, along with different understandings of service support for 'independent living' between 'mainstream' and user-led service providers. This makes for an uneasy relationship between user-controlled organisations and traditional statutory and voluntary service agencies – a situation potentially further complicated by local and national economic and political constraints.

The range and type of services offered by user-controlled services are appraised in Chapter Six. Discussion starts from disabled people's identification of the fundamental 'needs' or requirements for independent living. This is followed by a review of the pattern of service provision, and the character and implications of monitoring procedures. Fieldwork data reinforce suggestions that user-led organisations face a continuous struggle to ensure the availability of sufficient and appropriate resources – funding, staff and premises – to undertake their desired service role.

Debates about uneven access to user-controlled services for disabled individuals with diverse support needs are then explored in Chapter Seven. It foregrounds users' experiences using mainstream (statutory and voluntary), professionally led services and draws comparisons with disabled people's experiences of user-led services. User assessments of the latter's role in promoting social inclusion and independent living, including support for direct payments users, are examined to identify possible conflicts between the aims and achievements of user-controlled service organisations.

Early disability activists expressed concerns that clashes would arise from any attempt to play the role of service provider and political advocate for disabled people's rights. In Chapter Eight, two basic questions are posed: first, how far have disabled people's organisations maintained their role in political campaigning and advocacy? Second, how far, and in what ways, has their service provider role constrained their political activities? Local organisations reported different ways of responding to these dilemmas.

Chapter Nine sets outs the main issues and themes from previous chapters regarding user-led organisations and the implementation of a social model approach to disability against a background of New Labour's endorsement of independent living. The chapter explores such key issues as the potential for closer links between user-led organisations and statutory and voluntary service providers; the possibilities for countering the entrenched dominance of professionals in service provision; and the potential for user-led organisations to build alternative support services for independent living.

Finally, in Chapter Ten, we stress that the social inclusion of disabled people remains a central priority and that it is crucial to maintain the impetus towards greater user involvement in the development and delivery of support services for independent living in the community. However, such action is not by itself sufficient: it must be complemented by significant progress in dismantling the wider social and environmental barriers and discriminatory attitudes in British society.

TWO

Traditional approaches: disability policy and the welfare state

Introduction

This chapter provides an overview of social policies that have influenced the lives of people with impairments, and how these have changed historically across different political and economic contexts. First, we outline available assistance from the 17th to the early 20th century for individuals broadly categorised as 'sick and infirm'. This ranged from state poor relief and charitable aid, to 'informal' support from family members and the local community. Into the 19th century, there was increasing resort to segregation in institutions. By the start of the 20th century, with poverty increasingly regarded as a social problem requiring collective action, Poor Law relief was being supplanted by an alternative state-regulated package of social security, old age and war pensions, and National Insurance benefits.

Second, the consolidation of the welfare state in the 1940s is reviewed. This promised a major change in the direction of social policy, with an emphasis on the principle of equal citizenship that included a range of measures directed at disabled people. In practice, state services failed to make the anticipated advances in the social and economic conditions of disabled people, and the reliance on the voluntary sector and 'informal carers' continued. Third, the dominance of a 'personal tragedy' and medicalised view of 'disability' in policy reforms and service provision is highlighted. This was legitimised by the ascendancy of a scientific medical profession. Its emphasis on individual cure and rehabilitation endured through the 20th century, although at its end policy makers began to acknowledge a contrary perspective, promoted by disability activists, which stressed the social barriers to inclusion.

In the final section, we outline the reforms since the 1970s to the welfare state and public sector provision. Initiatives from both Conservative and New Labour governments promoted a 'mixed economy of welfare' and consumerism, along with novel forms of governance, but these failed to deliver major progress in overturning the social exclusion of disabled people.

Historical perspectives on disability policy

Most notably during the 16th century, the state became a site of continuing public debate about how to resolve the competing demands of 'at least two distributive systems, one based on work and one on need' (Stone, 1985, p 15). Primacy was given to sustaining economic production, and the Poor Law Act of 1601 provided an enduring, decentralised basis for distributing relief payments to those in extreme poverty and unable to provide for themselves. This group comprised a significant number of individuals broadly classified as 'sick and infirm' (Pelling, 1998; Borsay, 2005).

Thereafter, the growth of a capitalist wage economy fuelled political conflicts over a 'culturally legitimate rationale for nonparticipation in the labour system' (Stone, 1985, p 22). The widely cited distinction between the 'deserving' (or unemployable individuals including sick and infirm people) and 'undeserving' ('able-bodied') poor deemed capable of employment was difficult to agree in practice. Indeed, 'economic and social crises created a class of able-bodied poor who could not find work or earn enough when they did' (Pelling, 1998, p 63). Moreover, 'sick and infirm' people were forced to carry on working as long as they could, perhaps gravitating to 'more appropriate' employment. Resort was also made to other 'creative' strategies, such as individuals moving between households, for example, where orphaned young people were given lodging by older 'infirm' people in return for domestic support (Pelling, 1998).

A further 'safety net' was provided by diverse 'customary rights' – spanning 'regular doles, clothes, fuel, rent, medical relief, institutional provision' (Hitchcock et al, 1997, p 10). Even so, there was considerable suspicion that not all those claiming poor relief had genuine grounds. Hence, local justices were expected to assess the 'moral character' of applicants, and the capacity of families to provide some of the necessary assistance (Borsay, 2005, p 146). By the early 19th century, a renewed campaign against the poor relief system as both costly and destructive of the work ethic resulted in the Poor Law Amendment Act of 1834. It sought to deny relief outside an institution and set benefits at a 'less eligible' level or below the income of an 'independent labourer of the lowest class'. A growing proportion of the 'deserving' aged and infirm population was forced to enter the widely stigmatised workhouses (Roberts, 1973), while the pressure on other disabled people to find work intensified (Williams, 1981).

State-organised poor relief was part of a wider system of assistance that included a large voluntary sector of charitable and mutual aid organisations, and an informal sector of family and friends, as well as a small commercial sector, such as private 'madhouses' (Porter, 1987). Their contribution was considerable: with suggestions that assistance from the voluntary sector alone exceeded the amount received from poor relief (Innes, 1994; Daunton, 1996). This was enlarged by 'a philanthropic bonanza that swept across Britain in response to political unrest and moral disquiet' at the end of the 18th century (Borsay, 2005, p 142). At the same time, membership of Friendly Societies expanded rapidly among the working classes. This mutual aid typically offered payments to contributors forced out of work because of sickness or injury, although the same societies often discriminated against new applicants on grounds of ill health or impairment (Borsay, 2005, p 141), just as charities took special measures to identify 'undeserving' claimants (Fido, 1977).

Overall, the industrial capitalist system emerging in the 19th century intensified the marginalisation of the 'sick and infirm' population. For example, structural changes exerted an important, if uneven, impact on the opportunities for paid employment. Thus, the rise of mechanised and factory-based production encompassed:

> a highly unfavourable change from the slower, more self-determined methods of work into which many handicapped people had been integrated. (Ryan with Thomas, 1980, p 101)

Yet it was the pursuit of economic rationality and profitability generally in an increasingly market-oriented economy and society that proved the more serious barrier to the paid work opportunities for people with impairments. Where work was obtained, it was mostly unskilled work, street trading or working at home (Gleeson, 1999).

Such trends exacerbated the representation of people with impairments as a 'social problem' – not capable of making a proper economic contribution and a 'burden' on their family and local community. Their perceived 'unruly' and 'degenerate' character legitimised a range of institutional solutions – prisons, workhouses and asylums. The number of workhouse inmates in Poor Law institutions in England and Wales rose substantially from the mid-18th century to a high point of one million recorded in the 1871 Census. Moreover, people with impairments constituted a rising proportion of those incarcerated in specialised institutions (Williams, 1981).

The 'insane' were among the first to be singled out for institutional segregation. However, the early 19th-century therapeutic optimism about asylum treatment was replaced by an overtly custodial regime in later decades, with the enforced incarceration of growing numbers of 'lunatics'. The asylum system provided physical and symbolic confirmation of the declining tolerance of 'the awkward and unwanted, the useless and the potentially troublesome' (Scull, 1979, p 240), although the continuing importance of family support should not be underestimated (Walton, 1980). Over the 19th century, the asylum population rose from 2.3 to 29.6 per 10,000 (Scull, 1979, table 8). By its final decades, the so-called 'idiot' (or 'mentally subnormal') population was being similarly targeted:

> Specialised institutions appealed to humanitarians who felt that the helpless would be 'better off' inside them; to eugenists who hoped incarceration would prevent the unfit from breeding; to the medical elite who were themselves becoming more specialized; and to a vague public sense of propriety which disliked mixing the deserving with the disreputable poor. (Crowther, 1981, p 90)

Impairment and disease attracted more and more 'scientific' interest, particularly the supposed deviation of specific groups from 'normality' (Davis, 1995). This was reinforced by further claims, for example, associated with Social Darwinism, that 'mental handicap' was linked to sexual and criminal deviance, and in the case of the 'mongolian idiot', with racial degeneration (Ryan with Thomas, 1980). Such eugenic thinking influenced the Mental Deficiency Act of 1913. It set out a process for identifying, certifying and, where necessary, compulsorily detaining 'mental defectives' in specialist institutions or 'colonies'. In practice, all manner of social deviance was taken as justification for incarceration, particularly individuals from the 'lower classes' (Jones, 1972, pp 176-8).

The hegemony of the 'institutional solution' extended across the life cycle. Legislation in the late 19th century and early 20th century stressed the need to segregate blind, deaf-mute, mentally and physically 'defective' children in special residential schools. These were thought to offer the best chance of preventing such individuals from becoming a burden on the rest of society. Analogous thinking characterised the work of charitable organisations such as the Council for the Care of Crippled Children (Drake, 1999).

However, by the start of the 20th century, a more interventionist state role was taking shape, particularly in the expansion of a safety net for those in poverty. This confirmed growing political support for arguments that poverty was a social problem requiring government action rather than a moral defect suggesting individual responsibility and treatment. Trades union and working-class campaigns in response to the increasing number of workers who acquired impairments as a result of work accidents led to a series of Workmen's Compensation Acts from 1897 onwards. This established a highly selective system based on how the injury or disease was acquired. An insurance-based system of compensation was introduced in the National Insurance Act of 1911 although again far from comprehensive. The 1914-18 World War motivated further legislation covering such areas as injury compensation, regulation of charities for wounded members of the armed forces, help for disabled ex-servicemen to find work, and war pensions. These measures reinforced the centrality of medical criteria for rehabilitating people with impairments, and eligibility for welfare benefits (Drake, 1999, 2001).

Through the first few decades of the 20th century, British social policy moved away from its focus on providing food and shelter in the workhouse or through outdoor relief. A distinctive publicly administered social security system began to take shape. Nevertheless, the voluntary sector contribution remained an important feature of disabled people's lives well into the 20th century, encouraged by the first piece of legislation specifically targeted at disabled people – the Blind Persons Act 1920 – and a significant growth in partnerships with local government (Lewis, 1995, 1996).

Overall, the 'sick and infirm' looked for assistance from a variety of sources: income from work, welfare benefits, family and friends, and charity (Borsay, 2005, p 140). Yet, while the link between poverty and segregation in an institution was weakening among the population as a whole, this was less apparent for people classified as having a 'severe' impairment.

Disability and the welfare state: 1940s to 1970s

The welfare state legislation of the 1940s rested on social democratic claims of equal citizenship and entitlement to services and benefits. Its innovativeness was based on 'three separate but overlapping types of settlement: the political-economic; the social; and the organisational' (Clarke and Newman, 1997, p 1).

At the *political-economic* level, the dominance of Keynesian macro-economic policy on governments in the immediate post-1945 years was crucial. At its heart was a commitment to full employment that proved critical in winning agreement for, and maintaining, the welfare reforms. Policies were designed to promote a national pooling of risk. This helped confirm the political and ideological bases of the welfare state, which became the litmus test of a 'caring' society: with all citizens guaranteed basic social needs, irrespective of the ability to pay (Marshall, 1950). In practice, the political-economic settlement was a compromise between this 'state-guaranteed citizenship' and 'market-driven' inequality (Clarke and Newman, 1997, p 1).

The *social* settlement incorporated notions of family, nation and work (Williams, 1992, pp 211-12). 'Family' and 'work' in this context were based on the 'norm' of a wage-earning male maintaining other family members. This, in turn, recognised various groups of dependants, children and older people, married women, plus those who are in ill health or have impairments (Langan and Clarke, 1993, p 28). The effect of such exclusionary assumptions was to 'naturalise' social divisions, not only of gender and 'race', but also 'the distinction between the able-bodied and the "handicapped"' (Clarke and Newman, 1997, p 4). This confirmed disabled people as the unfortunate victims of disease and injury and was used to legitimate their continued segregation and treatment of their 'special needs', and as objects of charity.

The *organisational* settlement encompassed 'two modes of co-ordination: bureaucratic administration and professionalism' (Clarke and Newman, 1997, pp 4-8). Public service norms and values in administration reinforced claims that the new system would be more 'neutral' – impartial and even-handed – in the way it dealt with the different sections and interests in the population. Bureaucratic norms complemented professional expertise in identifying and 'treating' social problems (Cousins, 1987), but this went with a significant degree of professional autonomy among service providers, while a number of 'new' professions sought similar privileges (Hugman, 1991). While the welfare state was embedded in professional expertise and 'care', this was subsequently contested by the state and service user groups.

Overall, the interests of disabled people were a low priority within the 1944-48 legislative programme. There were general promises that the rebuilding of the post-war society and economy would be more inclusive and that where this was not possible disabled people would benefit from the much enhanced package of medical rehabilitation and social welfare support (Drake, 1999, 2001). However, there was a stark lack of symmetry between the aims of social citizenship and the policy reforms and their outcomes – across such crucial areas for social inclusion as education, social relationships, leisure activities, employment, social security, housing, transport and the built environment (Barnes and Mercer, 2003). In practice, the professional and bureaucratic domination of the organisation and delivery of social and health 'care' services confirmed the continuing segregation and dependence of disabled people.

For example, access to the paid labour market has traditionally been a key indicator of citizenship. This was re-emphasised in the 1944 Disabled Persons (Employment) Act. Similarly, the 1944 Education Act argued for equal educational opportunities and the inclusion of disabled children in mainstream schools. Yet, in the following decades, disabled children and adults were still confronted by wide-ranging barriers and discrimination. The general experience was one of segregation into 'special schools' and 'sheltered workshops' or unemployment, with few prospects of earning their living, or living much above the poverty line.

Furthermore, for those unable to find paid work, the safety net of welfare benefits established in the National Insurance and social security reforms of the 1940s discriminated against disabled people – particularly those who had a lower employment record, older people and married women. In addition, benefits varied according to the cause and effects of the impairment. While those individuals with war and industrial injuries were entitled to a pension, other disabled people had to rely on national assistance/Supplementary Benefits. Moreover, such financial relief was far from 'generous', and made little allowance for the extra costs of living with an impairment, including the purchase of necessary equipment aids. Again, the complexity of the claiming system and the stigma attached to welfare benefits effectively put off many potential recipients (Simkins and Tickner, 1978).

With the passage of the 1948 National Assistance Act, the Poor Law system was formally abolished. It transferred responsibility for the provision of residential accommodation for disabled people to local authorities, while allowing for the involvement of voluntary organisations. However, the Act did little to overturn the general bias in favour of residential 'care', despite arguing that:

welfare services should ... ensure that all handicapped persons ... have the maximum opportunity of sharing in and contributing to the life of the community ... so that their capacities are realized to the full, their self-confidence developed, and their social contacts strengthened. (Ministry of Health, 1948, para 60)

Potential non-residential services included practical assistance in the home, transport, sheltered employment and recreational activities. Domiciliary or domestic services (home helps, meals-on-wheels) and the provision of aids and equipment developed very slowly. The lack of a statutory duty on local authorities, and of funding, was decisive (Younghusband, 1978). In contrast, social services departments mostly provided segregated, institution-based services such as day centres, workshops and residential homes.

There was a similar uneven response to the requirement to identify and register disabled people, and provide accommodation for those 'in need of care or attention which is not otherwise available' (Ministry of Health, 1948, section 21). Some authorities built special residential units, others located disabled and older people together, or paid maintenance charges for individuals to live in a private or voluntary sector residential home. Another option was to locate younger disabled people in special rehabilitation units attached to hospitals – thus reinforcing the medicalisation of 'disability' and institutional solutions. However, the Act also permitted cooperation between local authorities and the voluntary sector and this encouraged a growth in the provision of non-hospital residential accommodation for 'younger' disabled people (Davies, 2002). Most notably, Cheshire Homes began in 1948 with the Le Court home in Hampshire and by 1980 had expanded to 74 homes with over 2,000 residents (Evans, 1993).

The lack of local authority services for disabled people led to an expansion in the number and role of voluntary agencies in the 1950s and 1960s (Drake, 1996). Charities concentrated on 'ameliorative, palliative and consolatory activity' (Drake, 1999, p 151), including the newly formed Spastics Society (since renamed Scope). Most addressed the 'special needs' of disabled people, ranging from the Disabled Drivers' Association to the Winged Fellowship Trust (which arranged holidays for 'severely disabled' people and their families). Along with longer-established charities, these were 'generally perceived as altruistic enterprises' for the 'care' of disabled people, and occupied an 'all but unimpeachable' place in British society

(Drake, 1996, p 150). Moreover, through the post-1945 decades, their activities increasingly overlapped with local authority social services departments' provision – from residential homes and sheltered workshops to day centres. While the promotion of social, economic and leisure activities allowed disabled children and adults to lead less isolated lives, the charitable sector reinforced public impressions of the dependency and special needs of disabled people (see Chapter Three).

Moving to the community

Despite early optimism in official quarters that the quality of life experienced by those in institutions was moving from that of 'master and inmate' to one closer to that of 'hotel manager and his guests' (Ministry of Health, 1950, p 311), most disabled people remained fearful of the prospect of being forced into one of these 'human warehouses' (Townsend, 1962, p 36).

Public criticism of large-scale institutions reached a peak in Britain in the 1960s and 1970s, fanned by a series of scandals in long-stay 'mental handicap' and 'psychiatric' hospitals (Martin, 1985). Institutional life was characterised as staff dominated, with a clear gulf between 'them' and 'us'; batch living, with inmates experiencing little autonomy or respect but depersonalisation and a very subsidiary role and status (Goffman, 1961; Morris, 1969). Residents had little opportunity to exercise choice over how to spend their day; how to organise their personal time; what to eat and when; who they talked to; and how to maintain a personal identity and esteem. They experienced isolation and separation from the rest of the local community (Peace et al, 1997, pp 50-1). This 'warehousing' approach concentrated on prolonging physical life, so that for most people, entry into the institution became a 'point of no return', or a 'social death sentence' (Miller and Gwynne, 1972) (see also Chapter Four).

The Seebohm Report (1968) argued for a major reorganisation of local authority social services, and echoed the claims of many disabled people that they were forced into institutions because of the lack of alternative community support services, and the difficulties experienced by their reliance on family and friends as 'carers' (Carter, 1981). Such concerns attracted parliamentary attention, which led to the Chronically Sick and Disabled Persons (CSDP) Bill introduced by Alf Morris after he came first in the Private Member's ballot in 1969. This was described by another Member of Parliament, Jack Ashley, as a 'charter for the chronic sick and disabled' (Topliss and Gould, 1981, p 30), although considerable revisions had to be made before it reached the statute book. The 1970 CSDP Act (CSDPA) required local authorities to provide disabled people with those services deemed 'permissive' under the 1948 National Assistance Act, to publicise them, and to raise the level of services to at least equivalent to that of the currently 'best' authorities. It also obliged authorities to identify those individuals with severe physical and mental impairments living within its boundaries. Specific targets included public sector/council housing (where a third of disabled people lived), while social services departments were expected to fund, albeit within available resources, alterations and aids, and improve other social 'care' services, along with recreational facilities, such as holidays, radio and television.

However, local authorities were slow to take action, due in part to ignorance of the Act, but also to continuing opposition, as well as insufficient central funding. At the same time, the Ministry of Health outlined a 10-year Hospital Plan in 1962 that anticipated halving the long-stay population (particularly in 'psychiatric' and 'mental handicap' institutions) by 1976 and eliminating it completely by the end of the century. The therapeutic and financial advantages of 'community care' were widely accepted. However, the decarceration of so many inmates in a relatively short period greatly increased the pressure on already inadequate 'care in the community' services. One unforeseen outcome was the significant level of homelessness among former 'psychiatric' patients.

More generally, there was a lack of accessible housing for disabled people, and low incomes exacerbated these difficulties (Martin and White, 1988; Martin et al, 1989). At the same time, there was a rise in the numbers of disabled people under 65 years of age living in small residential homes and hostels, particularly individuals classified as having 'mental health problems' or with 'learning difficulties'. As a result, living in the community was an isolating experience for many disabled people (Oldman and Quilgars, 1999).

Throughout this period, the shortage of alternative or adequate support services forced many disabled people into a position of total dependence on other family members, particularly mothers or spouses. At the same time, it exposed a conflict of interest between the family 'carer' and the disabled person. From the family perspective, 'caring for' a disabled relative often exacted a heavy price: leading to restricted employment opportunities, financial hardship, and deteriorating ill health and inter-family relationships.

Disability as a personal tragedy

Before bringing this review of policy up to the present, it is instructive to take stock of the dominant influence exercised by an individual, medicalised approach to 'disability'. This took root after the scientific medical profession was granted a monopoly position by the state in matters of health and illness (Turner, 1987) during the second half of the 19th century. The authority of medical knowledge extended from the diagnosis and treatment of disease to impairment. It focused on bodily 'abnormality', disorder or deficit, and the way in which this 'causes' a 'disability' or functional limitation. For example, people with hearing and visual impairments or people who have cerebral palsy may experience difficulties with mobility. In practice, the 'disability' becomes the individual's defining characteristic and identity and shorthand for a general incapacity. The individual is regarded as a victim, and dependent on the 'care and attention' of others, in what has been aptly summarised as a 'personal tragedy' approach to disability policy and services (Oliver, 1983, 1990).

The classification of diseases and impairments has become increasingly complex, fanned by the multiplication of medical specialisms, such as psychiatry and rehabilitation (Armstrong, 1983). As well, through the 20th century, a veritable multi-million pound 'disability business' took root with key interest groups spanning professionals and allied practitioners, drug companies and residential homes across the public, voluntary and private sectors (Albrecht, 1992). The expansion of allied health and social 'care' practitioners, such as occupational therapists, physiotherapists and social workers, as well as educationalists and psychologists, has been particularly remarkable. As a consequence, having or acquiring an impairment attracts attention from a wide range of different professional experts who determine the individual's 'special needs' and how these should be met. There is also a veritable army of 'personal care' staff with relatively little training who 'look after' the disabled person, by supplying help with basic activities of everyday living, such as eating and drinking, washing, going to the toilet and getting dressed. A further addition to this extensive list is the continuing high number of informal 'carers' – families and friends – providing a variety of 'care' and support.

The medical profession is also crucial in determining entitlement to social 'care' and welfare services and benefits (Blaxter, 1976; Brisenden, 1986). One way has been to translate the individual's 'abnormality or loss' into a particular level of incapacity. For example, the National Insurance

Benefit Regulations in the 1960s advised that the loss of fingers and a leg amputated below the knee constituted a 50% 'disability', while the loss of three fingers and the amputation of a foot or the loss of an eye translated into a 30% rating (Sainsbury, 1973, pp 26-7). However, this way of determining entitlement to services and benefits often proved very contentious. How many everyday activities should be covered, and should these be weighted equally? Again, should allowance be made for changing capacity over time and between social contexts (Sainsbury, 1973; Townsend, 1979)? These and other issues preoccupied the Office for Population Censuses and Surveys (OPCS), renamed the Office for National Statistics (ONS) in 1997, when it was asked by the government to undertake the first national survey of 'disability' in Britain in the late 1960s (Harris et al, 1971), with a follow-up in the 1980s (Martin et al, 1988).

The most influential intervention in these debates was the World Health Organization's (WHO, 1980) *International Classification of Impairments, Disabilities and Handicaps* (ICIDH). This defined the key terms as follows:

- *Impairment:* 'Any loss or abnormality of psychological, physiological or anatomical structure or function' (p 27).
- *Disability:* 'Any restriction or lack (resulting from an impairment) of ability to perform an activity in the manner or within the range considered normal for a human being' (p 28).
- *Handicap:* 'A disadvantage for a given individual, resulting from an impairment or disability, that limits or prevents the fulfilment of a role (depending on age, sex, social and cultural factors) for that individual' (p 29).

While 'impairment' refers to those parts of the body that do not work 'properly', 'disability' centres on what people cannot do, particularly basic skills of everyday living. The novelty of the WHO schema lies in its definition of 'handicap'. This conveys the impact of impairment and disability in creating difficulties in carrying out social roles, while acknowledging that these vary across social groups and cultural contexts. However, academic and government research has been disinclined to pursue the analytic potential of social 'handicap' in explaining the manifest social exclusion of disabled people across social and economic life. Instead, social policy and social welfare services have remained rooted in an individual, medicalised explanation.

There is a close correspondence between this ICIDH approach and that followed in the OPCS national surveys of disability conducted in Britain between 1985 and 1988. The latter selected as the main areas of functional limitation: locomotion; reaching and stretching; dexterity; seeing; hearing; personal 'care'; continence; communication; behaviour; and intellectual functioning. Scores in these areas provided an overall measure of 10 levels of severity of 'disability'. The OPCS surveys were based on a sample of disabled adults and children who lived in both 'communal establishments' and private households. The 'entry criteria' were extended in comparison with its previous national study (Harris et al, 1971) to include those with a 'mental illness and handicap' and those with less severe impairments (Martin et al, 1988). It calculated that there were 6.2 million disabled adults in Britain: a majority was over 60 years of age, with more disabled women than men. Increasing age was also closely associated with 'severity of disability', although almost a third of disabled people were ranked in the two 'least severe' categories.

The ICIDH and OPCS definitions and measures of disability have generated considerable debate. First, this approach relies primarily on medical criteria, and use of a bio-physiological definition of 'normality'. Yet 'scientific' identification of boundary lines is sometimes contentious: for example, at what point does blood pressure or body weight and shape move from 'normal' to 'pathological'? In practice, the meanings and consequences associated, for example, with having a visual or hearing impairment are not automatic but situationally and socially mediated. Spectacles are a necessary aid for many people with a visual impairment, but their use is no longer regarded as a mark of a disabled person. More generally, the notion of bio-physiological 'normality' remains heavily laden with non-disabled assumptions.

Second, 'impairment' is identified as the cause of both 'disability' and 'handicap'. This renders people with an accredited impairment dependent on professional experts to define their needs and appropriate service provision and rehabilitation. It also rationalises a reliance on others for 'care' or charity. Little significance is attached to disabled people's own experiences of disadvantage, or the social creation of disabling barriers and hence the possibility of overcoming these by political action and social change.

Third, the disabled person must accept a social identity as in some way 'not normal' or 'defective'. Individuals are expected to adjust to their situation and develop appropriate coping strategies. This is a feature of psychological studies that explore the impact of an impairment on a person's emotional and psychological well-being. For example, Weller and Miller (1977) outline a four-stage process of personal adjustment through which people accommodate to a severe spinal cord injury. The initial reaction of *shock* and horror is followed by *denial* or despair that any recovery is possible, leading to *anger* at others, and finally to *depression* as a necessary preliminary to coming to terms with their diminished circumstances. Hence, the presumption of a fifth stage, termed 'acceptance' or 'adjustment', which may not be reached until one or two years later. Again, the 'victim-blaming' orientation means that those who stray from the prescribed adjustment process are at risk of being criticised for being in a state of 'denial' and in need of psychological rehabilitation (Oliver, 1983).

These and other criticisms led to the production of a revised version of the ICIDH (WHO, 1999). The *International Classification of Functioning, Disability and Health* (since known as the ICF) sought to bring together the medical and social approaches to disablement into an all-inclusive 'bio-psychosocial model of disability'. By separating 'impairments', 'activity limitations' and 'participation restrictions', it establishes a framework that identifies those aspects that are properly the subject of medical intervention from other areas where social and environmental barriers are the major factors (WHO, 1999, 2005). However, the ICF has been criticised for giving precedence to impairment as the primary cause of limited activity and participation, and the continued linkage of disability as a health issue (Finkelstein, 1998; Pfeiffer, 2000). Furthermore, the ICF has yet to achieve a notable impact on those undertaking government (or other research) surveys in Britain, at least in the ways statistics on disabled people and social exclusion are collected.

Changing policy perspectives on disability since 1979

In the last two decades, the pre-eminence of the individual, medicalised approach to 'disability' has been contested by an alternative, socio-political analysis of the reasons for the social exclusion of disabled people in contemporary society (see Chapter Three). This has now gained formal recognition in government discussion papers and debates among social welfare professionals central to the implementation of disability policy and service provision (Beresford, 2004).

New Right

At the same time, the proper role of the state in social welfare policies became the subject of renewed political controversy in the final quarter of the 20th century. The election in 1979 of a 'New Right' (neo-liberal), Conservative government, headed by Margaret Thatcher, signalled a radical shift in political and economic thinking. The welfare state, which had been regarded as an instrument for dealing with social problems, was now identified as one of its main causes. This led to calls to restructure or 'roll back' the state, with cuts in state expenditure to reduce taxation, and revitalise market forces and competition in the delivery of welfare services as a way of enhancing their efficiency and effectiveness. This reverted the policy emphasis back towards market-driven citizenship.

The central aim, as far as social welfare policy was concerned, was to expose the management of the public sector to the presumed discipline of the economic marketplace and by generating competition between service providers for 'clients' (Griffiths, 1988). This market orientation was based on a 'supermarket' model in which the power of individual consumers was greatly enhanced by increasing the range of options to 'exit' (that is, shop elsewhere) as opposed to pursuing their citizenship rights through their democratic 'voice' (Hirschman, 1970). In the case of welfare services, competition between service providers was regarded as increasing consumer choice and service quality and delivering better 'value for money'. Consumers acquired a countervailing power compared to professional and service provider interests in determining service choices and priorities. In addition, the encouragement of active consumers was regarded as a means of reversing individual welfare dependence and passivity.

Conservative government thinking on the significance of market competition and consumerism underpinned the 1990 National Health Service and Community Care Act (NHSCCA). It stressed the importance of market forces and competition and the necessity of introducing private sector practices and discipline into the public sector provision of health and social 'care'. The central targets were 'economy, efficiency and effectiveness' (Exworthy and Halford, 1999; Sanderson, 1999), the so-called 'holy trinity' of neo-liberalism (Clarke, 2004, p 132). These were allied to welfare pluralism, or a 'mixed economy of care', with market competition between the public, private and voluntary sectors enhancing individual choice, opportunity and rights. Alternatives to public sector provision included private residential homes and voluntary sector provision in day centres. Considerable significance was also attached to the responsibilities of the family and other 'informal' or unpaid 'carers'.

In this new scenario, the state was assigned a very different role – through the creation of quasi-markets, privatisation (including charging for those services previously free at the point of delivery), contracting out, and new inter-organisational and social partnerships (Clarke, 2004). The government's White Paper *Caring for People* proclaimed the overall aim of 'community care' as 'promoting choice and independence' while emphasising giving 'people a greater individual say in how they live their lives and the services they need to help them to do so' (DH, 1989, p 4). This was reiterated in subsequent policy guidance:

> The rationale for this re-organisation is the empowerment of users and carers. Instead of users and carers being subordinate to the wishes of service-providers, the roles will be progressively adjusted. In this way, users and carers will be enabled to exercise the same power as consumers of other services. This redressing of the balance of power is the best guarantee of a continuing improvement in the quality of service. (DH, 1991, p 9)

There was an extra emphasis on the role of local authority managers in assessing individual support needs, designing a 'care' plan and purchasing services on behalf of service users, within available resources. In addition, the implementation of the 'care' plan was monitored and the overall process reviewed (DH, 1991, p 41). However, assessment of user needs remained under professional control and suspicion remained that this served as a rationing device, while access to services was further limited by people's capacity to pay, and 'eligibility criteria' based on an individual (medical) model of disability.

Nevertheless, a specific priority identified by disabled people was not included in the NHSCCA. Disabled people's organisations had been campaigning since the 1980s to overturn the 1948 National Assistance Act prohibition of cash payments by local authorities directly to individual service users to enable them to buy their own personal assistance instead of using local services. However, it was not until the passage of the 1996 Community Care (Direct Payments) Act that local authorities were finally allowed to make direct payments to selected groups of disabled users (Glasby and Littlechild, 2002). Although the Act contained a number of significant restrictions on eligibility, it began the process of allowing disabled people more opportunities to exercise meaningful choices in their everyday lives (see Chapter Three).

Another key policy emphasis was listening to and involving users in the organisation and delivery of services. Thus, the NHSCCA built on earlier initiatives, such as the 1983 Mental Health Act Code of Practice, which encouraged user access to information, and the 1986 Disabled Persons (Services, Consultation and Representation) Act. Although not widely implemented, this Act placed a duty on local authorities to consider the needs of disabled people (plus 'carers') for services under the CSDPA, particularly the provision of information, and confer with 'appropriate' organisations of disabled people.

The type and level of user participation envisaged was geared to consultation and data collection exercises seeking service user feedback on the planning, management and operation of health and 'community care' services. The Department of Health anticipated few serious difficulties, and suggested that any imbalance in the service provider–user relationship:

> can be corrected by sharing information more openly and by encouraging users and carers or their representatives, to take a full part in decision-making. (DH, 1991, p 18)

Consultation with service users quickly became an ever-present feature of social policy reforms (Cook, 2002). As an illustration, the 1994 *Framework for Local Community Care Charters in England* (DH, 1994) referenced the involvement of users and 'carers' in the assessment of needs, inspection of residential homes and other services, and future service planning. Associated initiatives included the introduction of 'charters' between users and various public services, with rights to information, complaint processes and redress (see Chapter Five).

New Labour

The New Labour government elected in 1997 promised a modernising 'third way' between Labour's 'old Left' and the Conservative 'New Right'. In fact there have been strong continuities with Thatcherism and its neo-liberal project to realign economy, state and society. Moreover, private and voluntary organisations were allowed to take on a much greater role in delivering services, and a range of stakeholders became involved in processes of consultation and co-production (Needham, 2003; Clarke, 2004).

Thus, the 'Best Value' process was introduced to enhance service standards underpinned by the most efficient and effective means, which included recognition of local community and user involvement. *Modernising Social Services* (DH, 1998) emphasised local user satisfaction surveys. The 2001 Health and Social Care Act and 2002 National Health Service Reform and Health Care Professions Act outlined a new user involvement structure. Nevertheless, there was continuing criticism about the lack of meaningful impact on either the decision-making process or its substantive outcomes (Lister, 1998). A typical conclusion was that services remained under the control of managers and professional providers.

New Labour's modernisation strategy also gave a vanguard role to a new managerialism and the ethos and practices of the private sector. Professional 'tribalism' was portrayed as a barrier to organisational efficiency and effectiveness (Flynn, 1999). In response, scrutiny, inspection, evaluation and audit emerged as solutions to problems of maintaining 'arm's length control' (p 129). Tight, centralised control gave way to the delegation of operational autonomy to local managers but this was constrained by strict performance targets. Yet, one consequence of the prioritisation of explicit standards and performance measurement, and efficiency in resource allocation, was to restrict considerably user influence over service provision.

More widely, there has been an elevation of 'pragmatic decision making' (Clarke, 2004, p 133) – 'what counts is what works' – as a virtue compared with 'ideological' politics. The government attempted to rewrite the relationship between the state and its citizens – building on the 1995 Disability Discrimination Act. It claimed the mantle of the 'people's champion' in siding with 'consumers' over 'producers', and encouraged 'partnerships' and collaboration between user organisations and the voluntary, private and statutory sectors in developing and delivering services (Glendinning et al, 2002). Significantly, support for direct payments was extended under New Labour. Again, this harmonised with a market orientation in its emphasis on greater user choice and better-quality services. Conversely, the marketisation of social 'care' encouraged not only competition between service providers but also among service users (Rhodes, 1999).

New Labour further sought to revitalise governance by setting up many new agencies, although it stopped short of a decisive transfer of power. Social welfare initiatives included the establishment of a General Social Care Council (GSCC), and the Social Care Institute for Excellence (SCIE). In England, the 2000 Care Standards Act launched a new regulatory body, the National Care Standards Council (NCSC), with responsibilities that include social 'care' services, and taking over the inspection and regulation of services from local authority and health inspection units (NCSC, 2003). Since April 2004, the NCSC has been incorporated in the Commission for Social Care Inspection, along with the Social Services Inspectorate (SSI) and the SSI/Audit Commission Joint Review Team with an expanded remit over the 'social care industry'.

New Labour also stressed its commitment to bring about the inclusion of hitherto excluded groups, with a priority on participation in the labour market. 'Welfare to work' and 'New Deals' were extended to disabled people, as a way of increasing the number who might enter paid employment. A specific goal was to produce a major reduction in the proportion of disabled people 'excluded' from the labour market. Most recently, the Prime Minister's Strategy Unit (PMSU, 2005) signalled a major shift in New Labour policy towards disabled people by endorsing the principle of 'independent living' and the importance of user-led organisations in its achievement (see Chapter Nine).

This represents at least a notable modification in political vocabulary, with a move away from the language around 'exclusion' to 'inclusion', as well as a downgrading of external barriers (or at least the claim that these were addressed in anti-discrimination legislation), and a refocus of policy intervention on measures that sponsor greater individual responsibility in the economic and social arenas. It remains to be seen how far there is a notable realignment of 'practical governance' rather than a new form of 'regulation' of service user choices.

Review

Historically, disabled people without any means of support were viewed as part of the 'deserving' poor and hence entitled to state poor relief or charity. With the gradual industrialisation and urbanisation of British society, there were increasing attempts to contain and regulate the 'unruly' elements of the population, notably through the withdrawal of customary rights and outdoor poor relief and the enforced segregation within institutions.

This 'disability' divide was increasingly policed by a growing number of medical and allied professionals. They secured, with state approval, the dominance of an approach to disability that concentrated on individual functional limitations or perceived 'defects' as the rationale for a service concentration on medical rehabilitation and welfare dependence.

Nevertheless, the historical reliance on the voluntary and 'informal' sectors endured, even as there was a growing state involvement in providing health and 'social care' services through the 20th century. Even then, the welfare state assembled in the 1940s offered a much devalued form of social citizenship to disabled people. They were typically relegated to 'special needs' policies and benefits. By the late 1970s, this welfare state itself underwent major reconstruction first by Conservative and then New Labour governments. An emphasis on market competition, a mixed economy of 'care', consumerism, and the obligations and responsibilities of citizenship – albeit with the conspicuous introduction of the 1995 Disability Discrimination Act – provided a very different context for disability policy, offering new possibilities but also constraints.

A central factor in political debates around disability policy in the last quarter of the 20th century has been the rise of an active Disabled People's Movement. In Chapter Three, we will review its challenge to the individual, medicalised approach to 'disability' and campaigns to dismantle the barriers to disabled people's social inclusion and for support services that confirm their social citizenship rights.

THREE

Disability activism and the struggle for independent living

Introduction

Through the last quarter of the 20th century, disabled people developed a remarkable challenge to the dominant understanding of disability. It has involved the politicisation of disability with the setting up of many new grass-roots organisations around the country, the involvement of an increasing number of disabled people in campaigning activities, and the production of a crucial body of writings by disabled people and their allies advancing a socio-political analysis of disability. Moreover, these interventions have recently begun to exert a discernible impression on government thinking and policy (Barnes et al, 1999).

This chapter begins by examining the emergence of this new disability politics, with specific reference to the goal of 'independent living', and the development of user-led or user-controlled organisations and services. The rise in social and political protest was linked to the denial of citizenship rights and the wide-ranging experience of inequalities, and the failures of social policy to effect change. In the case of the Disabled People's Movement, the early momentum was established by campaigns around 'independent living'. Second, we examine the specific impact on the new disability politics in Britain of a radical shift from a medical to a social model of disability – pioneered by organisations of disabled people. This stressed the social and environmental barriers to the inclusion of people with accredited impairments. In the following two sections we detail the criticism by disabled people of existing, mainstream services for disabled people, and then finally, trace specific initiatives by disabled activists to pioneer more participatory and collaborative approaches to service support and assistance, particularly user-led organisations.

Towards a new disability politics

A notable feature of the burgeoning number of protest movements emerging in the 1960s and 1970s was their location in new lines of social division and conflict. Interpretations differ about whether these were stimulated by realignments in capitalist societies, or the social and cultural dynamics of an emerging postmodern society (Touraine, 1981; Scott, 1990). What is less in dispute is that these protests included the rise of the Independent Living Movement (ILM), most prominently in the US, and the generation of a politicised Disabled People's Movement around the world.

In Britain, disability theorists argued that welfare state 'universalism' was a cruel distortion: their experience was of being marginalised, pathologised, and generally excluded from mainstream society. Welfare institutions, far from diminishing these divisions, were implicated in their perpetuation, by their reliance on a medical approach that highlighted their functional limitations and need for rehabilitation or 'normalisation'. Disabled people began to reject this biological rationale for inequality and emphasised instead the social, economic, cultural and political bases to their discrimination and oppression.

There have been lively debates about whether the Disabled People's Movement should be classified as a 'new social movement', although any conclusion is weakened by the lack of agreed criteria for determining its novelty or 'innovativeness' (Oliver, 1990; Fagan and Lee, 1997). Some commentators concentrated on their presumed capacity to resist bureaucratic regulation (Melucci, 1980), and their allegiance to more direct forms of democracy (Habermas, 1981). Others queried the basic disjuncture between 'old'- and 'new'-style protest. Indeed, the roots of disability protest in Britain stretch back at least to the 1890s, when low pay and poor working conditions led to the formation of the National League of the Blind and Disabled (NLBD) and the British Deaf Association. These organisations instigated a series of campaigns through the first half of the 20th century (Pagel, 1988). Nevertheless, while conventional political activities continued, there was an upsurge in more radical analyses of disability and political interventions by what were regarded as the failures of pressure group politics to win important policy reforms.

Historically, organisations *for* disabled people, voluntary agencies and charities, dominated disability politics, and how disability policy is viewed. As indicated in Chapter Two, their priorities have been challenged by organisations *of* (that is, controlled and run by) disabled people. These include:

- the ethos and focus of voluntary action (reinforces dependency);
- hegemony, governance and resources (opposite of user control of lives);
- structures and practices within voluntary groups (too cosy a relationship with the state, too little concerned with user empowerment);
- the use of (personal tragedy) imagery by charities in fundraising; and
- the political inertness of the voluntary sector (reliant on significant government funding/patronage, while successive Charities Acts encouraged political passivity/neutrality) (Drake, 1996, p 152).

As a result of criticism from disabled people, some organisations for disabled people, such as MIND (National Association for Mental Health), have been persuaded to adopt a more critical political stance or to change their names – the Spastics Society turned into Scope – and promote more positive messages in line with a social analysis of disability.

The Independent Living Movement

In America, the ILM was instrumental in advancing the new disability politics in the 1960s (Martinez, 2003). DeJong (1979, 1981) located its emergence in the efforts of groups of disabled people to improve their lives as well as the actions of rehabilitation professionals to recruit more and more users into vocational programmes. It took inspiration from contemporary social movements such as 'civil rights, consumerism, self-help, demedicalisation/self-care, and deinstitutionalisation' (DeJong, 1979, p 435). Hence, independent living comprised both a social movement and a new 'analytic paradigm' (p 435).

It was the actions of Ed Roberts and other disabled students at the University of California in Berkeley that first attracted national prominence with campaigns for self-managed accommodation, with the aim of making themselves 'independently dependent'. Subsequently, the 'Rolling Quads' were allowed to access California's Aid to the Totally Disabled programme to recruit, train and fire their own 'care attendants'. In 1971, a marked increase in the number of off-campus users triggered the establishment of the first Centre for Independent Living (CIL) at Berkeley in 1972. Its broad goal was to facilitate the integration of disabled people into the community by providing a comprehensive system of support services

(Centre for Independent Living, 1982). Such initiatives in the US attracted considerable interest and visits from disabled activists from Britain and across Europe in the 1980s.

The momentum behind the establishment of CIL-type organisations was maintained through the next two decades and a research survey in 1978 recorded over 450 programmes providing 'independent living' services. Yet only 12 met the original Berkeley definition of a CIL: a non-residential, community-based, non-profit programme, controlled by users, which provides services directly or coordinates these through referral services. Activities ranged across peer counselling, 'attendant care' referral, civil rights and benefits training, job and housing referral, independent living skills, assertiveness and self-management training. More than two thirds of the organisations served multiple impairment groups. About half of the programmes were staffed primarily by disabled people, with some others managed by a disabled person. By the late 1990s, there were more than 300 CILs in the US (Charlton, 1998, p 132).

However, DeJong noted that the ILM was dominated by individuals from a few impairment groups: 'those with spinal chord injury, muscular dystrophy, cerebral palsy, multiple sclerosis and postpolio disablement' (1979, p 435). 'Younger', white, middle-class adults were also over-represented among ILM activists. A further contradiction arose with the increasing impact of the ILM campaigns. This sparked a move from street campaigns into conventional political activities but raised difficult questions over political strategy and tactics. Should CILs remain 'grass-roots' advocacy or campaigning organisations or become 'mainstream' service providers or agencies? Should CILs seek external accreditation, and assume the additional responsibilities as a service provider to enhance their organisational legitimacy and potential funding sources (DeJong, 1988)?

By the 1990s, some commentators argued that while CILs had been in the vanguard of disability politics:

> Most CILs do not hire politically active people, do not have organizers, and have no strategic view of how to effect social change. Many executive directors of CILs and disability rights groups are apolitical, outside narrowly defined disability related issues. Most disability rights groups avoid demonstrations because they are considered outdated, or because they would alienate funding sources. (Charlton, 1998, p 122)

Disability activism in Britain

In Britain, early disability activism centred on small groups of disabled people living in residential institutions. These promoted debate about disability and appropriate collective action. Their approach to independent living stressed self-determination, choice (where and how to live) and control over support services (who assists, how and when), and the removal of disabling barriers in mainstream society (Brechin et al, 1981; Hasler et al, 1999).

The term independent living refers to all disabled people having the same choice, control and freedom as any other citizen – at home, at work, and as members of the community. This does not necessarily mean disabled people 'doing everything for themselves', but it does mean that any practical assistance required should be under the control of disabled individuals – 'independence is created by having assistance when and how one requires it' (Brisenden, 1989, p 9).

An early move towards self-organisation, rather than independent living support, was taken in 1965 with the formation of the Disablement Income Group (DIG) by two disabled women, Megan du Boisson and Berit Moore. In the late 1960s DIG became a focus for political activity, particularly a comprehensive disability income, although it was increasingly taken over by non-disabled 'experts'. From the 1970s, there was a notable growth of organisations controlled and run by disabled people such as the Union of the Physically Impaired Against Segregation (UPIAS), the Liberation Network, and Sisters Against Disability (SAD). As in the US, these offered a 'powerful source of mutual support, education and action' for disabled people campaigning against discrimination and the oppression of disabled people (Crewe and Zola, 1983, p xiii). In addition, the British Council of Disabled People (BCODP), which was established in 1981, grew rapidly and by 2000 had a membership of 130 organisations of disabled people (BCODP, 2001).

Yet, similar concerns surfaced that disability politics was not fully inclusive of all interests within the disabled population. For example, specific impairment groups and their organisations, such as mental health system survivors and people with 'learning difficulties', remained on the periphery (Beresford and Campbell, 1994). Again, the elevation of disability issues on to the political agenda led to many disabled activists and organisations of disabled people entering the mainstream political and policy process. Fears were expressed that:

> To get too close to the Government is to risk incorporation and end up carrying out their proposals rather than ours. To move too far away is to risk marginalisation and eventual demise. To collaborate too eagerly with the organisations for disabled people risks having our agendas taken over by them, and having them presented both to us and to politicians as theirs. To remain aloof risks appearing unrealistic and/or unreasonable, and denies possible access to much needed resources. (Barnes and Oliver, 1995, p 115)

As disabled people are one of the poorest and most disadvantaged sections of the population, material issues have been central to disability politics. The Disabled People's Movement has highlighted demands for equal pay and working conditions, and channelling more resources to the social and welfare system. Equally significant has been the emphasis on culture as a site for political struggle. The affirmation of a positive disabled identity poses a direct challenge to the negative representation of impairment and the stigmatisation of difference in the media and realm of culture more generally. This radical challenge – the politics of identity – to established cultural ideas and values has been advanced in tandem with struggles over the redistribution of income and wealth.

The advancement of disabled people's interests by underlining the claim to 'rights, not charity' was initially more associated with the civil rights campaigns in the US, following the inspiration of black civil rights struggles, particularly through the 1960s (Hahn, 1987; Shapiro, 1993). In contrast, early disability activism in Britain concentrated on overturning local policy and pressing for new legislation at the national level. This is partly explained by the lack of a written constitution or a tradition of human rights campaigning or legislation (at least until the 1998 Human Rights Act). It was also a reaction to the involvement of national charities in conventional political lobbying (Imrie and Wells, 1993). Nevertheless, by the late 1980s, the language of 'rights' had become embedded in disabled people's campaigns.

On both sides of the Atlantic, disabled people's organisations adopted 'direct action' tactics. For example, large demonstrations were held against charity shows and Telethons, while the formation in 1993 of the Direct Action Network (DAN) provided an organisational base for continuing local and national direct action (Pointon, 1999). Such activities challenged popular notions of a passive or 'grateful' disabled population (Shakespeare,

1993). Even so, it was always a minority of disabled people that accepted a positive or politicised 'disabled identity' and became active in the Disabled People's Movement – a feature it shares with most other 'new' and 'old' protest movements.

The social model of disability

During the 1970s and, 1980s, disabled activists and their organisations voiced increasing criticism of the individual, medical model of disability. In developing what became known as a social or political approach to disability, disabled people in Britain argued that it is society that disables people with accredited impairments, and therefore any meaningful solution must be directed at socio-political change rather than individual adjustment and rehabilitation. A social model riposte to the individual, medical approach is that 'disability is not measles' (Rioux and Bach, 1994).

The UPIAS was in the vanguard of those calling for an alternative model of disability. In its manifesto document *Fundamental Principles of Disability* (1976), UPIAS placed the responsibility for disability squarely on society's failures:

> In our view it is society which disables physically impaired people. Disability is something imposed on top of our impairments by the way we are unnecessarily isolated and excluded from full participation in society. Disabled people are therefore an oppressed group in society. (UPIAS, 1976, p 14)

The close connection between impairment, disability and handicap is rejected in the UPIAS interpretation. While it broadly accepted the medical definition of impairment, the meaning of disability was turned on its head:

- *Impairment:* Lacking part or all of a limb, or having a defective limb, organ or mechanism of the body.
- *Disability:* The disadvantage or restriction of activity caused by a contemporary social organisation which takes no or little account of people who have physical impairments and thus excludes them from participation in the mainstream of social activities (UPIAS, 1976, pp 3-4).

Subsequent discussions among disabled people and their organisations have amended the reference to 'physical impairments' so that any impairment (including sensory and intellectual examples) falls within the potential scope of disability.

Whereas impairment is regarded as an individual attribute, disability is described as 'the outcome of an oppressive relationship between people with ... impairments and the rest of society' (Finkelstein, 1980, p 47). Once defined as a disabled person, the individual is stigmatised and social expectations about how, for example, those with a visual or hearing impairment should behave, or what they are capable of doing, exert an influence independent of their impairment. Moreover, the form of disability – as a social creation – demonstrates cultural and historical variation.

This reformulation of disability prompted Mike Oliver to coin the phrase the 'social model of disability' to refer to:

> Nothing more or less fundamental than a switch away from focusing on the physical limitations of particular individuals to the way the physical and social environments impose limitations upon certain groups or categories of people. (Oliver, 1983, p 23)

Hitherto, 'disability' was 'naturalised' as individual sickness or pathology in comparison with 'able bodied' or healthy 'normality'. As a result:

> personal tragedy theory has served to individualise the problems of disability and hence leave social and economic structures untouched. (Oliver, 1986, p 16)

In contrast, from a social model perspective, disability is equated with 'disabling barriers and attitudes'. Instead of concentrating on the link between the underlying medical condition and typically functional limitations, the social model redirects attention to, for example, the 'defects' in the design of the built environment or transport systems that restrict social inclusion (Oliver, 1990, pp 7–8), and 'which we had the knowledge and ability to alter' (Topliss and Gould, 1981, p 142). Hence, measures of disability would focus particularly on the physical, social and economic disabling barriers experienced by disabled people and the impact of anti-discrimination policies.

In advancing this alternative to the personal tragedy model, a very different set of key questions are posed, such as: 'What is the nature of disability?

What causes it? How is it experienced?' (Oliver, 1996a, pp 29-30). The search for answers heralds the development of a more comprehensive social *theory* of disability:

> the social model of disability is not a substitute for social theory, a materialist history of disability nor an explanation of the welfare state. (Oliver, 1996a, p 41)

Thus, the social model's references to 'disabling barriers' demand an intensive and extensive examination of the processes and structures associated with social oppression and discrimination: whether at everyday levels, or in the workings of the state and social policy. Forms of domination also raise complex issues relating to culture and politics: but not simply as sites of domination, but as arenas of resistance and challenge by disabled people.

The social model focuses on the experience of disability, but not as something that exists solely at the level of individual psychology, or even interpersonal relations. Instead, it encompasses a wide range of social and material factors and conditions, such as family circumstances, income and financial support, education, employment, housing, transport and the built environment, and more besides. At the same time, the individual and collective conditions of disabled people are not fixed, and the experience of disability therefore also demonstrates an 'emergent' and temporal character. This spans the individual's meaning and experience of disability, in the context of their overall biography, social relationships and life history, the wider circumstances of disabling barriers and attitudes in society, and the impact of state policies and welfare support systems.

Hence, this politicisation of disability represented a new discourse around citizenship and rights (Drake, 1999). The construction of a social model of disability together with the formation of organisations of disabled people provided a basis for political resistance (Campbell and Oliver, 1996). The emphasis shifted from 'charity to rights' and from social exclusion to inclusion with the replacement of a culture of dependence and pity by one based on acceptance as equal citizens.

This is not to deny the significance of impairment in people's lives or the relevance of medical interventions to the experience of impairment, but rather it underscores the lack of interest or the extraordinary silence from those adhering to a medical approach to the existence or impact of disabling social and environmental barriers. It is for such reasons that advocates of a social model approach have concentrated on those social barriers that are constructed 'on top of' impairment, and which can be affected by economic, cultural, political and social changes (Abberley, 1987).

Yet the claims of the social model should not be exaggerated:

> The social model is not about showing that every dysfunction in our bodies can be compensated for by a gadget, or good design, so that everybody can work an 8-hour day and play badminton in the evenings. It's a way of demonstrating that everyone – even someone who has no movement, no sensory function and who is going to die tomorrow – has the right to a certain standard of living and to be treated with respect. (Vasey, 1992, p 44)

Critiques of traditional community services

Failures and shortcomings in the organisation and delivery of mainstream statutory and voluntary sector services have been a major stimulus to disability activism. Critics charged that 'social care' policy remained locked into a traditional medical and individualised approach to personal 'care' and rehabilitation. From this perspective, for a person to have a 'disability' meant that they are unable to do things for themselves. It followed that the criterion for judging community services is how well disabled people are 'cared for' rather than whether they are enabled to lead more independent lives.

This criticism of mainstream services built up through the second half of the 20th century, despite attempts to improve community services. This objective was particularly associated with the passage of the 1970 Chronically Sick and Disabled Persons Act, which sought an expansion and upgrading of support services for disabled people to live outside institutions, including meals on wheels, aids and adaptations, day centres, respite 'care' and greater contact with social workers, occupational therapists and physiotherapists. As an illustration, in 1959 there were about 200 day centres in England and Wales, but by 1976 this figure had risen sharply to over 2,600. Local authorities provided slightly less than half of these facilities (47%), followed by area health authorities (26%) and voluntary agencies (23%) such as MIND and Age Concern (Carter, 1981).

Without these developments, many disabled people would no doubt have been forced into segregated, institutional settings. Nevertheless, the organisation and delivery of services for disabled people was constrained by inadequate funding and shaped by professional assumptions that people with accredited impairments needed to be 'cared for' (Oliver, 1990; Hugman, 1991). As a result, disabled people remained in a 'culture of dependence', and were treated as if they were unable to make their own decisions or choose the aids and services they needed (Hunt, 1966; Shearer, 1981; Humphries and Gordon, 1992).

The traditional service orientation was reinforced by government policy, which stressed the necessary contribution of family and 'informal carers' – the majority of whom were female – in 'looking after' the disabled person (Parker, 1993). This reliance on family and friends contained a considerable potential to break down into conflict because:

> it exploits both the carer and the person receiving care. It ruins relationships between people and results in thwarted life opportunities on both sides of the caring equation. (Brisenden, 1989, p 10)

Overall, the failings and limitations of state and provider-led welfare provision, included:

- low standards, with complaints of lack of respect, neglect and abuse – in the community as well as in residential settings;
- a failure to ensure equal access and opportunities to engage in everyday activities;
- the presumption of service provider control and user passivity/ compliance; and
- a lack of accountability, with little recognition of the rights of service users (Morris, 1993a, 1994).

Traditional assumptions about gender and ethnicity roles attracted further criticism that, for example, disabled women have more difficulty accessing services than disabled men (Rae, 1993), and that disabled people from minority ethnic groups require less service support because of the greater involvement of family members (Begum, 1993, 1994).

A common failing highlighted by disabled users was that services were not delivered in ways that enabled individuals to have control over everyday activities:

in many areas of their lives, disabled people's experiences do not accord with the lifestyle expectations of their contemporaries. For example, many disabled adults do not have the right to decide what time to get up or go to bed, or indeed who to go to bed with, when or what to eat, how often to bath or even be in control of the times when they can empty their bladders or open their bowels. (Oliver, 1996b, p 48)

Hence, disabled people who were dependent on local domiciliary services often declared that they were 'isolated' or effectively 'institutionalised' in their own homes, without the chance of leading an outside social life or developing social relationships beyond their family members. These experiences were reinforced by the language used:

We need to reclaim the words 'care' and 'caring' to mean 'love', to mean 'caring *about*' someone rather than 'caring *for*', with its custodial overtones. (Morris, 1993a, p 42)

The language of 'care' legitimised the over-protectiveness of professionals and other family members, the denial of education and employment opportunities or capacities, the undermining of self-esteem, such as not recognising an individual's role as mother in the family, and the failure of non-disabled people to acquire appropriate communication skills.

A vivid illustration is contained in Barrie Fiedler's (1988) review of the Living Options Project set up in 1984. This entailed an action research study covering 30 voluntary organisations involved with the availability of housing and support services for people with severe physical impairments. It found that the majority of disabled participants were assisted at home by relatives or friends with little or no backing from statutory services. Others were located in hospitals or residential homes. The shortcomings of residential homes were replicated in domiciliary services. Although identified as a 'priority group', the ambitions of this group of disabled people for 'independent and ordinary lifestyles' were largely frustrated:

provision was largely ineffective, uncoordinated and patchy and was meeting the needs of very few disabled individuals. (Fiedler, 1988, p 86)

A major exception that offered disabled people a very different prospect was the establishment of the Independent Living Fund (ILF) in 1988. Previous campaigns by disabled people were revitalised by changes to the Supplementary Benefit system introduced in the 1986 Social Security Act. It was set up to enable a small number of disabled people for a five-year period to help with their personal assistance requirements. In practice, the number of applications and the funds awarded went far beyond government expectations, which severely misjudged disabled people's priorities for service support (Kestenbaum, 1993; Morris, 1993a, 1993b).

A series of government reports and research studies identified a range of shortcomings in the community 'care' policies implemented since the 1970s. The Audit Commission (1986) concluded that services for the main 'priority groups' – 'the elderly, mentally handicapped, mentally ill and younger disabled' – demonstrated similar failings to those identified 20 years previously by the Seebohm Report (1968). These included fragmentation, low quality and an absence of innovation.

The 1990 National Health Service and Community Care Act (NHSCCA) outlined important policy changes to address such 'failures' (see Chapter Two). The emphasis was on a new system of community 'care' planning designed to achieve closer cooperation between health and social services authorities and the private and voluntary sectors, and encourage a more 'user-centred' approach. Local authorities were required to organise 'packages of care'. Individual needs and circumstances (involving assessment of impairment-related functional limitations, family situation and financial resources) were the subject of detailed assessment by social workers. 'Case' or 'care' managers were then appointed to coordinate services and budgets. A further aim was to deliver a 'level playing field' in the funding of residential and domiciliary services (Morris, 1993b, p 4). The separation of provider and purchaser functions within authorities was identified as the key to increased consumer choice between services.

However, although this was supposed to be an empowering experience many disabled people felt they had few opportunities to challenge professional assessments or decisions (Evans, 1993; GMCDP, 1995). The stress on 'care' replicated previous dependency-creating service provision. Disabled people called for a shift from service-led to needs-led assessments, so that services do not flow from what is available or thought best by service providers, but from the priorities of the disabled user. The 1986 Disabled Persons (Services, Consultation and Representation) Act had provided the right to an assessment of needs, and these had to be met by social services departments under the terms of the 1970 Chronically Sick and Disabled Persons Act. Moreover, the Social Services Inspectorate agreed that the assessment should be participatory and 'recognise that some users may be the best assessors of their own needs and solutions' in their everyday lives (SSI, 1991, p 15). It also reiterated criticism from disabled people that the assessment process should be separated from the allocation of resources and available funding (Oliver, 1983; Oliver and Zarb, 1992), but with little tangible effect.

Disabled people's organisations continued to campaign for a more decisive shift towards 'democratic decision making' in order to:

'• maximise the opportunity for service users to be involved in assessment, care management, service delivery as it affects them as individuals…;
• create opportunities for service users to be present at all stages of decision-making which affect groups of service users: that is, in planning, purchasing, service delivery, inspection, monitoring and evaluation' (Morris, 1994, p 45).

The critique of hierarchal power relations in social 'care' was also developed 'from within'. In particular, a focus on 'anti-oppressive' practices in the social work literature demonstrated the potential overlap with users advocating a radical change in the role of health and social welfare professionals (Dominelli, 1998; Wilson and Beresford, 2000). In some instances, 'front-line practitioners within administrative systems of assessment and care management enjoy relative autonomy' (Ellis and Rummery, 2000, p 107). This discretion in the social welfare system might be exploited to advantage disabled users (Davis et al, 1997), but equally it might block 'progressive' moves, for example, towards support for independent living.

Additionally, some have expressed concerns that disabled people will become 'victims' of the inter-professional rivalry characteristic of the health and social 'care' divide (Glendinning et al, 2000). Other researchers have identified a continuing disregard or even ignorance of the social model of disability and independent living among front-line 'care' staff (French, 1994; Abberley, 1995, 2004). This has resulted in considerable frustration and dissatisfaction with the assessment process (Maynard-Campbell and Maynard-Lupton, 2000; Mottingly, 2002; Rummery, 2002).

Overall, organisations of disabled people charge that traditional mainstream service provision has not translated ideals of support for users into tangible progress towards independent living (Barnes, 1993; Kestenbaum, 1996). First, there is a focus on incapacity rather than helping/ supporting disabled people to exercise their citizen roles and choices. Consequently, the welfare system produces dependency. Support for independent living is not regarded as a form of social and economic investment. Second, disabled people are expected to fit into services instead of services being fitted to the person; policy, professional and service boundaries lead to service fragmentation that militates against working together on behalf of disabled users. From a disabled person's perspective:

> It is very difficult to be positive about many aspects of the experience of receiving personal assistance in the form of a service from social or health authorities. Some people appreciate it when responsibility for organising and employing carers is taken on by a local authority but generally the picture is one of a failure to respond adequately to personal assistance requirements and real difficulties in the relationship between service users and service providers. (Morris, 1993a, p 26)

In contrast, campaigns initiated by organisations of disabled people have been grounded in an alternative set of political priorities to:

- improve disabled people's quality of life;
- extend the support they receive to enable them to live independently, outside institutions, particularly by providing personal assistance;
- campaign against discrimination and 'disabling barriers' and for the human and civil rights of disabled people; and
- act collectively to achieve these goals (Morris, 1994).

Building user-led services

User-led services offered an example of disability praxis – with the integration of the socio-political analysis of disability and the practice of independent living. The controlling role was taken by disabled people (whether current service users or not). The initiation and direction of their own organisations became a key indicator of disability activism, far beyond being involved in consultations about traditional social 'care' services. This links with the priority given by organisations of disabled people to the provision of appropriate and accountable support in general and more specifically to personal assistance as the necessary foundations to enable disabled people to live independently and on equal terms in mainstream society (Oliver, 1990; Morris, 1993a).

The impact of the Disabled People's Movement in making a reality of user-controlled services since the 1970s has been immense, but it is also necessary to recognise the promotion, sometimes for different reasons, by the neo-liberal agenda for political change:

> User-controlled services have emerged out of people's desire to have more say, out of their anger, but the reality of why there's such an interest in user-led services is the government's wish to encourage a consumerist perspective. (Oliver, cited in Morris, 1994, p 10)

Historically, user-led organisations in Britain demonstrate many differences as well as similarities – in their origins, organisational structures and processes, and their specific aims and objectives. Early pioneers of self-help and user-led action include the Spinal Injuries Association (SIA), Project 81 and the Derbyshire Coalition of Disabled People (DCODP). The SIA was one of the first user-controlled service provider organisations in the UK. It was established in 1974 with a paid general secretary and 300 members. Although membership always included disabled and non-disabled people, from the outset its management committee comprised only people with spinal cord injury. Its basic philosophy was that disabled people's problems were 'social rather than personal' and therefore concentrated on combating:

> [p]oor housing, poverty, unemployment, lack of information, rather than the need for help with coming to terms with their disabilities. (Oliver and Hasler, 1987, p 117)

The SIA embarked on the development of a range of independent living-type services. These encompassed information, welfare, link and counselling services. Information services included a quarterly, but later a bi-monthly, newsletter, pamphlets and books dealing with medical and social 'care' issues (SIA, 1981). A social model approach advocated by Mike Oliver (1981, 1983), who was a member of the SIA management committee during the 1970s and 1980s, was adopted by the welfare service (D'Aboville, 1991). The link and counselling services were based on the assumption that information is crucial but more likely to be accepted if offered (as soon as possible after the acquisition of an impairment) by someone in similar circumstances.

In 1978 the SIA organised a Counselling Conference where participants identified three key issues:

> The first is the need for counselling; this was generally acknowledged, and has now been expanded, to include the counselling needs for families with a disabled member, and of people who had left hospital and perhaps been living in the community for some time. Secondly, was the usefulness of peer counselling; paralysed people and their families felt they could derive greatest help from other people in a similar situation. Thirdly, and most crucially, the need for close supervision and support for voluntary counselling were underlined. (Oliver and Hasler, 1987, p 119)

In response to concerns about the lack of support for informal 'carers' and the difficulties encountered accessing appropriate help when away from home, the SIA launched its own personal assistance service known initially (following American terminology) as the 'Care Attendant Agency'. Experienced personal assistants (PAs) visited members' homes on a short-term or live-in basis. Subsequently, the SIA started training programmes for PAs and these have considerably influenced how 'care' agencies work with people with spinal cord injuries (Bristow, 1981). Nonetheless, funding cuts forced this scheme to close in 2001. Other projects included a financial support service for families visiting disabled relatives in hospital, a legal claims service, a telephone counselling service, an independent living advocacy, peer and community support services, and accessible holiday accommodation. In November 2003 the SIA had over 6,000 members and 26 paid employees – 10 of whom were disabled people including the Executive Director (SIA, 2004).

Disabled activists in Derbyshire played a pivotal role in the development of Britain's user-controlled services. An early example was the Grove Road integrated housing scheme in Sutton-in-Ashfield. This was conceived and developed by disabled people, with Ken and Maggie Davis taking a lead role, while they were still living in a residential home. Beginning in 1972, the initiative took four years to develop. It involved detailed and sometimes difficult negotiations with housing associations, the district council, the local authority social services department, architects and planners. They relocated into a small block of six flats. From the outside, the complex looked quite ordinary, but the three ground floor properties featured designs and adaptations now commonly associated with 'Lifetime Homes' or 'wheelchair-accessible' housing. Furthermore, the three first-floor flats were to be let to non-disabled families willing to provide appropriate support to their disabled neighbours (Davis, 1981).

The Grove Road scheme was a direct reaction to the dire experience of institutional living. It provided an opportunity for disabled and non-disabled people to live in the community in a housing complex specifically designed to promote 'inclusion'. It demonstrated that, over time, people with 'severe' physical impairments could live independently in a community-based setting, given the right kind and level of support (Davis, 1981). Indeed, the first set of disabled residents subsequently decided to transfer into their own homes in order to achieve even greater choice and control in their lives.

Another milestone in building independent living support arose from the activities of a group of disabled people living in the Le Court Residential Cheshire Home at Liss in Hampshire. To draw attention to the designation of 1981 as the United Nations' International Year of Disabled People, they set up 'Project 81: Consumer Directed Housing and Care' in 1979. After three years of intensive discussions with their county council, and support from key managers, an innovative arrangement of 'indirect payments' was agreed. It allowed local authority funding of an individual's institutional 'care', subject to an assessment, with individual cash payments in lieu of the institutional services received. The money was paid into a trust fund (with a local authority or voluntary organisation) on behalf of the user and was used for personal assistance to enable the disabled person to live in the community (Evans, 1993). Disabled people's campaign for the legalisation of direct payments gathered momentum through the 1980s, supported by research commissioned by the BCODP and Help the Aged, and the establishment of the Direct Payments Technical Advisory Group (Zarb and Nadash, 1994; Barnes, 1997; Glasby and Littlechild, 2002).

The 'Project 81' group was also responsible for setting up the Hampshire Centre for Independent Living in 1985. It was a user-led organisation committed to the principle that services should be available to disabled people, regardless of their impairment and social and cultural background. User control was regarded as crucial to developing disabled people's individual and collective expertise in promoting independent living.

In 1976, disabled activists in Derbyshire set up the first local Disablement Information and Advice Line (DIAL) run and controlled by disabled people. DIAL Derbyshire was significant because it was designed for disabled people as a whole, not a specific impairment group, as with the SIA information service. It was rooted in the experiences and accumulated knowledge of being a disabled person. Although access to information was acknowledged as important in the 1948 National Assistance Act, it was not until 1970 that the Chronically Sick and Disabled Persons Act required local authorities to publicise their services to potential users. However, subsequent surveys revealed the continuing paucity of information assistance, particularly for those living in rural areas (Barnes, 1995; Moore, 1995).

DIAL Derbyshire began as a telephone advice service by disabled residents of Cressy Fields, a residential home and day centre. It received a small grant from Derbyshire County Council. It was operated by volunteers from a converted cloakroom, but exerted a much wider influence on the Disabled People's Movement (Davis and Mullender, 1993). Similar services were soon established in Manchester, London and other parts of the UK. By 1978 a steering committee had been formed from representatives of local DIAL groups to form a National Association of Disablement Information and Advice Services, now known as DIAL UK. By 1980 DIAL Derbyshire had dealt with over 5,000 queries.

> DIAL Derbyshire had become a base, a focal point of disability activity, and it took the gradual process of disabled people 'coming together', which had been developing for over twenty years, an important stage further. (Davis and Mullender, 1993, p 8)

The network of local information and advice services continued to mushroom so that there were almost 130 local DIALs in 2001, although DIAL UK was subsequently taken over by non-disabled professionals (Oliver and Barnes, 1998).

The growth of local action led to the formation of the DCODP in 1981. Four years later, the Derbyshire Centre for Integrated Living (DCIL) was established, and secured the development of the 'seven needs for independent living':

- information (know what options exist);
- counselling and peer support (for encouragement and guidance by other disabled people);

- housing (appropriate place to live);
- technical aids and equipment (to generate more self-reliance);
- personal assistance (controlled by the disabled person/employer);
- transport (mobility options);
- access (to the built environment) (Davis, 1990, p 7, adapted).

These 'seven needs' provided an 'operational framework' for DCIL, by which the social model of disability could be implemented in everyday practice. This stage-like scheme drew on the collective experience of the Disabled People's Movement and the struggles to achieve an independent lifestyle in the community outside the confines of a residential institution or dependence on family and friends.

Once meaningful progress had been made towards satisfying these support needs, other 'secondary' needs would arise before the disabled person could begin to achieve a full participation in the wider society. Following this line of action, in 1989, Hampshire Coalition of Disabled People added four more areas – employment, education and training, income and benefits, and advocacy – to extend the list to 'Eleven Basic Needs'.

CILs in Britain also developed links with their counterparts in other European countries, notably Sweden and Germany. These have their origins in the first International Conference on Independent Living in Europe that took place in Munich in 1982. It brought together European and North American disability activists and provided a valuable exchange of information and expertise. The first national conference in Britain on independent living was held in 1987.

Wider European interest led to disabled people forming the European Network on Independent Living (ENIL) at Strasbourg in 1989. Access to personal assistance (with a choice of different models for delivering adequately funded personal assistance on a 24 hours and seven days a week basis was proclaimed a human and civil right. Moreover, it was argued that funding should be provided to allow training for the 'user' and the 'personal assistant', and 'must include assistants' competitive wages and employment benefits, and all legal and union required benefits, plus the administrative costs' (ENIL, 1989).

Review

The development of the Disabled People's Movement constituted a major challenge to conventional politics, with its politicisation of disability and emphasis on disabled people's citizenship rights. In Britain, the influence of a novel, socio-political (model) analysis of disability and the social and environmental barriers to social inclusion was crucial. It underscored a radical critique of traditional social 'care' and welfare services.

Hitherto, professionally led health and social support systems had failed to deliver the services necessary to support independent living. Mainstream social 'care' services, whether in the statutory or voluntary sectors, were criticised for perpetuating the dependence of disabled people and for their domination by service providers and a traditional approach to 'disability'. Nevertheless, in several important respects, the shifting political context offered new opportunities for the promotion of 'independent living' and user involvement in service organisation and delivery. In the case of user-controlled organisations, an impressive range of initiatives at the local level was weakened by relatively slow progress in the country as a whole. Furthermore, it is important to note that user-led services are not by themselves going to bring about the overall aim of overturning the whole range of barriers to living ordinary lives in the community.

In summary, the readiness of governments to address disability issues and the incorporation into the mainstream of local organisations providing services for disabled people have opened up new possibilities but also raised unanticipated political dilemmas for the Disabled People's Movement. These possibilities and concerns will be explored in more detail in later chapters, but the immediate task is to examine ways of doing disability research and the specific research strategy and design for our own study of user-led organisations in Britain.

FOUR

Researching user-led organisations

Introduction

In the last quarter of the 20th century, the critique of established ways of theorising disability was extended to mainstream social research. The starting point was the refocusing of analyses of disability on the ways in which social barriers rather than individual limitations contributed to the exclusion of disabled people from everyday life. In turn, this socio-political approach stimulated the adoption of a research paradigm that similarly challenged the social oppression of disabled people.

This chapter begins with a review of disability theorists' criticism of traditional ways of researching disability, particularly its theoretical standpoint and the disempowering role of 'research experts'. Second, we explore the key features of an alternative approach to doing disability research in line with a social model framework: what has been termed 'emancipatory disability research' (Oliver, 1992). This stresses its commitment to the central outcomes of the empowerment of disabled people and political change, while also informing the process of conducting research. However, as explored in the third section, the emphasis on political partiality has often deflected attention away from important debates about the choice of methodology and methods and their implementation when undertaking disability research. The final section describes the *Creating Independent Futures* project on user-controlled organisations. It covers the overall research strategy and design, including the main data sources, sampling, data collection and dissemination techniques.

Taking issue with 'conventional' disability research

In the early 1960s, a group of disabled residents at the Le Court Cheshire Home in Hampshire asked academic researchers at the Tavistock Institute to investigate their living conditions – apparently stimulated by the anticipated benefits of applying social psychological insights to residential living (Miller and Gwynne, 1972, chapter 2). Little did the residents realise how severely their hopes would be dashed.

The trigger for their invitation was a dispute with management that had continued since the late 1950s over residents' attempts to counter the disempowering effects of institutional living and exercise more control over their lives, such as choosing their own bedtimes and television viewing, whether they should be allowed to drink alcohol, or have open relations between the sexes. While the residents sought to confirm a more liberal regime that involved them in the running of Le Court, this was confounded by changes in senior staff such as the Matron and Secretary (Mason, 1990). Conversely, some staff and members of the management committee welcomed the restoration of discipline into the running of the home and a downgrading of regular consultation with the residents. The researchers were fascinated by the research issues raised in this clash of perspectives on residential life.

It was not until 1966 that the researchers obtained funding from the Ministry of Health to conduct a pilot study. This envisaged an intensive investigation of attitudes and behaviour in five different residential institutions, with an action research component to follow through the implementation of changes as if 'real-life laboratories' (Miller and Gwynne, 1972, p 22). Le Court was placed at the centre of this phase, although the research was affected by periodic 'crises' with changes in senior staff and continuing concerns about consultation over how the home was run. The fieldwork at Le Court was completed at the end of 1967.

One of the residents, Paul Hunt (1981), bitterly condemned the researchers – Eric Miller and Geraldine Gwynne – describing them as 'parasite people'. For their part, they stressed that their role as researchers was to maintain a 'balanced outlook' and to avoid being 'captured by a permanent bias' and taking sides in the conflicts between residents and management (Miller and Gwynne, 1972, p 8). The residents concluded that the researchers had sided with their oppressors and were simply looking after their own professional and career interests. They described the researchers' primary aim as to make repressive institutions 'work a little better' (Hunt, 1981, p 40). In short, the 'research experts' could not see beyond a medical approach to disability in which:

> the root cause of the whole problem is in our defective bodies
> and not in the social death sentence unnecessarily passed on us.
> (Hunt, 1981, p 41)

This trenchant attack on academic research consultants for reinforcing existing prejudices and discrimination against disabled people became a central reference point for later writers exploring a new direction for disability research. Mike Oliver, in particular, expanded on this theme in specifying the following stark choice:

> do researchers wish to join with disabled people and use their expertise and skills in their struggles against oppression or do they wish to continue to use these skills and expertise in ways in which disabled people find oppressive? (Oliver, 1992, p 102)

More generally, recent research on 'disability' may be divided into two main areas. First, large-scale national surveys, conducted by the Office for Population Censuses and Surveys (OPCS) (Harris et al, 1971; Martin et al, 1988), and as part of a study of poverty in the UK (Townsend, 1979), have documented the prevalence of 'disability' within the general population and the difficulties associated with impairment in key areas of daily living. These studies were designed to inform discussions around possible policy changes, particularly in the social security system and 'social care' services so as to reduce the number of people living in poverty. Second, there has been a considerable amount of small-scale, mostly academic research into 'chronic illness and disability' by sociologists and psychologists. These concentrated on how individuals experience and 'cope' with their illness or impairment or its symptoms/functional limitations (Bury, 1997; Barnes et al, 1999). In general, both approaches to disability research have largely downplayed or ignored the impact of 'disabling' social barriers. There are exceptions: for example, Peter Townsend (1979) and Mildred Blaxter (1976) both highlighted the wholly inadequate service support for disabled people.

Most of these studies affirmed their attachment to 'scientific' ideals of 'objectivity' and 'neutrality'. In contrast, disability writers took their standpoint from critical social theory (Oliver, 1992; Rioux and Bach, 1994). In the most widely cited contribution in Britain to establishing the credentials of an emancipatory paradigm for doing disability research, Mike Oliver (1992) locates it firmly within critical theory. This included anti-imperialist/racist and feminist attacks on positivist and, to a lesser degree, interpretive research on the grounds that these had failed to challenge the status quo.

Doing disability research from an emancipatory standpoint entails adoption of a social model perspective on disability as a form of social oppression. It presumes that researchers are openly committed to advancing disabled people's political struggles, by seeking to 'give voice' to their experience and acting generally to overturn disabling barriers in society. The early emphasis was on 'conscious partiality' (Mies, 1983, p 22) by the researcher, and granting epistemological privilege to a specific social group. This praxis orientation required the researcher to become a close participant in the political struggles and to function as a catalyst for exploring the interplay of theory, practice and action (Touraine, 1981).

The value–neutral approach has been dismissed as 'politically naïve and methodologically problematic' (Back and Solomos, 1993, p 182). This view accords with our assumption that disability research should strive to produce a radical critique of the disabling society. This invites criticism that politically committed researchers reveal or confirm little other than their existing perception of social reality, and that they exclude from the outset the potential significance of other perspectives, actions and beliefs (Silverman, 1998). In response, disability researchers have acknowledged the significance of stating clearly their ontological (the character of social reality) and epistemological (how the social world is known) positions and ensuring that the choice of research methodology and data collection strategies are rigorous and open to scrutiny.

The starting point for our research project was an open commitment to confronting and seeking ways to transform the structures and processes that oppress and exclude disabled people from the mainstream of society. We did not presume that 'objective partisanship' (Gouldner, 1965, 1971) was without its difficulties or contradictions, but tried to address such issues, such as examining potentially counterfactual data or explanations.

Disability research from a social model perspective

The foundation of emancipatory disability research is the adoption of a social model approach. Hence, it concentrates on the social and environmental barriers to the inclusion of people with an accredited impairment in mainstream society and gives centrality to disabled people's own experiences and knowledge (Oliver, 1990).

However, the social model has been criticised for downplaying differences in the experience of oppression within the disabled population. Initially, a 'standpoint' position prevailed in which disabled people's experiences and knowledge claims were generalised across all groups but the research spotlight has shifted to explore differences in the experience of oppression, particularly on the basis of age, gender and 'race'. This has undermined the notion of a homogeneous category of 'privileged' knowers and turned the spotlight on competing discourses, voices and experiences within the disabled population (Corker, 1999). Additionally, the presumed commonality in experience and knowledge claims have been challenged by specific groups such as Deaf people, people with 'learning difficulties' and 'mental health' system users/survivors (Beresford and Wallcraft, 1997). (In this and subsequent chapters, capitalising 'Deaf' refers to those people with a 'severe' hearing impairment who self-define as a distinct linguistic and cultural group.)

Again, the structuralist leanings of early social model accounts triggered criticism that disability research should widen its ontological gaze from 'public' barriers to incorporate the feminist maxim that the 'personal is political' and thus incorporate the experience of both impairment and disability (Morris, 1992). However, any discussion of disabled people's experiences remains contentious where it does not concentrate on a critical analysis of the 'inner workings of the disabling society' (Finkelstein, 1999a, p 861), and threatens to be entrapped in limited or restrictive service provider agendas.

Research gains

Disability researchers have argued that their goal is to expose disabling barriers as part of the wider politicisation and empowerment of disabled people (Finkelstein, 1999a), and the achievement of tangible 'gain' (Oliver, 1997). This elevates political outcomes to centre-stage in judging disability research. Indeed, Oliver specifically downgrades his own study entitled *Walking into Darkness* (Oliver et al, 1988) precisely because of its lack of a definite impact on service provision. However, the reasons why local and national policy makers accept research findings and recommendations are diverse and rarely within the control of the researchers (Maynard, 1994). In practice, research may 'succeed' or 'fail' at different levels, or have an unintended impact, with any judgement liable to variation over time, or well after the research project has been completed.

Alternative criteria for judging emancipatory research include whether it facilitated the self-empowerment of disabled people in terms of 'individual self-assertion, upward mobility and the psychological experience of feeling powerful' (Lather, 1991, p 3). Here, empowerment and emancipation are used interchangeably and defined in terms of revealing social barriers, changing perceptions of disability, and generating political action. Conversely, the disability literature is replete with apologetic 'confessions' that researchers have been the chief beneficiaries of their work – what Finkelstein (1999a, p 863) has aptly labelled 'Oliver's gibe'.

Further difficulties often arise when attempting to construct a research 'balance sheet'. Even among researchers pursuing a social barriers approach, the definition of oppressor and oppressed and their respective gains are not always easily agreed. Thus, it is not necessarily a zero-sum contest with one 'winner' and 'loser', while among the winners/losers some gain/lose more than others. Again, oppressors and oppressed are not always easily distinguished or stable categories across different social contexts, and the former may include some disabled people in selected contexts.

Accountability

A further goal of disability research is that it should be accountable to disabled people (Barnes, 2003). The preferred alternative has been to ensure that control is vested in a small group led by representatives of disabled people's organisations. Thus, the emancipatory credentials of the British Council of Disabled People (BCODP) anti-discrimination project rested on its design within a social model approach and accountability to disabled people through an advisory group in which disabled people and members of organisations controlled by disabled people were in the majority. This group met every two months to review progress. The first five months were spent discussing the aims and objectives of the research with key figures in Britain's Disabled People's Movement, while data analysis and drafts of chapters were circulated to the advisory group and representatives of disabled people's organisations. Comments and recommendations for amendments were discussed at advisory group meetings (Barnes, 1991, pp xi–xix).

A further aspect to accountability is the wide-ranging dissemination of the research products in a variety of accessible formats to stimulate campaigns and legislative action. The BCODP project produced various articles in journals, magazines and the popular press and an eight-page summary leaflet – produced in Braille and on tape for people with visual impairments. In this way the research had an opportunity to contribute to the further politicisation of disabled people.

Social and material relations of research production

Disability researchers stress the significance of transforming the social relations between researcher and research participants, and the material relations of research production such as the reliance on external funding bodies (Oliver, 1992, 1997; Zarb, 1992; Lloyd et al, 1996). Often, the expectations and constraints from funders reinforce traditional research hierarchies and values (Moore et al, 1998).

The emancipatory potential of disability research is equated with disabled people being 'actively involved in determining the aims, methods and uses of the research' (Zarb, 1997, p 52). This requires that researchers forgo their traditional claims to autonomy. However, some disability writers express alarm that there are signs of a new breed of disability research 'expert' who adopts an approach similar to that of other 'disabling' professionals (Finkelstein, 1999a). The aspiration to break down the traditional hierarchy and build researcher accountability to disabled participants raises a number of key questions about the nature of control and how it is implemented:

(i)   Who controls what the research will be about and how it will be carried out?
(ii) How far have we come in involving disabled people in the research process?
(iii) What opportunities exist for disabled people to criticise the research and influence future directions?
(iv) What happens to the products of the research? (Zarb, 1992, p 128)

A continuum spanning 'weak' to 'strong' direction by disabled people may be identified. In practice, instances of disabled participants assuming full control are rare, but this has been claimed in some research studies involving groups of 'mental health' survivors (Chamberlain, 1988). An important example is the Strategies for Living project, a user-led programme of work supported by the Mental Health Foundation, which carried out six local user-led research projects between 1998 and 2000. The primary concern of many of these projects 'is on alternative and self-help approaches to mental health', a focus that developed out of extensive nationwide consultation with user groups and was complemented by a UK-wide Strategies for Living study in which 71 people with 'mental health problems' were interviewed about their strategies for dealing with the experience of emotional distress. Each of the six project reports demonstrates an innovative example of 'mental health' research that is articulated, designed and carried out by people with personal experience of mental or emotional distress.

> The projects distributed around England and Wales were supported through small grants (for costs), training in research skills and ongoing support to the researchers during the main period of the research. The combination of topics and research approaches has been highly innovative and had the advantage of being independent of existing statutory mental health services and thus the particular agenda attached to those services. (Nicholls, 2001, p 3)

Examples of the projects undertaken include 'An Investigation into Auricular Acupuncture' by Carol Miller (2001) and 'Research Project into User Groups and Empowerment' by Sharon Matthew (2001).

Another notable example is the work conducted by Shaping Our Lives, a national research and development project run by service users, including disabled people, older people, people with 'learning difficulties' and users and survivors of 'mental health' systems and support services. Formed in 1996, Shaping Our Lives has conducted extensive user-led research on service users' experiences of 'social care' services (for example, Turner, 2003).

In other cases, there has been an emphasis on 'co-researchers and co-subjects' (Reason, 1988, p 1, 1994). This indicates a reflective dialogue with neither side dominating the other (Lloyd et al, 1996). Some believe that participatory options are the most realistic aspiration in the present political and economic context (Ward, 1997; Zarb, 1997) although a few are adamant that these offer something less than full control by disabled people (Oliver, 1992).

In practice, not all research participants have the time or inclination, even if politically aware, to take control of research production. Swain's experience illustrates a more general experience whereby disabled participants tend to defer to the 'research experts', particularly in areas perceived as technical matters, such as devising research questions, collecting and analysing data, and even disseminating research. Instead of seeking a reversal of the social relations of research production, disabled participants sought to build a 'working partnership' that would generate 'mutually beneficial outcomes' (Swain, 1995, pp 104–5). Even a prior understanding of the politics of disability and disability research does not necessarily make for an effective research group (Ellis, 2000).

Nonetheless, participatory research has been given a major boost by the active support of the Joseph Rowntree Foundation, which has been a long-term major supporter of social and disability research (for example, Morris, 1993a; Zarb and Nadash, 1994). More recently, the National Lottery's Community Fund has also emphasised user participation in its research, while a similar focus has been developed in NHS-funded research programmes.

Even so, what happens when disabled people insist on individualistic accounts of 'disability' or undesired policy recommendations (Barnes and Mercer, 1997a, 1997b)? Again, the structural constraints and inequalities between researcher and researched are not easily eliminated, particularly if the researchers are not used to having their authority challenged (Lloyd et al, 1996; Moore et al, 1998). Furthermore, disability researchers have been reticent to acknowledge power relations and hierarchies within research teams, mostly by assuming that a consensus position is inevitable.

While the use of Braille, large print and cassettes for people with sensory impairments has become more widespread, equivalent support for those with 'cognitive' impairments has been far less widely recognised (Ward, 1997; Goodley and Moore, 2000). This has been raised extensively in studies undertaken with people with 'learning difficulties', where some of the most imaginative attempts to develop collaborative approaches have been implemented. Research has moved a considerable distance since the early 1990s towards recognising their reliability as informants who are the 'best authority on their own lives, experiences, feelings and views' (Stalker, 1998, p 5). This has generated a number of innovative methodological approaches, often adopting 'advocacy' models, with people with learning difficulties acting as research advisers through to conducting their own research with researcher support (People First, 1994; Cocks and Cockham, 1995; Sample, 1996; March et al, 1997; Ward, 1997; Rodgers, 1999; Chappell, 2000; Walmsley and Johnson, 2003; Williams et al, 2005).

Methodology and methods

In this discussion, 'methodology' refers to a theory of how research should be conducted (Harding, 1987), while 'methods' comprise the specific techniques for data collection, such as surveys or participant observation, and analysis. Early disability research writings tended to conflate methodology and methods or regard methods as a subsidiary, technical area. The contrary argument pursued here is that methodology and methods are both crucial to doing disability research.

Instead of universal criteria for evaluating all empirical studies, standards tend to diverge across 'quantifying' and qualitative approaches. In the positivist, or quantifying tradition, the emphasis is on:

> internal validity (isomorphism of findings with reality), external validity (generalisability), reliability (in the sense of stability), and objectivity (distanced and neutral observer) ... (while those within the interpretive paradigm stress) ... the trustworthiness criteria of credibility (paralleling internal validity), transferability (paralleling external validity), dependability (paralleling reliability), and confirmability (paralleling objectivity). (Guba and Lincoln, 1994, p 114)

More recently, this debate has been supplemented by issues around achieving 'authenticity' raised in post-structuralist accounts (Lincoln and Guba 2000).

The broad intention is to make transparent how the research unfolds, from design through data collection, analysis and recommendations. Yet, the application of formal tests of 'quality control' promoted by mainstream research has often disregarded the specific circumstances of conducting disability research from a social model perspective, including perhaps disabled researchers and working with disabled participants (Sample, 1996; Stalker, 1998).

For the most part, social model research has concentrated on participant validation. This may mean disabled people identifying research questions, collecting data, and analysing and disseminating findings. In practice, taking fieldwork data back to respondents for verification of what they said is widely regarded as a key marker, whereas collectivising the process of data collection and analysis is much rarer. Achieving meaningful participation requires additional time and resources. Only two of the 30 key activists who provided in-depth interviews for Campbell and Oliver's (1996) study of disability politics took up the offer to 'validate' interview transcripts or read the draft manuscript. Oliver candidly admits that 'we neither had the time, energy or money to make it a wholly collective production' (Oliver, 1997, p 19).

Another benchmark used by some feminist researchers has been the claim that the validity of their data stems from the quality of their relationship with participants. Friendliness, openness, and general close rapport with participants have acquired a confirmatory status. Yet such declarations are imprecise indicators of 'quality assurance'. There are also ethical issues in exploiting an individual's willingness to reveal 'private' thoughts or relationships in order to enhance the 'quality' of the research data (Shaw, 1999). This suggests the importance of a much greater sensitivity to how researchers (whether disabled or not) directly and indirectly influence the research process (Davis, 2000).

Some qualitative researchers have stressed the importance of choosing a disabled person as interviewer (Vernon, 1997), but few develop this claim to indicate how far any matching process should be extended to cover, for example, age, gender, social class and type of impairment:

> Having an impairment does not automatically give someone an affinity with disabled people, nor an inclination to do disability research. The cultural gulf between researchers and researched has as much to do with social indicators like class, education, employment and general life experiences as with impairments. (Barnes, 1992, pp 121-2)

Notwithstanding such arguments, there are significant barriers to overcome in undertaking the role of a disabled researcher (Oliver and Barnes, 1997; Zarb, 1997). The organisation of the research must be able to accommodate individual support needs, although this is not easy when research trips are dependent on use of an inaccessible built environment and transport system. The uncertain trajectory of some impairments adds a further challenge to project management. Grant funding bodies are not as sensitive as they should be to such constraints in allocating more time and resources for disability research.

There have been few attempts to involve research participants, beyond a small advisory committee, in collectivising the processing and analysis of data. The exceptions are mainly restricted to small-scale, interview-based studies, with initial conclusions taken back to participants for comment. Even then it is not always made clear why a 'second opinion' is accepted, or whether participants are allowed to change 'errors of fact' but not of 'understanding'. More generally, disciplinary and theoretical perspectives may divide participants and researchers by influencing what the researcher 'hears' and how it is interpreted. This leads to difficult decisions about whether or how far researchers are entitled to 're-author' lay accounts to indicate what they 'really meant' when reporting their views and experiences (Shakespeare et al, 1996; Corker, 1999).

Initially, exponents of emancipatory disability research expressed uncertainty about the relative merits of quantitative and qualitative research methods (Oliver, 1997). The widely-cited BCODP study of discrimination (Barnes, 1991) and of direct payments (Zarb and Nadash, 1994) drew heavily on data generated by the quantifying approach. Subsequently, most disability research projects have had small-scale, qualitative designs, emulating the general trend in social research. This is justified on the grounds that quantitative methods are inherently exploitative of research participants, relying, as with the OPCS surveys, on postal questionnaires and structured interviews that for critics reinforce the division between research 'expert' and lay disabled respondent (Oliver, 1990; Abberley, 1992). In comparison, the qualitative emphasis on inter-subjectivity and non-hierarchical relationships is often uncritically embraced, as if it guarantees hearing the 'authentic' voice of participants.

Disability researchers have also ignored the growing claims within feminism that experiential studies have done much less than quantitative studies to document women's social oppression (Oakley, 2000). Certainly, the 'qualitative turn' has discouraged researchers from devising 'participant-centred' structured interviews and surveys that might be used to facilitate resistance to disabling barriers and attitudes (Kelly et al, 1994; Maynard, 1994). It is also very noticeable that a host of specific methodological issues such as sampling, data processing and constructing concepts and explanations have been disregarded by disability researchers. Even a sympathetic review of disability research in the mid-1990s concluded that:

> none of the advocates of the paradigm have yet laid claim to the achievement of truly emancipatory research *within the context of a field study*. (Stone and Priestley, 1996, p 706, emphasis in original)

There has been a particular silence within the disability research literature on methodological issues, including the appropriateness and merits of specific methods of data collection, processing and analysis (Mercer, 2002). The next section attempts to redress that balance by examining the research project at the heart of this book.

The *Creating Independent Futures* study

The project at the heart of this volume was initiated by the BCODP Research Committee in 1998 and developed in conjunction with the National Centre for Independent Living (NCIL). Its central aim was to assess the development of Centres for Independent/Integrated/Inclusive Living (CILs) and similar user-directed service organisations (see Chapter One).

The research project was overseen by an Advisory Group. It comprised the (then) co-directors of NCIL Jane Campbell and Frances Hasler, John Evans, a representative of the BCODP Independent Living Committee, Peter Beresford, a university researcher active in the 'mental health' system survivors' movement, plus the research project coordinators from the Disability Research Unit at the University of Leeds – Colin Barnes and Geof Mercer – together with the full-time research officer appointed for the study, Hannah Morgan.

The project was funded for two years from January 2000 and comprised four stages: (1) establishing research themes and questions; undertaking a postal survey of user-controlled organisations; (2) visits to nine case study organisations, including interviews with a range of staff; (3) in-depth interviews with service users of the case study organisations and analysis of the data collected; (4) return visits to case study sites to present and explore findings; and dissemination of the overall 'findings and recommendations' in an end-of-project national conference.

In addition, for a further 18 months from January 2003 through to June 2004, the authors monitored key issues and developments in user-led organisations, as well as maintaining contact with and collecting relevant data from the case study organisations.

Stage One

First, a literature review was undertaken covering a variety of sources, including published material, newsletters from disabled people's organisations, and internet documents, in order to identify research issues and information sources.

Second, four seminars were held – in London, Birmingham, Glasgow and Newcastle – during March and April 2000 with representatives from user-led organisations in the UK. CILs and user-led groups were identified using the NCIL *Personal Assistance Support Schemes Directory* (1999) and

BCODP membership data. This produced a list of 75 organisations. Each was contacted and invited to participate in one of the regional seminars, with 48 organisations sending representatives.

Each seminar comprised a brief presentation of the research aims followed by small-group discussions of the main issues facing user-controlled initiatives, including what participants thought differentiated these from other forms of service provision. Discussion summaries were circulated to all participants for comment. These were reviewed by the Advisory Group, which identified four broad research themes: (1) the role of the social model; (2) control and accountability structures and processes; (3) finance and employment issues and policies; and (4) the character and extent of service provision.

The information gathered from the literature review and seminars was used to form the basis for a postal questionnaire. This was designed by the Leeds research team and sent to all user-led organisations. It covered the following topics:

- organisational structure;
- wider organisational links and networks;
- resources;
- activities and services;
- campaigning; and
- longer-term ambitions.

The questionnaire comprised both closed (fixed response) items (with tick boxes) and open-ended questions for more detailed responses. Accessible questionnaires were available in a variety of formats – large print, Braille, disk and e-mail.

By this time, 85 user-led organisations had been identified and these were contacted by telephone to discuss the aims of the project and seek their involvement. In total, 69 organisations returned a completed questionnaire – a response rate of 82%.

Stage Two

The Advisory Group selected nine 'case studies' for a more in-depth study from those organisations completing the postal questionnaire. The choice was based on three main criteria: length of time in operation; size of the organisation; and geographical location. Stage One discussions suggested that it was important to examine both established and more recent organisations because these might demonstrate a different profile of activities, and perhaps philosophy of independent living. Similarly, service activity was expected to vary according to the number of users and staff employed. Finally, research participants confirmed the importance of exploring the influence of national location and contexts – between England, Scotland and Wales – as well as between urban and rural locations.

The final list of nine organisations included: Cardiff and Vale Coalition of Disabled People (CVCDP), CIL de Gwynedd (CILdG), the Centre for Independent (now changed to 'Inclusive') Living in Glasgow (CILiG), Derbyshire Coalition for Inclusive Living (DCIL), Disability Action North East (DANE), Greenwich Association of Disabled People's Centre for Independent Living (GAD), Lothian Centre for Independent (now changed to 'Integrated') Living (LCIL), the Surrey Users Network (SUN), and the West of England Centre for Inclusive Living (WECIL). These represent contrasting 'types' of user-controlled organisations (see Chapter Five for a description of their origins).

Interviews

Data collection in the case study sites consisted of a range of documentary evidence, such as constitutions and mission statements, and minutes of Annual General Meetings (AGMs), together with semi-structured interviews with individuals involved at different 'levels' in the development and delivery of services. This resulted in 32 individual and 10 group interviews with individuals who normally work together. The interviewees comprised 30 women and 26 men. They included those with experience as members of the controlling body, managers, clerical and reception staff, voluntary workers, and representatives of key funding bodies.

The interview schedules were based around the key themes identified in Stages One and Two, and highlighted each organisation's responses to the postal questionnaire. The 42 individual and group interviews lasted between one hour and two-and-a-half hours. These were all recorded on tape and transcribed in full. The transcriptions were then returned to the interviewees for verification and any other comments. Given the focus on encouraging participants to 'tell their own story', these qualitative data were processed and analysed using a 'constant comparison' approach (Glaser and Strauss, 1967). The identification of categories entailed analysis between and within participants' accounts. Two of the researchers examined these data in order to identify key themes and their presence and consistency across participants and research sites (Silverman, 2001).

Stage Three

This entailed further visits to the nine case study organisations in the early months of 2001 to explore the users' experiences of services. Specific issues included the perceived difference between mainstream and user-led services, and views about political campaigning. Did users share the same priorities as the officers of the case study organisations?

Interviews

The selection of users from the case study organisations did not form a representative sample. As membership and user lists are confidential, the choice of interviewees was determined by each organisation. In some, a request for volunteers was placed in the local newsletter, while others sent letters directly to everyone involved in the organisation. Some also approached individual users either to supplement the number of participants or to seek a broader picture of their user group – particularly individuals from social groups under-represented in user-led organisations, such as people with 'learning difficulties', 'mental health' system users/survivors and individuals from minority ethnic groups. Overall, 85 interviews were completed, of which 76 were with individuals and the rest in small groups.

One of the case studies – DANE – stands apart because it is solely an information provider to other disability and related organisations. In consultation with the group's administrator, it was decided to target recipient organisations. Seven agreed to complete a postal questionnaire, and a telephone interview was arranged with two organisations. These nine interviews produced an overall total of 85 interviews in Stage Three.

In most instances, the recruitment of individuals for interview was relatively 'painless' but 'research fatigue' proved hard to overcome in one organisation. It had recently been the subject of an in-depth evaluation of its direct payments scheme, and despite careful lobbying, only four individuals agreed to be interviewed against a target of 10.

Respondents chose their preferred method of interview, whether individually, in pairs or as part of a focus group. Individual participants had the option of face-to-face, telephone or e-mail interviews. Sign language interpreters and personal assistance support were provided if requested.

Most people (26) chose the face-to-face interview option, while 12 interviews were conducted by telephone or e-mail. Thirty-six people participated in focus groups. Given the spread of impairments across participants, attempts were made to match the interview style to the needs of the individuals involved (Barnes and Mercer, 1997b; Williams et al, 2005). Again, all interviews were tape recorded and the transcription returned to participants for comments. Data were processed and analysed in a similar fashion to that described earlier for Stage Two interviews. Participants were offered a nominal fee plus reimbursement of necessary expenses. Several declined this offer or suggested that the money be donated to the host organisation.

Interviewees were asked to complete a number of basic biographical questions relating to gender, age, impairment, living circumstances and ethnicity in order to establish a profile of the interviewees. The final sample comprised a slight majority of females (53%). Almost half of the sample fell into the middle age range of 35-54 years, with only four people (5.3%) aged 18-24 years, and five people over 65 years of age. Thirty-six participants (46%) lived with their partner, family or friends and 33 (47%) lived alone, with the remaining six (7%) living in residential homes.

Individuals were asked to describe their impairment(s) based on four criteria – physical, sensory, 'learning difficulties', and 'mental health' system users/survivors. A clear majority, 65, described themselves as having a physical impairment. Eight people reported emotional distress and/or were 'mental health' system users, and a similar number indicated they had 'learning difficulties' and another eight sensory impairments. Eleven of the total reported more than one impairment. A further item asked interviewees to record their ethnic identity, in their own words. The overwhelming majority (93.3%) described themselves as one of the following: English (48%), Scottish (24%), British (10.7%), Welsh (9.3%) and Irish (1.3%). The remainder (6.7%) identified as African Caribbean, White European or Jewish – confirmation of the very low involvement of disabled people from Asian and African Caribbean groups.

Stage Four

This final stage of the project brought the data collection, analysis and dissemination processes together. This comprised visits by the three members of the Leeds research team to each of the case study organisations that took part in the Stages Two and Three in order to present them with preliminary research findings. Everyone involved at each site was invited to attend and discuss, make suggestions and generally comment on the study and whether it reflected their views and experiences.

At the end of each stage, the activities and 'findings' were put together as a report that was then circulated to all participating organisations. In order to promote accessibility to the research, all four of the reports were placed on the project website – as they were produced at roughly six-monthly intervals (Barnes et al, 2000, 2001, 2002; Morgan et al, 2001).

The final aspect in the dissemination of the project was to hold a national conference in Manchester in December 2001 to present the overall findings and generate comments and discussion from participants. Attendance at this event was free to participants, while the proceedings were circulated as an end-of-project report free to all participating organisations (Barnes et al, 2002).

Review

This chapter builds on arguments that research is both a means to an end and an end in itself – that is, it should involve users as well as seeking to advance disabled people's inclusion more widely in society. The emphasis is on a meaningful dialogue between researchers and research participants. Emancipatory disability research is not a unitary project or group of projects, but rather an ongoing process determined by disabled people and their organisations. Equally, the disabling world of social barriers will not readily succumb to individual emancipatory projects, but such unashamedly partisan research has an important part to play in challenging disability. Furthermore, because it has no agreed set of epistemological and methodological guidelines and standards, disability research should be similarly transparent in its research design and methods.

Much has changed since the early 1990s in the field of disability research. There can be little doubt that the social model of disability and the emancipatory research paradigm have had a demonstrable and significant impact on organisations and researchers currently engaged in doing disability research. A decisive space has been created within the research establishment for researchers to pursue an emancipatory agenda. This is not an easy option but nor is it an 'impossible dream' (Oliver, 1997). The argument presented here suggests that when directly linked to disabled people's ongoing struggle for change, doing emancipatory disability research can have a meaningful impact on their empowerment and the policies that affect their lives.

We now turn in Chapter Five to examine the fieldwork data collected as part of the *Creating Independent Futures* study.

FIVE

User-led organisations: building an alternative approach

Introduction

This chapter begins the review of the fieldwork data collected as part of the *Creating Independent Futures* project. First, we examine disabled activists' dissatisfaction with the ways in which successive governments promoted consumerism, via the marketisation of services, particularly the ideas and practices associated with user involvement and consultation. This is contrasted with the commitment of organisations of disabled people to a democratic or participatory approach. Second, we trace the diverse origins and growth of user-led organisations, looking in detail at nine case study sites. In the third section, we consider the adherence of user-led organisations to a social model of disability and how this is translated into the development and operation of user-controlled services. Finally, the discussion turns to the organisation, management structures and resources available to user-led services with reference to the key themes identified by research participants. These are: control, accountability, inclusion, and the tensions arising from organisational attempts to reconcile the principles of the social model of disability with the realities of operating within a service provider context that does little to recognise disabled people's experience of social exclusion.

Attention centres on the uneasy and sometimes fraught relationship between user-controlled organisations and traditional statutory and voluntary service agencies, and the dilemmas and compromises that arise when trying to implement a user-led philosophy and apply a social barriers approach to disability within a policy context still dominated by individualistic medical model thinking, and amidst other local and national political and economic constraints.

From user consultation to user-led services

It is important to stress, at the outset, an important distinction between the *consumerist* approach, sponsored by both Conservative and Labour governments since the 1990s, and that taken by the Disabled People's Movement, which adheres to a *democratic/participatory* approach. Each has a distinctive philosophy that underpins contrasting policy practices (Beresford and Croft, 1993; Wistow and Barnes, 1993).

The democratic approach emphasises that people have a right to participate, to be heard, to exercise choice, to define problems, and to decide on appropriate action. Increased service participation forms part of a wider citizenship project, increasing democratic participation and revitalising governance for disabled people and society generally (Beresford, 1993). The historical denial of any significant participation of disabled people in running voluntary organisations (Robson et al, 1977; Drake, 1994), as well as statutory services, has been sustained despite claims of a shift towards more user involvement by the mainstream sectors during the 1990s.

The official encouragement of user involvement in the health and 'social care/welfare' sector has concentrated on a consumerist approach. This does not usually include strategic policy-making and service planning, but 'street-level' service organisation and delivery. Users have been involved in planning or advisory meetings, management groups, monitoring and inspecting service provision. They are engaged as service users or as 'representatives' of specific (mostly impairment) categories, perhaps with a range of such groups involved. Consultation may take a number of forms – from surveys and workshops to focus groups.

Another area for involvement has been in the use of, or eligibility for, mainstream services. Social services have a statutory duty to assess whether an individual should be offered a service, as well as 'care planning' to identify service objectives and what precisely will be delivered and how, with subsequent reviews also undertaken. 'Care plans' may range across different support systems (services provided at home, day services, residential provision) and be directed at a range of objectives, such as enhancing independence, developing skills or providing protection. Traditionally, the degree of consultation and involvement has been minimal although it has been encouraged over recent years (Barnes and Wistow, 1994a, 1994b), most significantly with regard to the growth of direct payments. Across these various elements, the spotlight is on the user experience of involvement, as it:

> seeks either to improve service quality by enhancing responsiveness to expressed need or preference, or to enhance users' control over design, management, delivery and review. (Braye, 2000, p 11)

Disabled service users suggest that under the consumerist approach mainstream services have become more responsive but they remain largely under the control of service providers and professionals, with considerable reluctance to engage with a 'disabling barriers' approach to disability. Participation entails, at most, 'being involved in the running of welfare services they might prefer not to receive' (Beresford, 1993, p 18). As Barker and Peck (1987, p 1) vividly point out: 'survivors of the mental health system are no more consumers of services than cockroaches are consumers of Rentokil', and that their experience had not changed significantly a decade later (Peck and Barker, 1997). An additional, widely neglected area was the notion of 'appropriate' support services for people with the label of 'learning difficulties' (Brown and Smith, 1992; Chappell, 1992).

Many managers and professionals have been resistant to the idea that user involvement is a social and political right. As a result, marginalised groups generally and disabled people in particular have found it difficult to achieve meaningful participation in mainstream services (Bewley and Glendinning, 1994; Lovelock and Powell with Craggs, 1995; Bowl, 1996). The process of publicly expressing concerns is too readily equated with effective influence.

> Service users have become accustomed to being invited to participation that is tokenistic, where agendas, dominated by professional or agency jargon, are confined to existing services or predetermined decisions, in which their experience is denied or minimised, and their representativeness challenged, without training or recompense for their involvement. They have become used to influencing processes without influencing outcomes, to having their participation 'managed'. (Braye, 2000, p 23)

What then are the main barriers to disabled people's involvement in 'social care' services? To start with, organisational constraints range from too little time for meaningful discussion, low access to senior staff, the value of disabled people taking on the preparatory training of service users, and the need for clear guarantees of confidentiality and codes of practice on conducting business and monitoring outcomes. Concerns are also expressed that user representation is too closely regulated by managers (Fletcher, 1995; Ross, 1995; Bott and Rust, 1997). Devaluing assumptions about the capacity of some disabled groups to participate and the reluctance to accept self-advocacy have restricted user involvement to a much diminished form (Braye and Preston-Shoot, 1995). Furthermore, the policy process is often so complex and bureaucratic that non-participation is too easily rationalised.

The physical and cultural environment for organisational consultation can also replicate wider experiences of institutional discrimination (Barnes and Mercer, 2003). This can generate feelings of 'internal oppression' or 'psycho-emotional' barriers to participation (Thomas, 1999) because of lowered self-esteem and self-confidence in formal social activities and interaction. Yet, individual participation in service provision is a stage to achieving both wider social justice and personal empowerment (Thompson, 1997).

There is ample evidence of low awareness among managers and professionals of disabled people's support needs – such as wheelchair access, British Sign Language (BSL) interpreting, accessible documents, and the specific difficulties in reaching and retaining disabled minority ethnic group members (Turner et al, 2003). This has led to more recognition of the importance of appropriate training for service user involvement. Important aspects include: assertiveness/'speaking up' courses, guidance on decision-making structures, negotiating skills, legal issues and rights under current legislation. It takes time to change people's thinking and deeply embedded processes and structures. User involvement also generates conflicts around what counts as knowledge in social 'care': as is evident in the distinction between users' views of appropriate services and management demands for evidence-based good practice (Beresford, 2000; DH, 2000; Edwards, 2002).

A further factor in disabled people's criticism of existing consultation schemes is that many local authorities have been very reluctant to engage with organisations controlled by disabled people, certainly in contrast with more favoured organisations for disabled people and groups of 'carers', if not individual disabled people recruited through their own contacts

(Beresford and Campbell, 1994; Bewley and Glendinning, 1994; Lindow and Morris, 1995). A similar reluctance characterised the implementation of direct payments (Glasby and Littlechild, 2002). Established non–user-led agencies have typically been around longer than user-led agencies, are mostly staffed by 'professional' service providers, and usually have access to far greater funding resources (Oliver, 1996b; Barnes and Mercer, 2003).

The growing market orientation of health and 'social care' services in both the statutory and voluntary provider sectors has also restricted the operational autonomy of managers by imposing strict budgetary controls and performance targets. Hence, the formal commitment to consultation and the implementation of user-led agendas is substantially reduced in practice.

Another major constraint on what sort of user involvement is established stems from professionals' claims to expertise and self-regulation. This too often produces schemes where user involvement is minimised if not denied at the point of taking decisions. The many professions working with disabled people have their own language, set of values and practices that separate practitioners from the majority of disabled people (Davis, 1993; Morris, 1994). This division between the expert-provider and lay-user has been particularly reinforced by the medicalisation of disability and its associated impact on professional training and practice (Begum, 1994; Wates, 1997; Oliver and Sapey, 1999).

Disabled people's interest in both the process and outcomes of the participation exercise reflects two main concerns: that services help them achieve the outcomes to which they aspire, and that services are organised and delivered in ways that they find empowering (Begum and Gillespie-Sells, 1994; Turner et al, 2003). While conventional discussions have tended to separate outcomes from the process of service participation, service users suggest they are closely interrelated. Their desired participation spans the achievement of desired outcomes and being fully involved in defining, developing, monitoring and evaluating services (Beresford et al, 1997; Turner, 1998). Hence, the expectation among disabled people, and particularly those engaged with user-controlled organisations, that more open and democratic processes will characterise their service support role.

The foundation is provided by the rejection of the medical model of disability (including 'mental illness') and the organisation and delivery of services along social model lines. This presumes that user-led services will be much more responsive to the needs of users and much more flexible in deciding when service support is required. In broad terms, the objective of a user-led service organisation is to greatly enhance the choice and control that disabled people have over their everyday lives. In moving forward, it is assumed that user-led services will routinely involve disabled service users in decisions and that those charged with the management of the services will be (democratically) accountable to disabled users (Morris, 1994, pp 7-8).

The point to which disabled people's organisations repeatedly return is that the move to a more equal and democratic society demands a bottom-up approach to politics and policy making. Its potential is demonstrated by the emergence of assertive and organised user groups such as those based on mental health system users (Survivors Speak Out) and people with 'learning difficulties' (People First) (People First, 1994; Campbell, 1996). If mainstream service managers and professionals will not or cannot embrace meaningful user participation, then user-led service organisations have to show the way forward.

The growth of user-led services

Responses to the postal survey of user-led organisations indicate (Figure 5.1) that the 'take-off' point for self-organisation took place in the 1970s and 1980s, with a further and more substantial expansion through the 1990s. Only two of the groups in existence in 2001 could trace their beginnings back before the 1970s. These started out as organisations for disabled people

Figure 5.1: Establishment of user-led initiatives

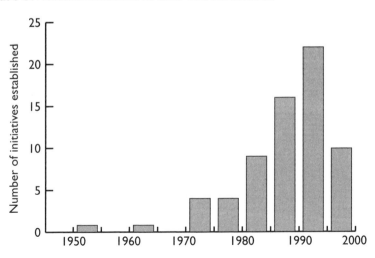

Source: Barnes et al (2001, p 14)

although they subsequently adopted the principle of user control as disability campaigns grew in the 1980s. Thus, the Greater London Action on Disability (GLAD) was established in 1952 as the 'London Association for the Welfare of the Physically Handicapped'. In the mid-1980s, local disabled activists campaigned with demonstrations and a sit-in at the GLAD offices in 1988 for disabled people to take over control of the organisation. This culminated in a decision by the members at GLAD's Annual General Meeting (AGM) in 1990 to change the constitution so that disabled people would have charge of the organisation. As a result, in the late 1990s, three quarters of the management committee were disabled users of GLAD's services, and most of the remainder were disabled representatives from other London-based organisations (Hasler, 2003).

A similar pattern is evident in Greenwich Association of Disabled People (GAD). It began in 1974 as the 'Greenwich Association for the Disabled' from an initiative led by the principal of a local college of further education. Although disabled people were involved in the general running of the organisation from the outset, and made a significant contribution to GAD's early development, it was only in 1983 that its constitution was formally changed to ensure that disabled people controlled its management committee. The vast majority of user-led organisations in the *Creating Independent Futures* study were established with this format.

Initially, in the early 1980s, user-controlled organisations were developed by groups of disabled people leaving residential care who were seeking practical solutions to overcome the absence of statutory or voluntary agency support for independent living in the community. These included Britain's first two Centres for Independent/Integrated Living (CILs) in Hampshire and Derbyshire.

The Derbyshire Centre for Integrated Living (DCIL) was set up as a registered limited company in 1985 after extensive discussions within the Derbyshire Coalition of Disabled People (DCODP), other disabled people's groups and the local council, on what form the new CIL should take (Davis and Mullender, 1993) (see Chapter Three). DCIL's approach to service provision involved a close working relationship with the local authority and this was reflected in the choice of 'integrated' rather than 'independent' living in its initial title. The local authority was represented on DCIL's management committee and although often difficult the relationship worked reasonably well until March 2000, when a shift in the political and economic climate resulted in the merger of DCODP and DCIL under the title 'Derbyshire Coalition for Inclusive Living' and the severing of formal links with the local authority. In a further confirmation of its user-controlled stance, the DCIL's management committee was restricted to DCODP members. The new title was chosen because it was felt that the term 'Centre' was misleading since DCIL had always provided county-wide services, while the notion of 'integrated' living made some disabled DCIL users uncomfortable:

> 'People I met wondered perhaps were we prisoners coming out of jail ... needing integrating back into society? ... I didn't think it was very relevant to disabled people.' (Jean) (participants' names have been changed to protect confidentiality)

Similarly, a group of disabled people explored ways of setting up a CIL in Bristol in the late 1980s. The first initiative was a 'county-wide' Avon Coalition of Disabled People in 1989. Following local government boundary changes, this was re-designated as the West of England Coalition of Disabled People (WECODP), with members establishing the West of England Centre for Inclusive Living (WECIL) in 1995. Unlike in Derbyshire, the Coalition and WECIL have remained separate organisations.

There was an even more substantial expansion of user-controlled organisations during the 1990s. It was facilitated by the 1990 National Health Service and Community Care Act and the subsequent 1996 Community Care (Direct Payments) Act. These encouraged optimism among disabled activists about the potential for organisations directed by users. Indeed, of the 69 organisations that responded to our survey, 44 (64%) began operations during the 1990s.

Another scenario was where small groups of disabled people started campaigning on disability issues, and then began to explore the possibility of setting up a service provider organisation. This was the case with the Cardiff and Vale Coalition of Disabled People (CVCDP). It was formed in 1991 as the 'Glamorgan Coalition of Disabled People' by four disabled people looking for an alternative to the existing impairment-specific organisations and their concentration on charitable fundraising activities. As a founder member explained:

> 'We felt that what was needed was an organisation, directly representative of disabled people that looked at [and] addressed issues rather than the actual conditions that people had.' (Rita)

A formal constitution was agreed in 1993 and the Coalition subsequently received funding from Glamorgan County Council. In 1996, following local authority reorganisation, the group adopted the name Cardiff and Vale Coalition of Disabled People to reflect its new location, and also enable it to access funding from both the Vale of Glamorgan and Cardiff local authorities.

In other parts of the country disputes within and between local groups undermined the prospect of user-controlled services. In such situations some local authorities tried to fill the gap by setting up 'consumer groups' or forums led by non-disabled people or representatives of organisations for disabled people. The 1990 National Health Service and Community Care Act proved a primary stimulus to action. However, according to a disabled participant in one local forum:

> 'It was a campaigning group *for* disabled people; it hadn't come from the grass roots. It was the council coming along saying we need to be consulted: there needs to be a group that we can consult with and we're seen to be consulting with. They would appoint a development worker and set up huge public meetings and they'd say "we need to hear from you". They would usually invite people who were using their services to these meetings. It was kind of safe, and it was people who were wanting improvements in council services, not radicals saying "let's start from scratch".' (Maggie)

While disabled people were deeply involved in user-led initiatives, the specific driving force varied between disabled people's organisations, individual disabled people and disabled local authority staff. Additionally, the period in which user-controlled services emerged was crucial. In the 1980s and early 1990s there was often a protracted period of negotiation, which reflected the innovative character of the work being undertaken, with little experience to draw on from other local authorities or groups of disabled people.

Several other case study organisations, including the Lothian Centre for Independent Living (LCIL) founded in 1991, the Centre for Independent Living in Glasgow (CILiG) established in 1995 (although both subsequently changed their names, see Chapter Four), and the Surrey User Network (SUN) set up in 1997, owe their initial development to the activities of disabled people working within or with local authorities. The following example typifies this experience:

> 'It was two people who happened to be employed by the council … disabled people saying "we've seen the crap services, that people are fitted into … and we want to do something about it".' (Maureen)

Research participants emphasised more generally the importance of allies at different levels within local authorities in order to secure a continuing commitment to supporting user-controlled services:

> 'The elected members [of the local council] were very pro these types of organisations and they've passed that down through the staff of the local authority as well. So that's the headquarters, we've got pretty good relationships. And also with local social work teams; but that depends … some are very good and some are not so good.' (Mary)

Indeed, most of the organisations surveyed were linked in one way or another to local authority or other public sector agencies, notably health authorities or health 'care' trusts. For instance, the CIL de Gwynedd was established jointly in 1999 by 'Camrod', a local disability forum, and the local authority social services department in North Wales, following a survey that identified a growing need for this form of provision. Although independent of local authority control, its social services department was represented on the CIL de Gwynedd's management committee. In an example of similar developments beyond the case study organisations, Coventry Independent Living Group established a formal attachment to the local authority through the social services department. Despite being described as a 'user-led independent living scheme' that delivers an array of services designed to enable disabled people to determine their own lifestyles within the community, Coventry Independent Living Group does not have a constitution, its management committee is not controlled or run by disabled people, and its chief executive is appointed by the local authority.

Only one of the case studies – Disability Action North East (DANE) – had no formal connections with statutory authorities. DANE had emerged from within Disability Gateshead, which was already a well-established user-controlled service provider. It was set up in June 1992 and funded solely as a campaigning organisation.

> 'The whole point about DANE was to create networks and links and to get people to think about disability ... it would take a lead in campaigning ... it would be the organisation that would upset people.' (Steve)

It was felt by members of DANE that by avoiding any formal connections with local or statutory authorities it could be more critical of local and national policies and practices without the threat of sanctions such as the withdrawal of core funding (see Chapter Six for further discussion of these issues).

Networking was considered vitally important by all the organisations studied. Each new 'wave' of fledgling user-led organisations was able to draw on the ideas and experiences of those CILs already operational. Thus, many of those involved in setting up user-led organisations had undertaken fact-finding trips to other groups of disabled people in order to learn lessons and identify 'best practice' for supporting independent living.

> 'In the early days we went around to the various CILs, we went to Derbyshire and Hampshire.... So we did that but then we never did it any more really because I think we've been pretty introspective....We've had to work so hard trying to set up our services that we haven't been outside the four walls really. But we had loads of people wanting to come here and find out what we were doing. So we set up open days, which ran every two months or something, and lots of disabled people's organisations have come to these; 30 or 40 over the years.' (Rebecca)

These networking activities have been a key feature in the development of user-controlled services. Fifty-seven per cent of participant agencies had formal links with, or were members of, other local organisations. The majority had links with local organisations controlled and run by disabled people (75%) and with other voluntary organisations (62%). Additionally, around a third had ties with organisations of people with specific impairments (39%) and local groups for disabled people (31%). Smaller numbers were linked to organisations for people with specific impairments (21%), multiple impairments (15%) and 'carers' groups (15%).

Moreover, two thirds of the organisations surveyed had established links with national organisations of and for disabled people such as the British Council of Disabled People (BCODP), the National Centre for Independent Living (NCIL) and the Disablement Information and Advice Line UK (DIAL UK). Groups within Scotland and Wales were also brought closer together through the activities of Disability Scotland or Disability Wales. A small minority, typically the longer-established organisations, had formal links with European (16%) and international (10%) organisations. These included the European Network on Independent Living (ENIL) and Disabled Peoples' International (DPI). DCIL, for example, had established close links with groups of disabled people in a variety of European countries from Portugal to Russia.

Applying the social model of disability

Since its inception in 1981 the social model of disability has had an increasingly important influence on disability politics and policy in Britain. Nonetheless, it is not without its critics both within and outside the Disabled People's Movement (Thomas, 1999; GLAD, 2000; Shakespeare and Watson, 2002). However, as far as the disabled people involved in our survey of user-controlled initiatives were concerned, the academic debates around the social model have not made a deep impression. The following statements from two disabled activists in Wales capture a widespread view about what is the defining feature and significance of a social model approach to disability:

> 'We've all got different views on what the social model means and I think that's important as well, but it all comes down to one thing: it's society that disables us, not our impairments, and at the end of the day I think that's what's important.' (Myfanwy)

> 'The social model was something that was very important to us and important in helping each other explain our experiences ... and to share these among ourselves ... it was really useful, part of our strategy for lobbying, the other part was it was really a really good way of supporting people individually, and helping disabled people to come together collectively.' (Thomas)

There was also broad agreement among participants that the social model of disability was the basis upon which all user-controlled service providers should operate. Research participants in seminar discussions, in responses to postal questionnaires and case study visits, consistently favoured a broad interpretation that accommodated local diversity and priorities, including variation in the needs of different impairment groups, although there were conflicting opinions of how far this focus should go. However, most participants insisted that the fears that, for example, people with physical impairments would resist association with people with 'learning difficulties' were unfounded:

> 'I never felt that impairment per se was outside the remit of the social model.... I think issues, for example, about specific impairments, be it a visual impairment or a mental health system survivor, I think it can become too divisive to be involved in the specific needs of people with specific impairments. But I don't think there is any exclusion. I know if you go back 10 to 15 years there was … a feeling amongst some in disability organisations that people with learning difficulties should not be included, but I think … that has ceased to be a problem.' (Alan)

The social barriers approach had also given a substantial focus and momentum to campaigning and other overt political activities, although some also expressed their concern that the social model should not be 'set in stone':

> 'I think we're in danger of doing what I think we get accused of, which is sort of using it as a kind of mantra. In its essence, it's a very simple idea, but I think that it could be a much more interesting idea and developed in different ways and I think it's worth us looking at it and kind of challenging it and seeing how robust it is … that's what we should be doing, not just leaving it to you academics.' (Evan)

Nonetheless, some interviewees acknowledged that while their organisation had a clear commitment to a social model approach, the level of understanding varied among individual members. Indeed, one organisation had adopted the phrase 'applied social understanding' in place of 'the social model' when describing its approach to service provision. It was acknowledged too that the social model often meant little to service users who were not active in the Disabled People's Movement.

A key issue was how to translate the social model into practical policies. Organisations explored various options in how this was implemented, some more explicit than others. This could take the form of Disability/ Distress Equality Training (DET)-type courses (Gillespie-Sells and Campbell, 1991) or the development of services compatible with the 'seven needs' for the independent living of disabled people as outlined by the Derbyshire Centre for Integrated Living (DCIL) in the early 1980s (Davis, 1990). In general, organisations regarded the involvement of users in service planning processes as crucial to fleshing out their understanding of the social model into specific aims and objectives:

> 'I think it's more about [the] empowerment of disabled people; making them aware of their rights and offering more services.... It tries to promote the idea that people have the right to live independently; they have the right to access, education, employment and transport.' (Stella)

There was wide-ranging discussion among the research participants about what this meant in practice, and about the challenges of implementing a social model approach within a service provision context. It tends to be seen as a means of identifying potential 'disabling barriers'. They were very aware of the difficulties of relying on organisations such as local authorities or funding agencies that have little or no real commitment to the adoption of a social model approach to the organisation and provision of services (Stalker et al, 1999).

> 'We're forced into positions; like some people will ask us to define what groups of people we are working with and we haven't fully resolved that one yet.' (Graham)

Furthermore, local authority staff acknowledged that the organisation of statutory agency structures and procedures meant that both services and users were generally compartmentalised into rigid categories and groups and that practices often varied from area to area. Common examples included divisions between services for children, adults and 'elderly' people as well as departments dealing exclusively with people with impairment-specific groups such as 'physical and sensory disabilities', 'learning disabilities', and 'mental health'. Such policies create obvious difficulties for organisations that are attempting to implement a more holistic approach to impairment-related concerns, which strives to serve all sections of the disabled population regardless of impairment condition:

> 'I'm not sure that they [local authority staff] really understand [the social model]. The more you try to get it across to people and the more purist you sound, the more difficulties you get into in terms of encompassing all forms of ... impairments. It's difficult for us to talk about it and put it across to people who don't know anything about it.' (Mary)

For their part, although those individuals from local authority funding agencies who were interviewed expressed a broad policy or political commitment to the social model, many accepted that this was difficult to implement in everyday practice. In his comments on the general level of understanding of the social model within local authorities, one disabled social worker suggested that:

> 'Some of the officers are wholly committed to the social model in terms of people with physical impairments, but with something like sensory impairments or learning difficulty or mental health ..., it's like the social model just goes out of the window. Some officers simply don't have a clue what the social model is.' (Bert)

Another social service employee, who was also a member of a local user-led organisation, suggested that the level of commitment among local authority service providers had recently declined as a result of the growing emphasis on market competition and financial restrictions within these agencies:

> 'As I look back on the years before I came into post, it felt like the social model was informing the whole area of practice and certainly when it was created it felt very social model led. I have grave doubts nowadays. Increasingly, and I'm sure you'll find this all over the country, local authorities are budget led, financially driven, and individuals and senior managers are led

away from the social model because of that. We do see examples of good practice. By and large I see a backwards movement toward much more medical approaches.' (Sheila)

Furthermore, seeking to balance a philosophical or ideological commitment to the social model of disability with the day-to-day realities of service provision produces tensions and dilemmas for people working within user-led organisations. While the broad interpretation of the model gives organisations greater scope to reflect local diversity and priorities, this also allows latitude for some confusion and contrary interpretations by both user-controlled organisations and statutory agencies.

Accountability and user control

One of the primary justifications for services provided by disabled people's organisations is that they are more accountable to service users than traditionally run services. Almost every group in our sample had a written constitution and 82% had a mission or policy statement. Constitutions are usually broad legalistic documents, and a legal requirement for organisations with charitable or limited company status. In comparison, mission and policy statements are more detailed working documents that contain information about specific aims, principles and practice.

All the case study organisations are companies limited by guarantee. This means that more legalistic memoranda and articles have superseded many of the constitutions written when the organisations were founded. Hence, in several cases, principles and philosophy tend to be contained within a more general mission statement. The role of both the constitution and mission statement varied between organisations. In some the constitution (or memorandum of articles) was taken up with procedural detail, which had little day-to-day impact. Others contained more explicit statements of intent. It was also evident that organisations sometimes change or amend their constitution or mission statements in response to local needs. As one manager reported:

'We had a lot of projects that wanted to get involved ... but they weren't disabled people's organisations, even though they've got disabled people there. So we've changed the constitution slightly.' (Jennie)

Moreover, in 2000, the formation of the DCIL was used as an opportunity to agree a very different constitution. To ensure accountability to their respective memberships a lengthy process of evaluation and discussion was conducted within both the DCIL and DCODP organisations:

> 'We've done something like a four-year review on the Coalition [DCODP] side and an organisational appraisal on the CIL side, then a year of discussions and at least a year of getting the constitution confirmed and cleared through the Charity Commissioners.... It's important to keep referring back to make sure everybody's aware of what's going on.' (Derrick)

All but two of the organisations responding to our survey had a management or executive committee, sometimes called a board of directors, responsible for running the organisation. To ensure disabled people retained control, all the case study organisations specified in their constitution that disabled people should be in a majority on their controlling body. The actual figure varied from 51% to 100%, with five of the nine organisations restricting membership to disabled people. These ranged from service users to disabled representatives from other disability organisations and funding agencies.

For example, CIL de Gwynedd required 90%, CILiG 75%, while LCIL set a figure of just 51%. The management committee of SUN must all be services users. These might include 'users of children's and family services', although in practice, 95% were disabled people. CIL de Gwynedd's management committee was made up entirely of disabled people, including a representative from the local authority. WECIL's management committee included 80% users and the remainder representatives of other organisations, while disabled people constituted 90% and 75% respectively of CILiG's and LCIL's management committees. In addition to users, LCIL included representatives of the local authority and other organisations, such as Lothian Coalition of Disabled People.

Just over half (52%) of these management committees comprised disabled people only, while the remainder had a majority of disabled people that varied between 51% and 90% (Figure 5.2). Most of the disabled people on the management committees were service users. A third of the organisations surveyed had representatives of their funders on the management committee. Twenty-five per cent included representatives from local authorities and 6% from local health authorities. Seventeen per cent included 'carers' as members of their management committee.

Figure 5.2: Disabled people as a minimum percentage of the management committee

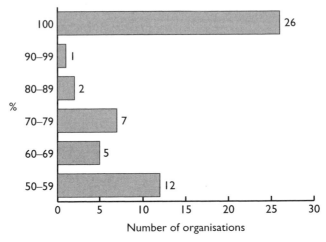

Source: Barnes et al (2000, p 16)

In each of the organisations studied membership of the controlling body is by election or re-election by members at the AGM subject to completing a qualifying period of service of between one and five years. In most organisations, members may also be co-opted as appropriate, but this must be approved by the membership at the AGM:

> 'People can be co-opted on to the board during the year and that has happened in the past. People come on prior to the AGM, and then they are formally elected at the AGM; they've maybe been co-opted to do a formal piece of work, but in terms of becoming formal directors that can only happen once a year from an election.... Anyone in the membership can nominate someone to be elected on to the board.' (Mary)

In general, management committees meet monthly or bi-monthly. Additionally, several organisations had sub-committees that focused on specific areas such as finance, personnel, policy and particular projects. Accountability is provided by a variety of mechanisms, including periodic service reviews, and consulting with members and users.

An overwhelming 93% of the organisations surveyed employ someone with overall responsibility for day-to-day management. The choice of title varied from director, chief executive, administrator to coordinator. In just over three quarters of the organisations, the person was appointed or elected by the controlling body. Members elect the manager in 14% of the organisations surveyed and in 5% the local authority or other funding body appoints the manager. Forty-five per cent of managers are appointed for three years or longer, but as many as 43% have a contract for less than two years. Of the case study organisations, all had managers who were appointed by and accountable to their management committee/board of directors and the membership. Six were long-term appointees and three were on short-term rolling contracts whose renewal depended on obtaining new funding.

In terms of accountability, organisations often identified more than one source. Around 80% reported that they were answerable to their members and about 46% to their service users (Figure 5.3). However, the distinction between members and users is imprecise in some agencies. Accountability for SUN is to its users, whereas DCIL is accountable to its members, although most are DCIL service users. Membership numbers varied considerably, from 40 in CIL de Gwynedd through to 612 in DCIL. For all organisations, only disabled people were eligible for full membership and voting rights or, where group membership was possible, organisations of disabled people. Several organisations enrolled non-disabled supporters.

Figure 5.3: Formal accountability of user-led organisations

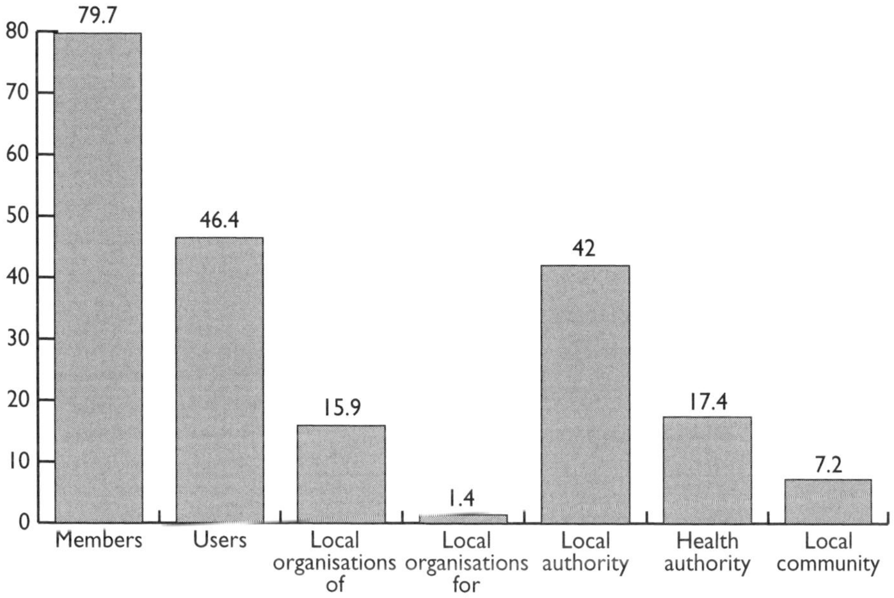

Note: More than one source allowed.
Source: Barnes et al (2000, p 17)

For example, DCIL reported 462 full members, 57 life members, 61 supporters, 31 group members and one family membership. In each of the case study organisations, only full members were allowed to vote or hold office. Some charge a nominal fee for membership, with different rates, for disabled or non-disabled, waged or unwaged persons.

Despite the emphasis on accountability, several respondents, particularly those disabled staff with deeper roots in disability activism, expressed concern about the relatively low levels of member participation, and the small minority who could be classified as 'active':

> 'I think the passion's gone…. Years ago people really wanted to get involved in the organisation. I don't know why it's changed … perhaps it's because more disabled people are working? … Maybe those that might have got involved have got jobs or are doing DET [Disability Equality Training] or consultancy, so they're not involved in running the organisation in quite the same way.' (Jennie)

Indeed, the current ratio of members to disabled people in the local population was often very low, with one case study organisation reporting that there were around 35,000 disabled people according to local authority figures, although the organisation itself 'had less than 100 members' (Evan).

This level of involvement has provoked some criticism of the representativeness of user-led organisations, and of the Disabled People's Movement in general (Bury, 1996; Shakespeare and Watson, 2002). A similar charge has been levelled against most social protest movements. Historically, Britain has operated as a 'passive' rather than a 'participatory' democracy (Beresford and Campbell, 1994), but it is not alone among industrial capitalist societies in this regard. There is, however, substantial evidence that traditionally there have been many environmental, economic and cultural barriers to social participation (Barnes et al, 1999; PMSU, 2004). Nonetheless, it was widely accepted by those in user-led organisations that a much higher level of involvement by disabled people was essential if its credibility and political 'clout' were to be maintained, if not extended.

Members and users apart, formal accountability centres on statutory and funding agencies such as local and health authorities and the National Lottery, particularly through service agreements or other forms of contract. Although all the nine case study organisations were reliant on statutory and other agencies for funding, only three (CVCDP, CILiG and LCIL) reported that this was matched by formal accountability. In each instance, this was to the local authority. However, in two of these cases the arrangement seemed to depend on long-term personal contacts between individuals in the user-led organisation and local authority staff. The absence of a formal service-level agreement (that is, a contract between the provider and user stipulating a particular type of service) was attributed to diverse circumstances such as local government reorganisation, financial cutbacks and staff turnover within local authority departments.

The lack of binding service-level contracts has both advantages and disadvantages for user-led agencies. Ongoing support from within local authority social service departments without a binding contractual obligation can mean that organisations are accorded a high degree of flexibility in terms of service development, monitoring and delivery, but it also means that local authorities have no legal obligation to support user-led initiatives. This creates an uncertainty that is a continuing source of unease:

> 'In terms of core costs, there is an element of concern; it's a year-by-year thing. I think we've been lucky in the sense that we haven't been too anxious about it because we know there's a vast amount of goodwill…. We get a lot of support from officers and councillors. But we know that can change; it's a very fickle, fragile thing.' (Evan)

Review

Government initiatives to promote consumerism and user consultation on the organisation and delivery of health and 'social care' services have been slow to impress disabled service users. Despite the burgeoning set of initiatives since the 1990s, the dominant feeling remains that their participation in service provision has been marginal, with little evidence of the redirection of services towards meaningful support for 'independent living'.

The gap between disabled people's expectations and their actual involvement in the statutory and voluntary sectors has reinforced claims from disabled people's organisations that the move to a more equal and democratic society demands a bottom-up approach to politics and policy making. Its potential is realised by the emergence of active user-led organisations. The growth of CILs and user-led organisations has been slow and uneven, but 'took off' in the early 1990s.

In building an alternative system of service support for disabled people, user-led organisations have stressed the merits of a social barriers approach, although it is acknowledged that its implementation is far from straightforward. Moreover, their accountability to disabled members and/ or users has been highlighted – as a 'badge of difference' from the statutory and voluntary sectors. Yet, a much higher level of involvement by disabled people generally is essential if the credibility and political 'clout' of user-led organisations is to be maintained and extended. Further progress also needs to be made by user-led organisations in securing a larger and more active membership and one that is also more representative of disabled users.

In the next chapter, attention turns to examining the range of services and support for disabled people and their families that have been developed by user-controlled organisations. Besides this, the discussion explores how far the type and level of service support has been constrained by the economic and political climate in which they operate.

SIX

Service design and delivery: opportunities and constraints

Introduction

This chapter focuses on the activities of user-controlled organisations as service providers and the associated constraints of a policy environment still dominated by traditional ideas about disability and dependence. How far and in what ways has service support for independent living worked out as intended in practice? This includes consideration of the 'seven needs' for independent living (and their subsequent extension) by user-led or user-controlled agencies. The discussion is grounded within recent trends in community-based services; in particular, the increasing emphasis on 'Best Value' with the goal of integrating high standards with efficiency and effectiveness in their achievement.

A specific requirement placed on service provider organisations over recent years has been the growing use of performance targets and general monitoring of their activities. This raises a number of issues for user-led organisations, particularly the cost of undertaking the monitoring process. It is resource intensive and is complicated by the often contrasting formats in which information is required by the various funding bodies.

The chapter concludes with a commentary on the precarious resource context in which user-controlled services currently operate, ranging over major concerns about: the level and continuity of funding, as well as its primary sources; the availability of staff, and particularly disabled people, with the appropriate skills and commitment to a social barriers approach; and the choice and availability of suitable physical premises. Hence, organisations under the direction of users operate in an often hostile service environment still dominated by an individualist approach – a challenge compounded by limited resources for action.

Delivering services in support of independent living

User demands for significant changes in services for disabled people provided by the statutory and voluntary sectors have been countered by arguments that local authorities and service providers operate under such tight financial constraints that they cannot possibly agree to the changes recommended. More recently, the policy rhetoric has shifted to an emphasis on a 'Best Value' approach, although it now seeks to incorporate the views of users in decisions about service provision:

> Better councils are more actively involving users in shaping changes, setting standards and monitoring progress. Best Value has encouraged politicians, users, and partners to collaborate in new ways to achieve good quality at the best price. (Audit Commission, 2002, p 5)

However, for organisations of disabled people, user involvement risks being turned into an exercise to give legitimacy to budget-driven service reforms rather than a means of recognising disabled people's rights as service users. Their emphasis on democratic participation means that user–led services will stand apart because they seek to maximise the contribution of individual service users and so facilitate opportunities to affect the course and outcome of decision making at all stages. The range of areas that has been targeted for action includes: self-assessment and definition of support needs, right to services, self-advocacy and representation, and greater choice and control of services (Morris, 1998).

A primary objective for disabled service users is to challenge ways of assessing service need and entitlement and disabling barriers and social exclusion more generally (see Chapter Five). Barnes and Wistow (1994a) identify various approaches by service users to influence service provision or the balance of power separating service users from professionals and policy makers and planners. The spread of strategies have been summarised as: fight it (campaigning to change services), fix it (giving advice to planners and providers), escape it (providing somewhere safe to run to), and replace it (setting up user–run alternatives) (Peck and Barker, 1997).

Used-led services have quite definitely indicated that they are in the business of 'replacement' – at least in the sense of providing a desired alternative service orientation and goals – although this position has been forced on organisations of disabled people by the unwillingness of statutory or voluntary services to move down the path of meaningful participation or support services for independent living. Hence, a crucial factor in making independent living a reality is for disabled people to be freed from their reliance on welfare professionals and 'unpaid carers'.

The specific policy encouragement for personal assistance through direct payments was one of the original 'seven needs' for independent living outlined by Derbyshire Centre for Integrated Living (DCIL) (Davis and Mullender, 1993). The other key aspects comprised: information; counselling and peer support; housing; technical aids and equipment; transport; and an accessible environment (Davis, 1990). These were derived from a social model analysis of disabling barriers and identified as primary targets for political action and service provision. They acted as a critical stimulus to thinking in user-led service organisations although their service aspirations were significantly circumscribed by economic and political constraints.

Until very recently, the central stumbling block was the prohibition, under the 1948 National Assistance Act, of direct funding to disabled individuals for the employment of a personal assistant (PA) – to help accomplish those things a disabled person was unable to do by themselves. These cover a diverse set of activities to enable a disabled person to achieve a more 'independent' lifestyle, such as getting in and out of bed, washing and dressing, assistance with housework and shopping, and other forms of practical help to participate in social and leisure activities. Indeed, an important indicator of user control and independent living has been the growth of direct (and indirect or third party) payment schemes. Direct payments schemes represent a break with both state and market approaches to personal assistance. As mentioned in Chapter Two, these started very slowly and hesitantly at the local level but have received increasing support from national governments since the mid–1990s. The introduction of the 1996 Community Care (Direct Payments) Act followed a long campaign by disabled people's organisations and their allies. It included the commissioning of research by organisations such as the British Council of Disabled People (BCODP) and Help the Aged, and the establishment of the Direct Payments Technical Advisory Group (Zarb and Nadash, 1994; Barnes, 1997; Glasby and Littlechild, 2002) (see Chapter Three).

Potentially, direct payments go far beyond a consumerist approach to welfare by investing the disabled 'employer' with the capacity to manage their personal assistance. As pioneered by disabled people's organisations, these are characterised by:

- self-assessment and self-definition of support needs;
- choice of who works with the disabled person, with the right to hire and fire;
- the disabled person defining what the personal assistant does and how; and
- recognition of the value and importance of support from disabled people's organisations – offering advocacy, independent information, training, advice and administrative backup – to enable disabled people to set up and run their own schemes (Morris, 1993a, 1994).

The development of direct or indirect payments to enable disabled people to employ their own PAs attracted continuing opposition from local authorities – both because of concerns about the legality of making cash payments to service users, and from opposition among service providers, and particularly social workers who often considered that the role of 'employer' of personal assistance was beyond the capabilities of many disabled people. However, direct payments received a dramatic stimulus with the introduction of the national Independent Living Fund (ILF) in 1988. Although subsequently revised, its flexibility and level of funding offered compelling evidence of disabled people's attraction to a scheme that enabled their organisation of PA support with reduced interference by the local authority.

The importance of support and assistance to lead 'ordinary lives' is cemented by giving the individual 'employer' control over their personal assistance and enabling the disabled person to operate as an 'active agent' in their own life. Moreover, the disabled employer is responsible for deciding what the person does and how (although this is constrained by the continuing rejection of self-assessment, some hostility to direct payments from service providers, inadequate funding and preconditions imposed by the local authority on how the funding may be used). Needless to say, personal assistance is not a sufficient condition for 'independent living' – that depends on a much wider dismantling of the barriers to social inclusion. Nevertheless, research studies suggest that direct payments are a practicable, cost-effective policy option, which is greatly preferred to traditional service provision by disabled people who have been offered the choice (Oliver and Zarb, 1992; Morris, 1993a; Zarb and Nadash, 1994).

Equally significant, the development of direct payments presents an obvious opportunity for local authorities to recognise the accumulated experience of disabled people's organisations – offering advocacy, independent information, training, advice and administrative backup – to give practical support and encouragement to disabled service users to take advantage of direct payments if they so wish.

The suggestion of the central contribution that organisations of disabled people can make to service developments makes it even more necessary to identify the 'current state of play'. To what degree have user-led service organisations provided greater choice and control over service support? Have user-led organisations made discernible progress in providing a pattern of services that are clearly differentiated from the mainstream sector? Obviously, user-controlled organisations must operate within a policy and economic context not of their making: which of these constraints have proven most onerous or threatening to alternative service provision? User-led organisations have now accumulated considerable experience in service provision and it is also important to identify particular examples of 'good practice' in the promotion of independent living.

Service patterns

Research participants did not expect user-controlled organisations to provide a set list of services, but stressed that service provision should be primarily dictated by local needs and priorities. Most organisations provide a range of services, as illustrated in Table 6.1. It is notable that almost two thirds (58%) of the organisations sampled provide Disability/Distress Equality Training (DET)-type services, over a third (38%) offer employment advice and support, and 30% include education-related information and

Table 6.1: Services offered by user-led organisations (%)

Service	Offered	Hope to offer
Information	82	65
Peer support by disabled people	67	13
Disability/distress/equality training	58	9
Personal assistance	54	8
Employment advice/training	38	12
Housing advice	36	15
Environmental access	32	13
Education advice/support	30	12
Transport	22	6
Counselling	16	20
Health/impairment related	15	9
Technical aids and assistance	13	6

Source: Barnes et al (2000, p 22)

advice in their portfolio of provision. Moreover, in the majority of cases (90%), it is the management committee that decides which services are delivered, although 55% indicated that service users are involved in this process. Funding bodies, including local (20%) and health (10%) authorities, also have a role in determining the shape of user-led provision. Indeed, this is a condition of funding for 33% of the responding organisations.

An increasing source of activity and of income at least up to 2001 for Centres for Independent/Integrated Living (CILs) is running support schemes to enable disabled people to use direct payments. These involve advice and information, advocacy and peer support, assistance with recruiting, training and employing PAs, a payroll service, and a register of PAs.

Of the case study organisations, the larger well-established examples, such as the West of England Centre for Inclusive Living (WECIL), offered a comprehensive range of services, while smaller agencies such as Disability Action North East (DANE) were set up with very specific objectives in mind. This was further influenced by the relationship with their main funding agencies and the availability of financial and human resources.

There were three areas covered by all nine case study organisations: information, peer support and DET. There are several sources for information needs, including local and national information providers both of and for disabled people (see Table 6.2). DCIL, for instance, collects information from the Citizens Advice Bureaux (CAB), Disablement Information and Advice Line UK (DIAL UK), the Disabled Living Foundation (a national agency specialising in data on technical aids and equipment) and the Royal Association for Disability and Rehabilitation (RADAR). More generally, information services span newsletters, telephone answering services, drop-in facilities, periodic meetings, seminars and conferences and websites. Cardiff and Vale Coalition of Disabled People (CVCDP) produces a quarterly newsletter and arranges various events, information days and training sessions.

Most did not have the space or the staff to provide a drop-in service, although some, such as WECIL's Disability Information and Advice Service, provide 'home visits'. This is most often related to 'help with form filling', which constitutes the bulk of their user enquiries. As the largest disabled user-controlled service provider in the UK, WECIL delivered information and advice to 2,583 disabled people in 2002-03 (WECIL, 2003, p 2). One way to focus services has been DCIL's strategy to locate four offices across the county. In addition, four of the organisations provide designated

Table 6.2: Services offered by case study organisations

Service	Organisations								
	1	2	3	4	5	6	7	8	9
Information	✓	✓	✓	✓	✓	✓	✓	✓	✓
Environmental access			✓	✓	✓				
Housing advice			✓	✓	✓				✓
PA services	✓		✓	✓	✓	✓	✓		✓
Peer support	✓	✓	✓	✓	✓	✓	✓	✓	✓
Counselling				✓		✓	✓		
Transport		✓		✓					
Technical aids/equipment				✓		✓			
Employment/advice		✓	✓		✓	✓			✓
Education/advice		✓		✓					
Health/impairment advice/support								✓	
DET		✓	✓	✓	✓	✓	✓	✓	✓

Key:
1. Cardiff and Vale Coalition of Disabled People (CVCDP)
2. Centre for Independent Living de Gwynedd (CILdG)
3. Centre for Independent Living in Glasgow (CILiG)
4. Derbyshire Coalition for Inclusive Living (DCIL)
5. Disability Action North East (DANE)
6. Greenwich Association of Disabled People (GAD)
7. Lothian Centre for Integrated Living (LCIL)
8. Surrey Users Network (SUN)
9. West of England Centre for Inclusive Living (WECIL)
Source: Stage One survey

information and consultancy services on environmental access, accessible housing, transport and technical aids and equipment. As it serves an overwhelmingly rural area, CIL de Gwynedd operated its own accessible transport service for users.

Seven of the case study agencies delivered services for PA users. These included PA user support and training programmes, emergency cover systems, registers and training programmes, and payroll services. The Centre for Inclusive Living in Glasgow (CILiG) provides one-to-one support for 30 people managing their own independent living packages and employing PAs. In 2002-03 it ran 81 training sessions for disabled people who employ PAs, a 41% increase on the previous year. The aim is to help people become good employers. Topics included recruiting, interviewing, assertiveness, health and safety and employment law. The programme also included an 'Information Day on Direct Payments' for people from minority ethnic communities. CILiG's Payroll Solutions scheme handles the bureaucracy involved in employing a PA for 21 direct payment users (CILiG, 2004).

As well as enabling disabled people to acquire the skills to become good PA employers, several organisations provide training courses for PAs. However, it has been found that some of those trained by the CIL leave the host organisation's PA register and go to work for one of the growing number of 'care' agencies springing up in response to the growing demand for skilled PAs. This had obvious benefits for those disabled people who do not have access to user-controlled services, although there were concerns it might result in a shortfall of PAs for the user organisation.

Peer support is a primary activity for all the organisations visited. Services might include employment and educational advice, community development work and advocacy. Three of the organisations – DCIL, Greenwich Association of Disabled People (GAD) and Lothian Centre for Integrated Living (LCIL) – provide facilities for peer counselling by disabled people. For example, during the year 2001-02 LCIL offered one-to-one support and advice to 92 people (LCIL, 2002). Only two organisations provided information on technical aids and equipment. This is probably because there is a well-established national network of 40 professionally led agencies, some confusingly called 'Independent Living Centres', that specialise in this type of service (Disabled Living Centres Council, 2004).

Several of the case study organisations provide information and advice on employment and education. In addition, six of these agencies train volunteers for work within the organisation. For instance, in 2002 seven out of 10 disabled people successfully completed the LCIL-sponsored Counselling and Psychotherapy in Scotland (COSCA) Certificate in Counselling Skills course (LCIL, 2002). For some individuals, this training has led to paid employment either within the organisation or elsewhere.

Typical activities for volunteers included working at reception, work in the information service, and clerical and administrative duties. Apart from the fact that this involvement often enhances the individual's self-esteem and confidence, several people approached volunteering as a 'trial run' for possible paid work. Sharon, for example, contacted her local organisation for information regarding access, then became a volunteer for the information service and, subsequently, left to take up part-time paid work:

> 'I was trying to find a place who could sort out a ramp for a friend of mine, and I found the number in the 'phone book,

phoned them [the CIL] up, and they sorted it out … I went into the office … and I saw a leaflet saying "volunteers needed"'. So I thought, well, I'll volunteer. I used to go for three mornings a week. I did three mornings a week for about three years. And then I got a part-time job working from home. So I had to give my notice in at [CIL]. I've never been back since in a voluntary capacity. But I do use the services a lot for information. I'm on the management committee for the local MS [Multiple Support] group.' (Sharon)

This also leads to a higher staff turnover. What is more, the selection of suitable trainees has important ethical and resource implications that are often difficult to overcome.

'We've got someone [a volunteer] we've been working with … who cannot read or write and there will be a point where we need to agree with [the management committee] whether there are any circumstances or impairments that are incompatible with the post. Now it does beg the tricky question, do we get him a PA to make it accessible for him or does it mean that the amount of work being done by the PA raises the question who the real practitioner is: so there's those sorts of gritty issues to get to grips with.' (Larah)

Moreover, one organisation, CILiG, has devised a work experience placement scheme for disabled jobseekers. Their 'Glasgow Disabled Person's Housing Service' provides housing information on the availability of accessible homes in the Glasgow area. In 2002–03 it received 627 enquiries, and provided one-to-one support for 262 people and helped 25 families to find appropriate accommodation. The related housing employment service, in its second year of operation in 2003, provided training and work experience with housing employers including housing associations and private sector providers for 16 disabled people. Of the 12 participants in year one, seven moved into full-time employment and one into full-time education (Carson and Speirs, 2004; CILiG, 2004).

Beyond these services, all the organisations visited provided DET courses of various types for a range of audiences including other statutory and voluntary agencies, professionals, 'carers' and disabled people. Furthermore, all the case study agencies were engaged to varying degrees in political activities, such as campaigning (see Chapter Eight). Other provision included support services for particular sections of the disabled population, including young disabled people and people with 'learning difficulties'. In some cases, as with CILiG and CIL de Gwynedd (CILdG), the organisation was able to offer conference and seminar facilities for use by other groups.

Service monitoring or control?

Over recent years the shift towards service-level agreements and a more formalised relationship with statutory agencies has resulted in an increase in the level of performance monitoring required. In many cases it is a precondition for funding. Even so, while all the organisations surveyed monitored the numbers of people using their services, the way in which the measurement is undertaken and the uses to which the data generated are used have been a source of continuing difficulty and dispute.

Two main criticisms were advanced. First, statutory agencies tend to focus on quantitative data rather than the more qualitative information preferred by some user-led service providers. While it is evident that all the organisations studied sought to be inclusive in their membership and user groups, several participants were acutely aware of the tension arising from a philosophical commitment to a social model approach, and the practical implications of demands for specific data collection and reporting on services. While some organisations favoured monitoring inclusiveness and the accessibility of their services, they did not want this to be classified by impairment groups:

> 'We want to be monitoring the accessibility, the processes by which we make our services and information accessible.' (Derrick)

However, other participants accepted the counterargument that there was a need to demonstrate that organisations receiving public money did indeed operate an equal opportunities policy as claimed.

Second, monitoring is resource intensive in terms of staff time and is further complicated where funding bodies require information in a variety of formats. This is a particularly complex issue for those organisations receiving funding from a range of sources or whose catchment area covers more than one local or health authority. One of the case study organisations, for example, provided services for two health and two local authorities, which employed different monitoring criteria. It took considerable time and effort to gain agreement for a single monitoring system.

Responses from different user-led organisations also suggested that collecting data was easier for some services than for others. For example, a wealth of information can be gleaned, both unobtrusively and sensitively, when providing services that involve ongoing interaction such as PA services, peer support, one-to-one counselling and training. This is far more difficult for telephone- or postal-based services.

> 'It's a difficult process because if we don't do the monitoring we're targeted by equal opportunities … so we're trying to do it informally as it's the only way you can find out…. When you have a lot of telephone enquiries … you can't sit at a desk saying are you A, B and C. It's just not possible.' (Andy)

> 'The majority of people are fine about it and if there are certain questions they don't want to answer, they don't have to, and we say that from the start…. It does sometimes feel like we are asking them an awful lot before they even get a chance to say what they want, and it is their 'phone bill. It does feel a bit lop-sided at times.' (Terri)

More generally, as Table 6.3 illustrates, there was some unease that potential users from particular groups were not being adequately supported by organisations controlled and run by disabled people. These include disabled people from minority ethnic groups, lesbian and gay disabled people and younger disabled people under the age of 25. In addition, people with the label 'learning difficulties' and 'mental health' system users/survivors were also identified as under-represented.

Traditional services are provided by a host of agencies in both the statutory and voluntary sectors, and there is no consistency across the country in terms of who provides what and for whom. Services provided by local authorities are usually divided along impairment or age-specific lines and funding for minority ethnic groups and on the basis of gender and sexual orientation are often distributed by separate equality units. Organisational links with local authority staff are crucial in determining what services can be offered in terms of funding and referrals. When discussing this issue, a manager of a well-established PA support service stated:

Table 6.3: Perceived under-representation of selected groups within user-led service organisations (%)

Group	%
Disabled people from minority ethnic groups	64
Gay and lesbian disabled people	54
Younger disabled people (aged 16-25)	51
Disabled young people under the age of 16	41
People with learning difficulties	37
Mental health users/survivors	31
Older disabled people (60+ years)	23
People with sensory impairments	22
People with specific impairments/conditions	15
People with physical impairments	10
Disabled women	10
Disabled people generally	9
'Carers'	9
Families with a disabled member	7
Professionals working with disabled people	3

Source: Barnes et al (2000, p 23)

'In terms of funding, the authorities we serve, they're all organised slightly differently. Often the funding for individual service packages comes out of individual team managers' budgets and they're split with different specific lines. That means that if someone comes through from mental health the funding comes out of that team.

The scheme's always been non-impairment specific.... It's always been open to all disabled people who are over 18 and we haven't had an upper age limit.... We haven't monitored by impairment which is part of I suppose coming from a social model background. Anecdotally there's been a low take-up of people with learning difficulties and people who experience emotional distress. I think a lot of it comes from the fact that direct payments were pioneered by disabled people with physical and sensory impairments.' (James)

Equally important, there is a growing number of voluntary agencies and groups, some of which are controlled and run by users themselves, operating at both the national and local levels that provide a range of services for particular user groups within the disabled population. Examples include the British Deaf Association, People First (organisations run by people with the label of 'learning difficulties'), MIND (National Association for

Mental Health) and Age Concern. In this regard, several of the organisations visited work with or support impairment-specific groups or provider organisations:

> 'We've been working with a local group of Deaf people to help them set up their own focus group forum for people with sensory impairments. In these areas again there are difficulties with people with multiple impairments ... we've not really got to them.' (Jason)

Furthermore, all the case study agencies have tried hard to make their services more accessible, while acknowledging the failure to establish a common ground with people with 'learning difficulties', as this statement from LCIL indicates:

> In response to the increasing number of people with learning difficulties or with different communication needs approaching LCIL all service areas have assessed their accessibility to this client group. Independent Living training materials have been produced in jargon free plain language and picture formats. The training programme includes counselling people with learning difficulties for counsellors and trainers working for LCIL and other agencies. (LCIL, 2002, p 6)

User-controlled services have for the most part yet to prove that they can reach out successfully to black and minority ethnic disabled people and other marginalised groups. The case study groups acknowledged their shortcomings in attracting and including disabled users from these minority groups, and were aware of the criticism of their record in this area. Some claimed that there was a 'reasonable' representation of some minority groups, even though it was recognised that service provision was not as geared to these minority needs as it should be:

> 'Statistically, it's probably about right. I think there's about 6% of our users are black people and [the area served] has a 6% black population but it doesn't feel like that, it still feels like it's under-represented.' (Rebecca)

Most participants identified a lack of resources as a major problem to developing more inclusive services, particularly in areas where there is a diverse minority ethnic population with several different languages:

> 'I know that when we were doing our leaflets in ethnic minority languages, it's so expensive to have it translated into nine different languages. So it's very hard and yet we do want to reach organisations of ethnic minorities. So we try to do a lot of networking and go out and meet people and meet their organisations and discuss what we do and what they do. Money's the biggest issue I think in terms of not having enough to do exactly as we would like.' (Terri)

Even then, some apprehension was expressed that raising the awareness of their services among under-represented groups risked generating a demand that could not be fulfilled. For example, in one location the take-up of direct payments is particularly low among disabled people from minority ethnic groups. While the organisation would like to target these groups it has already achieved the maximum number of direct payment users it is able to support with current funding levels. This viewpoint was echoed by several other agencies. As a consequence, disabled people from minority groups (as compared with service users as a whole) tend not to hold such a positive view of 'user-led' services relative to the 'mainstream' alternatives.

Resources: economic, physical and human

Funding

In a political climate increasingly dominated by the rhetoric of market forces, user-led initiatives have experienced marked difficulties in accessing adequate local authority funding, and have been forced to seek support from other sources, including income generated from selling services. This must be set against the often higher costs of providing fully accessible and flexible services to disabled people and their families.

Most draw funding from several sources, with only 10 of the 69 organisations surveyed dependent on a single funding body. Nonetheless, the main sources include grants from the local authority (83%), although over half of the organisations (55%) have won lottery grants, followed by support from health authorities. Additional sources include self-generated funding, income from services (35%) and membership fees (32%). The majority of organisations received core funding for start-up costs, developing and maintaining services, employing staff and administration. Yet, funding streams were typically short term, and two thirds of the organisations had less than two years of guaranteed income (Table 6.4). None of the case study organisations had financial security beyond three years, and in one case, core funding had less than a year to run. Needless to say, this severely inhibits long-term service planning and development.

Local authority support centres on service-level agreements and project grants. Organisations reported a gradual shift from grants to service-level agreements or contracts that last on average for two or three years. Some welcomed this trend because it provided greater certainty in organising services, but others expressed the exact opposite view, arguing that they offered no long-term security of funding while increasing the level of bureaucratic control and form-filling. A further criticism was that entering into formal contracts reduced the user-led organisation's ability to generate new services in line with user views.

According to one disabled social worker employed by a local authority routinely engaged in securing funding for a local CIL:

> 'Every year we look at the budget and every year I have to fight for my corner and there's always the question of, even if we've got a service-level agreement, we might have to cut. So, why do

Table 6.4: Major sources of funding over the last three years for the case study organisations

	Local authority	Health authority	Central government	Lottery grants	European funding	Charities	Membership fees	Service income
CVCDP	✓							
DCIL	✓	✓		✓		✓	✓	✓
DANE			✓					
CILiG	✓		✓				✓	✓
GAD	✓			✓	✓		✓	✓
CILdG	✓		✓		✓			✓
LCIL	✓		✓	✓		✓	✓	✓
SUN	✓			✓				✓
WECIL	✓	✓	✓	✓		✓	✓	✓

Source: Barnes et al (2000, p 21)

we have service-level agreements? What kind of security does it give an organisation?' (Katy)

Moreover, some organisations complained that their staff budget was not increased in line with the cost of living:

'The part of our base budget which covers our employment costs has been frozen at last year's level.... While we mirror social work terms and conditions, we pay nationally negotiated costs of living increases and increments, we don't get increased funding for salaries from the [local authority] for that.' (Evan)

For those organisations reliant on yearly based funding contracts the situation was even more precarious:

'The core funding is yearly, so we're never sure from one year to the next whether our projects will be funded. So April, March we might be sending out redundancy notices.' (Jennie)

Uncertainty over funding affects both employees and service users, and means that there is a continuing pressure to identify new sources. This creates a heavy demand on staff time and energy that is already overstretched. Nevertheless, most research participants felt that some sources of funding should not be pursued or accepted. Most opposition centred on drug companies and charities with a tradition of providing conventional individualistic medical-type services. In one instance, the suspicions about cooperating with some local authority social services departments were more exceptional:

'We learned early on that when you work with local authorities, to consult on community care services ... all of a sudden you realise that your name's appearing on documents that you don't approve of.... Organisations like Leonard Cheshire and Scope, if they wanted to give us money we'd just tell them to sod off.' (Darrell)

Another organisation adopted a more formal policy that required making a prior binding agreement about what each side should deliver:

'It [the Constitution] says … whoever you take money from there's got to be some sort of agreement associated with it. You make your position absolutely clear in that agreement and that's what we do. We write it down; this is what we believe in. This is the way we work.… If you're not happy with that we don't want your money. It's basically as straightforward as that.' (Rod)

The precariousness of funding highlighted the importance of networking in identifying potential new sources:

'Being on [the local authority social services] committee meant we could access more easily information about regeneration initiatives and that's where a lot of funding has recently come from; so there's a lot of self-interest in a lot of the decisions we make about where we want to be on which committee.' (Rebecca)

It was because of these difficulties that one of the case study organisations employed a professional fundraiser. Even then, there was a constant conflict between reconciling user-controlled principles with the reality of securing finances:

'We formally engaged a fundraising consultant, the board set up a fundraising committee … and we drew up guidelines for fundraising. So there were certain things … could not be done in terms of fundraising, like out canvassing in the street, shaking cans, that kind of thing.' (Mary)

A further significant dilemma is whether to charge for services, particularly those provided directly to individuals, such as advocacy or direct payments support. Despite some reluctance, seven of the case study organisations raised money in this way (Table 6.4). Indeed, some of the funding acquired by user-led agencies is regarded as pump-priming money for specific projects with the assumption that the service will prove self-financing. While there is often greater autonomy in spending income generated in this way, there were concerns that local authorities might use this as a reason to reduce future funding.

Location and premises

Eighty-nine per cent of the organisations had their own premises or offices. Of the remainder, 6% had no fixed premises, and 4% operated out of an individual's home. Forty-two per cent of groups had exclusive use of their offices, while 47% shared their premises/offices with other groups. These included voluntary organisations (61%), social services departments (15%), health authorities (3%), other disability organisations (3%) and private organisations (3%).

Finding and securing satisfactory office accommodation was another crucial issue. In practice, the choice of premises is most typically a compromise between accessibility and affordability. Too often, affordable and accessible accommodation is located in unsuitable locations such as former day centres or on the outskirts of towns with poor public transport links. For example, one large well-established user-controlled organisation had its main office far out from the city centre in a building adjacent to a segregated special school for disabled children, although the organisation was opposed to segregated educational provision:

> 'It's not where we want to be, it's miles away from anywhere....
> We've wanted to move ever since we got here. It was the only accessible place that we could find, so it's always been an issue.'
> (Rebecca)

The high cost of office space often forced a compromise. Thus, three of the case study organisations were housed in former social services buildings close to local authority departments. While such a location had occasional advantages in terms of networking and accessing information, its overall effect was negative:

> 'You're in somebody else's building here, no matter what we're promoting ... you still feel like squatters.... We're actually stuck in the social services buildings and they [social services staff] actively drop in and out.... People are frightened as well to come in because they think that there is an ulterior motive of us being next to social services.' (Barbara)

Subsequently, this organisation moved to a more appropriate location.

Several of the case study organisations shared premises with other groups in the voluntary sector – in one instance with DIAL and People First. This was often viewed positively as it provided firm links to the local network of voluntary agencies and groups providing services to other disadvantaged groups. In contrast, sharing premises with traditional organisations for disabled people and 'carer's groups' was a source of tension:

> 'There's people who think that we're too radical and we'd influence other disabled people; they don't feel comfortable with the two approaches.' (Jennie)

The type of building can also create difficulties. For instance, an organisation with offices in a converted Christian church found that some users from other faiths felt unhappy visiting. Another CIL had its main office in an area known as hostile to people from minority ethnic groups:

> 'This area is particularly racist and not somewhere that a lot of black people feel at ease coming to really.' (Rebecca)

An added dilemma is whether to concentrate all activities in one location or, as with organisations serving a more rural population, operate 'satellite' offices.

Paid staff and volunteers

User-led organisations have promoted the employment of disabled people. Despite this, in practice, the proportion of disabled employees varies significantly. It is influenced by a variety of factors including organisational philosophy and structures, funding, the range and type of services offered, and the availability of disabled staff. Organisations with a specific focus, such as information providers, generally employ fewer staff than those offering a wide range of independent living services (Table 6.5). It is also evident that some organisations are very reliant on volunteers.

The number of paid employees ranges from two full-time staff members at DANE to 32 full-time and five part-time employees at WECIL – one of the largest user-led service providers in the UK. Six of the organisations employ both disabled and non-disabled people, with another in the postal survey reporting 20 non-disabled employees, although a majority (55%) are formally committed to recruiting only disabled employees.

Table 6.5: Number of paid staff numbers in case study organisations

	Full-time disabled staff	Full-time non-disabled staff	Part-time disabled staff	Part-time non-disabled staff
CVCODP	4	0	0	0
DANE	2	0	0	0
DCIL	2	5	9	8
CILiG	7	1	0	2
GAD	4	0	4	0
CILdG	1	0	2	2
LCIL	3	3	2	2
SUN	2	2	1	0
WECIL	29	3	5	0

Source: Barnes et al (2001, p 25)

Some agencies, with close links to local authorities, maintained that recruitment should be solely on the basis of the 'best person for the job'. Conversely, some campaigning organisations, such as DANE, employ only disabled people. Those agencies providing a range of services for both disabled and non-disabled people tend to adopt a more pragmatic approach.

Six of the case study organisations employ non-disabled staff, across a range of posts from administrative staff to support workers (Table 6.5). Three agencies had non-disabled directors or managers. Although all were committed to employing more disabled people, individuals expressed concerns about the practicalities of doing this. Managers reported a conflict between operating in a competitive marketplace and obtaining the resources necessary to support disabled employees (as required by current employment support schemes):

> 'What's that professor called? [Stephen Hawking]; we couldn't afford his wheelchair, we couldn't afford to provide him with a speaking machine. We couldn't afford the six or seven personal assistants he has helping him write his lectures.' (Rod)

Moreover, there were often considerable difficulties finding disabled people willing to accept short-term, temporary contracts – primarily because of their impact on social security benefits. Similarly, some organisations encountered difficulties when seeking to recruit suitable replacements for existing employees on (sick) leave.

Agencies with a 'disabled only' employment policy continued trying to fill vacancies, or where resources permitted, offered training schemes for unqualified disabled applicants. Others adopted a fall-back position:

> 'Initial adverts ask for disabled people or if it comes to a point at any time when we've advertised several times and not managed to recruit a disabled person then we'll advertise and say 'disabled person preferred', but would accept a non-disabled person.' (Rebecca)

However, this policy only applied to non-managerial staff or to posts not requiring direct contact with the general public.

There was an added tension in promoting good employment practice against a backcloth of generally short-term funding:

> 'Everyone's got a permanent contract but they're aware that if the funding runs out then redundancy's an option. There might be a temporary contract, but we've got a policy that says when you can do a temporary contract ... only if it's a specific time-limited piece of work, like to cover maternity leave or secondment, other than that everyone's on a permanent contract.' (Rebecca)

Several of the case study organisations provided induction processes for new personnel, as well as further training for existing staff.

Three quarters of organisations employ voluntary workers, and of this group, three quarters are disabled people. In several organisations voluntary workers played a significant role in operational activities. While organisations reported occasional problems in terms of reliability and commitment on the part of some volunteers, these workers were generally highly valued, although there was general recognition of the need to formalise the role of volunteers with contracts, induction and training programmes.

Review

Despite government protestations of encouragement for independent living services, user-led service organisations have experienced a range of obstacles in their development.

Thus far, user-controlled organisations in general offer a diverse range of support services, but individual agencies have found it well-nigh impossible to sustain the full range of support provision advocated in early debates around the 'seven needs' for independent living. There has also been a failure to achieve the intended levels of inclusion of all sections of the disabled population, notably minority ethnic groups and different impairment groups, as intended.

In part, these difficulties link with the lack of resources available to user-led organisations – not just in terms of funding, but in the shortage of staff and the accessibility of premises – and the overall impact on service provision. Funding is a basic difficulty: both because of its low level and lack of continuity, which leaves little scope to engage in long-term planning. Inadequate funding is exacerbated by the problems in recruiting and retaining disabled staff as well as a severe shortage of accessible office accommodation in convenient locations and available at a reasonable rent. Overall, user-led organisations find themselves at a considerable disadvantage in competing with mainstream service providers.

Moreover, user-controlled organisations feel constrained by associated political demands to monitor and assess the activities of service providers. The main consequences revolve around the cost and resource implications, and an extra complication is introduced where different funding bodies with contrasting information requirements are involved. There are also complaints that the 'official' emphasis on quantitative data, including the emphasis on impairment-specific reporting, is counterproductive or divisive compared with what is felt to be the more revealing and sensitive qualitative information preferred by user-controlled service providers.

In the following chapter, we explore how these concerns are reflected in users' experiences of the services offered.

SEVEN

Service users' views and experiences

Introduction

This chapter, first, foregrounds users' experiences using mainstream, community-based support services. A contrast is drawn with disabled people's experiences of user-led services. The discussion concentrates on the perceived advantages and disadvantages of the two forms of provision. Second, consideration is given to the impact of current economic and policy contexts on the promotion of 'independent living'. As previously noted, the growing emphasis on market forces and user involvement in government policy statements has provided a fertile context in which user-controlled initiatives have developed. Although small in number, organisations controlled and run by disabled people have provided a range of services that represent an alternative option to traditional, professionally led provision.

Third, there is a more detailed examination of the key aspects about user-led services that users believe set them apart from mainstream statutory and voluntary services. These range over the process of assessment of support needs through the quality and range of services to central claims by organisations of disabled people that user-controlled agencies provide greater choice and control to individual disabled service users. More specifically, the development of direct payments over recent years has provided an important opportunity for disabled employers of personal assistants (PAs) to draw on the wide-ranging experience of disabled people working in user-led organisations.

The final section considers the responses of research participants to questioning about the drawbacks and shortcomings in their experience of user-led services, and whether there was a discrepancy between the aims and objectives of user-controlled organisations and actual practice, and if so, what might be the explanation.

Views on mainstream services

The disabled participants in the *Creating Independent Futures* study received a range of services provided by a variety of providers: statutory, private and voluntary. The majority, 68, had used or were still using services supplied by local authority social services departments. These included the allocation of a social worker and/or case manager, home adaptations, home helps, and day centre placements. These services were delivered by different divisions within local authority social services departments, such as those for 'physical and sensory disabilities', 'mental health', 'learning disabilities' and 'community care'.

Several people were also receiving services provided by health authorities, large charities, local voluntary organisations and private agencies. Health authorities offered in-patient 'care', occupational therapy and physiotherapy services (12 people). Residential home and day centre facilities were supplied by the larger established charities such as MENCAP, which describes its focus as 'learning disability', and the Leonard Cheshire Foundation. Some people used information, peer support and advocacy services delivered by local voluntary organisations. Others were reliant on 'home help' and 'carer'-type services delivered by private agencies. Some were also receiving funding from the Independent Living Fund (ILF) for personal assistance packages. Levels of satisfaction with service provision varied greatly. In order to understand users' perceptions of user-controlled services it is instructive to gain an insight into their experiences of other forms of provision.

There was a broad consensus that assessments for support should be user led and that the assessment process posed a major barrier to independent living. Eligibility for state-sponsored services was determined after an assessment conducted by local authority staff. Yet for disabled people this process has been widely represented as a major 'bureaucratic barrier' to independent living (Barnes et al, 1995; Maynard-Campbell and Maynard-Lupton, 2000).

Most assessments were professionally led and this allowed participants little meaningful input on the outcome. Many interviewees thought that traditional service providers were not really interested in their opinions or in offering a more holistic service tailored to the individual. Instead, service users felt like one person on a long list, and that there were insufficient numbers of staff to complete a detailed assessment of their support needs:

'[T]hey just don't work to the services that you require, that you want. They suit themselves, they don't listen to the person that they are attending to. Mind you, I suppose that they are short of staff and that's their way.... "look we've got other people to attend to", but that's not what people want to hear.' (Betty)

Furthermore, research participants were acutely aware that financial considerations, rather than the required level of support needs, were the determining factor in the 'care' packages received:

'It was a fight to get any sort of care package to begin with. Their assessments were budget led.' (Anne)

For research participants, this confirmed the significance of moving towards a system of self-assessment:

There ought to be no compromise regarding self-assessment; it is fundamental to the empowerment of disabled people. It is critical in terms of the assessment process that self-assessment is the starting point in enabling disabled people to determine their own lifestyles. (Evans, quoted in Barnes et al, 1995, p 2)

The Prime Minister's Strategy Unit (PMSU) recently acknowledged that many disabled people are able to self-assess their own support needs, and that those who are regarded as unable to take on this task should be provided with the necessary help to do so. What is more, in the few cases where resources have been allocated for self-assessments, there is no evidence that this has led to disproportionate demands on services. Thus, in one of the evaluations of self-assessment, it was concluded that service users took up less hours of an on-call support scheme than had been predicted (PMSU, 2005, p 71). A similar pattern has been identified in the implementation of direct payments with considerable variance across the UK, nationally, regionally and locally, in how assessments are conducted and the degree of user involvement in the assessment process (Riddell et al, 2004).

The end result is a far from adequate outcome for service users in terms of the actual support received. This covered the type of services available, what they actually provided, and the number of hours or days of support allowed. For example, the restrictions on what home helps are supposed to do were a common concern. Many of those interviewed talked about the difficulties that this posed, particularly in relation to lifting and handling and domestic tasks such as washing up and putting things away. Conversely, it was also reported that some helpers carried out tasks that they were not supposed to do.

Reliability or the lack of it was a regular complaint. Home helps, including agency staff and those working as volunteers, came in for particular criticism. Several people talked about the frustration of not knowing when, or sometimes even whether, staff would turn up. If service providers were short-staffed, individuals could often be kept waiting for long periods of time.

> '[Y]ou can't be pedantic and say I want them at one minute to eight because there might be 400 of you in an area and 40 people coming out to do the care. So you have to allow for this and be flexible. What happens in reality is that you're up at half past seven (in the morning) waiting for your care worker and sometimes at a quarter to one in the afternoon you are still sitting there waiting for her.' (Anne)

The lack of flexibility (no doubt exacerbated by a heavy workload and inadequate resources) in the administration and organisation of mainstream services was another frequent cause for concern. The timing of support was usually determined by service agencies. This was a particular problem for people whose health condition fluctuated from day to day as the level of help needed would often vary accordingly. Examples include people with multiple sclerosis or people experiencing severe emotional distress. Participants suggested that there was little flexibility within conventional forms of support to accommodate such needs.

Another frequently mentioned issue related to the helper–helped relationship. A major factor was the relatively high levels of staff turnover within mainstream organisations, good helper–helped relations were often difficult to establish and maintain. Having a different home help or support worker come into their home on a regular basis was a major cause for concern among those interviewed. Indeed, the anxieties associated with having different people unfamiliar with their particular needs undertaking intimate and potentially 'embarrassing' personal tasks such as toileting were especially acute for some participants.

'You didn't know who was coming to see you and a lot of different people come and they would come in and tell you what they would do, they didn't know what to do with me, how to lift me or anything.' (Eddie)

The quality of support received varied considerably. Individuals considered themselves 'very lucky' to have a 'good' social worker or home help. However, it was evident that participants resented the fact that the quality of support available was such a lottery. This was a particular issue where the support was provided by agencies that relied on voluntary helpers:

'When I think back to the volunteers, some of the volunteers ..., I mean some were excellent but it was pot-luck because I had no involvement in recruiting those volunteers, I just had to make do with who turned up.' (Sue)

Respondents also felt that their opinions and priorities were not taken seriously by conventional service agencies, and that they were expected to be grateful for the services they received. Several people commented on their lack of control over the services delivered by professionally led statutory and voluntary service agencies.

'There was no control ... I was very much worked on, I was an object more than a subject.' (Mike)

Many service users said that they had to be constantly on their guard to ensure an appropriate level of support and that this was an unnecessary and unacceptable drain on personal resources.

'You have to be constantly on top of it, but you don't have the energy sometimes. You're fighting bureaucracy all the time.' (Claire)

The organisation and bureaucracy associated with conventional service provision means that complaining is often very difficult. Research participants frequently argued that complaints were rarely dealt with satisfactorily. Where people had gone down this route they felt that little was resolved. Moreover, those who made such comments ran the risk of being criticised for being a 'trouble maker' or else felt that their complaint was dismissed as unwarranted without any real investigation having taken place:

> 'You're put down as a whiner, or you're a moaner, the fact that you mightn't have had a shower for three or four days – "well, it doesn't really matter dear, you're not really going anywhere today, are you?"' (Anne)

Promoting user-led services

Over recent years an emerging theme in government policy has been the emphasis on enhanced choice and control for service users. It is demonstrated in the stated commitment to: first, increasing the numbers of people using direct payments and related funding schemes, and second, expanding the number of user-controlled organisations. For example:

> The Government is committed to seeing an increase in the take up of direct payments as they are an excellent way for individuals using social services to gain control and independence over their own lives. (DH, 2005b, unpaged)

In *Improving the Life Chances of Disabled People* the PMSU states:

> Local organisations, run and controlled by disabled people will be a vital part of the implementation of a new approach to supporting independent living. (PMSU, 2005, p 75)

However, the number of people using direct payments and related schemes remains relatively small. Recent government estimates suggest that approximately 1.46 million people received community-based support during the year 2003–04 in England alone, 4% more than in the previous year. Despite this only 17,300 adults aged 18 and over were in receipt of direct payments from local authorities, although this represents an 80% increase on 2002–03 when the figure stood at 9,600 (DH, 2005c, unpaged). Furthermore, there are proportionately fewer service users accessing direct payments in Northern Ireland, Wales and Scotland (Riddell et al, 2004; Pearson, 2006). Again, the *Creating Independent Futures* survey identified only 84 user-controlled organisations providing services to disabled people (Barnes et al, 2000, pp 32-4). Employing a narrower definition, recent official estimates suggest that there are currently 22 fully constituted Centres for Independent/Integrated/Inclusive Living (CILs) or 'disability organisations either providing a similar role or working towards becoming a CIL' (PMSU, 2005, p 70).

Consequently most disabled people across Britain remain reliant upon a bewildering array of services delivered by a variety of statutory and voluntary agencies generally, but not exclusively, controlled and run by non-disabled professionals and dominated by a culture of 'social care' rather than 'social rights' (Goodinge, 2000; PMSU, 2005). A particular problem revolves around what the New Labour government referred to as the 'Berlin Wall' of blurred and contested boundaries between 'health' and 'social care' services (Hudson, 1999). Since the welfare reforms of the 1940s community-based support for 'sick' and disabled people has been divided between 'health care' for the former and 'social care' for the latter. This has resulted in a tangled web of legal, administrative and organisational involvement that often makes it difficult to locate those responsible for services (Glasby and Littlechild, 2002; Glendinning, 2006). Thus, despite the government's stated commitment to increase the numbers of people using direct payments via the 2001 Health and Social Care Act, this relates:

> only to certain local authority social services. This means that where an individual has an identified health need under the NHS that part of any care package cannot be delivered as a direct payment within the meaning of the legislation including where a local authority is acting under a partnership agreement. (DH, 2005c, unpaged)

The problem of accessing coherent and comprehensive community-based support is exacerbated by the continuing tendency in both the statutory and voluntary sectors to provide services on an impairment-specific basis. People with the label of 'learning difficulties', 'mental health' system users and survivors, older and younger disabled people, and people from minority ethnic communities are especially disadvantaged when accessing direct payments (Luckhurst, 2005). This gives added weight to the argument that mainstream services are too structured by professional interests rather than users' needs (Abberley, 2004; Beresford, 2004).

Furthermore, although user-controlled organisations have tried to address this problem, their success rate in terms of attracting the involvement of people across the disabled population in the development and use of user-controlled provision has been marginal and very uneven. This low coverage unfortunately mirrors the low involvement of minority groups among the disabled population in most community organisations, from both the statutory and voluntary sectors.

Accessing user-led services

It is notable that a majority of the service users interviewed were directed towards user-led service provision by professionals employed by statutory authorities.

As Table 7.1 indicates, 33 people, or almost half of the individuals interviewed, had been referred to user-controlled services by someone employed by local authority social services departments or the health authority. These referrals were predominately made by social workers. The proportion of referrals by professionals was consistently higher in those areas where there were strong links between user-controlled organisations and the local social services department or health authority, such as Cardiff, Glasgow and Surrey. Also, there was a clear correlation between referral by a social worker and the use of direct payment-related services. Typically, as one participant in an area with a well-established user-controlled organisation pointed out:

> 'I would say that that particular office at social services was quite proactive in helping me get in touch with the direct payment scheme.' (Peter)

However, there is no system of automatic referral to disabled people's organisations by medical and allied health 'care' professionals, even at the time of diagnosis. A number of people who had recently acquired an

Table 7.1: How users accessed user-led services

Type of access	Number
Referral by professionals	33
Word of mouth	19
Contact by the organisation	15
Referral by other impairment/disability organisation	4
Self-referral	3
Unknown	2
Total interviewees	76

Source: Barnes et al (2001, p 19)

impairment commented on the failure of health service professionals to provide information about disability groups and user-controlled organisations. This left them feeling isolated and unsure of the future:

> 'When I started to become ill and went down to the [hospital], he [the consultant] gives you a prognosis, I was left absolutely devastated. There was no information in the hospital whatsoever, and I wasn't in a state to ask. Basically I went home not aware of any group whatsoever.... You're by yourself, you don't know where to go.' (Ray)

Nonetheless, more than half of the user sample had started using user-controlled services because the organisation had contacted them or they had heard about it through discussions with family and/or friends. Fifteen of the 76 individuals interviewed had been contacted directly by the case study organisation either by telephone or through an outreach/development worker. Larger and established organisations had more users who had heard about their services from other disabled people, family and friends:

> 'I wouldn't have found out about [the local CIL] if I hadn't heard about it through friends.' (Alan)

For the older more established organisations the nature of user involvement was more complex. Some people had been involved from the outset, although almost half of the service users had only been involved with user-controlled services for less than two years – a pattern that can only be partly explained by the relative 'newness' of many user-controlled organisations.

Use of services

Research participants had experience of a range of services provided by the case study organisations. Table 7.2 illustrates the range and type of services used.

In discussion, comparisons between professionally led and user-led services highlighted two main themes: namely, choice and control. Participants were adamant that user-led organisations were far more responsive to their needs both in terms of what was on offer and how it

Table 7.2: Pattern of service use

Services	Number
Direct payments	39
Direct payments/PA employers' support services	38
Information	37
Training	31
Counselling	12
Volunteers	11
Total interviewees	76

Note: Several people used more than one service.

Source: Barnes et al (2001, p 21)

was offered. They felt that they had a greater choice of services and, equally important, more control over how they were delivered.

A significant reason underlying this pattern is that a majority of the research participants were involved either directly or indirectly with direct payments programmes. Those in receipt of direct payments (39 people) via the case study organisations confirmed conclusions from previous research studies that a PA can often bring about a significant improvement in the quality of disabled people's lives (Lakey, 1994; Zarb and Nadash, 1994; Glendinning et al, 2000; Stainton and Boyce, 2002):

> 'I have transferred from a social services' help at home to a direct payment scheme via the [user-controlled organisation]. We were struggling with the kind of help we were having.... [The independent living support worker from the organisation] came to see us with my social worker. We discussed the whys and wherefores, and we thought we would at least attempt to use this direct payment scheme.... From day one the impact was just totally different. It totally turned our lives around.' (Angela)

Thirty-eight people (50%) used direct payment/PA employer support services. Several of the case study organisations were unable to offer both direct payments schemes and PA employers' support systems. However, even where both were offered some people used one but not the other. Experienced users tended to use direct payments but not necessarily the support service other than as trainers or to offer peer support. Some people accessed direct payments from other agencies but attended PA employers' support groups run by the case study organisation:

'Nobody was available to help me with the Independent Living [Fund], to tell me how to go about paying anything or how to sort it. I was at my wits end when I discovered the [CIL]. M… [a disabled support worker] has been exceptionally helpful. I was over today to talk to her about the payment of Income Tax and National Insurance. I actually had to call the taxman. He didn't know anything about carers, about people like me employing carers. He had never heard of it before. They had me down as a director of a company [laughs]. They sent me all this bumf on tax and paying employees. I have one lady who is on Family Credit [a tax credit for people with families on low incomes] so I don't know how to go about paying her as a carer…. That is where M… comes in.' (Claire)

Other people used independent living support services in order to prepare the way for employing PAs. Almost everyone felt that this was a particularly important service given disabled people's lack of familiarity with employment issues. Another recurring complaint has been that social workers and other professionals question the competence of disabled people applying for direct payments (Witcher et al, 2000):

'I went to the social work side and it went so far, and basically it was binned at a certain level. I didn't get the support to follow it through, or the information. So I went back and challenged them and came down here to the CIL … and that's why I've been coming on the training schemes…. They bring you up to speed with what's necessary if and when you're on the payments scheme. How do you handle your personal assistants? How do you handle your payroll? How do you do your recruitment? They make sure you've got everything in line and order…. The CIL, it can keep you totally on the right track; not some of the time, most of the time.' (Arthur)

Many studies have drawn attention to the difficulties disabled people face accessing relevant information (Moore, 1995). The situation is especially acute for people with newly acquired impairments:

'It's the "catch-22" situation, in as much as when you most need it, when you become disabled or incapable of performing certain

functions, it becomes harder and harder to obtain information,
One might say "well you just need to go to the library or you
just need to call this office or that office", but if you've not
experienced that syndrome before it can be a very frustrating
and long process trying to get in touch with the people who
can help you.' (Paul)

Thirty-seven of the user respondents (49%) had deliberately sought out
information from the organisations visited. This included information
provided via the telephone, via the internet and, where resources permitted,
on a face-to-face basis. This applied to a full range of independent living
issues including direct payments, PA services, housing, employment, and
disabled people's rights:

'One of the things that they started to do was develop a resource,
a special library. This was particularly around independent living
issues and I suppose some of the broader issues that come from
that.... We used it a lot and referred disabled people to go and
use it, and also professionals who were working and advocating
and wanted to know more about the issues.

   The other thing that they did on the information side was to
set up different groups; a [disabled] women's group etc. We would
certainly refer a lot of people through to those groups. It was
useful for a lot of people to ... to have the opportunity not only
to get information, but also to meet with other people and
exchange information in that way. Conversations can create a
very dynamic exchange of information rather than leaflets.'
(Mavis)

In fact, all the case study organisations produced some form of newsletter
for circulation to members and users. These are regarded as particularly
helpful for people living alone or in residential homes:

'Previously I lived in [Home A] and then we were told they
were going to knock it down and rebuild it in a year's time. So
I had to move from there. When we moved I had to attend
some meetings all over the [local] area. I was a member of a
focus group and it was most interesting hearing other people's
points of view how they fared in their [residential] homes. Now

I get a regular magazine from [the CIL] which is most useful because it contains all the information that I need.' (Clive)

Almost half of the participants identified as both users and members of their local CIL. Eleven acted as volunteers – reflecting the attempts made to encourage users to get actively involved in the running of the organisation and the services offered.

Training facilities and courses were offered to service users by all the user-controlled organisations, and had been used by 31 (41%) of the interviewees. Examples included training in computer skills, art and drama, practical independent living skills, counselling and advocacy and as Disability/Distress Equality Trainers. Besides enabling individuals to acquire new skills and self-esteem, these training programmes gave some people the confidence to think about employment. The following statements from a disabled mother living in a remote rural community and a disabled man who runs a consultancy firm illustrate this point:

'I've done two computer courses, I did the initial one, it was just basics.… It was all about moving things around and getting to know your computer, which was brilliant. And then we had another course where people from the college brought in little laptop computers, we did documentation things, word based and processing. You get a certificate at the end of it, so that's good.… You feel you've achieved something. And, if you were able to go back to work, which unfortunately I'm not at the moment, it does give you the start to say "well look, I've got this under my belt", you know.' (Diane)

'The training I received enabled me to be a proficient deliverer of Disability Awareness or Equality Training. I've found the training very good.… I've more confidence, not just in myself but in the whole group. When we were looking to set up and do it, I wanted it done more professionally. I'd done it informally in the past with various other people and I wanted to take it a step further, get it on a more professional footing. So let's go to the experts … and get some training. We approached them. We approached them and there was a training package, so that was very good.' (Trevor)

Twelve of the interviewees were involved in counselling programmes – either as trainee counsellors or as users of the counselling services. This service was considered especially important and was based directly on users' individual and collective experiences. In recent years, there has been a considerable expansion of such programmes as more and more people seek professional help to resolve all manner of personal difficulties. Disabled people are no exception. The demand for counselling, particularly where it involved a disabled counsellor, was particularly valued by people who have recently acquired an impairment and/or only recently become aware of disability issues.

Nevertheless, disabled people are generally ill-served by the counselling industry (Lenny, 1993; Corker, 1995; Thomas, 1999). While some individuals find orthodox counselling services helpful, many are faced by 'counsellors who are unaware of their disablist attitudes' or of the lived experience of disability (Reeve, 2000, p 672):

> 'I initially rang up and spoke to a lady and from the very first telephone call I felt ... that I could trust her. She understood the emotions that I was going through, because no matter how much you talked, even my wife who's able-bodied, they don't seem to realise what emotions are boiling inside of you. They don't seem to understand what aspect you're coming from. I rang up and arranged to come down and speak to the lady here ... it's quite difficult to come to someone and say "there's something wrong with me".' (Steve)

> 'When I came here they gave me confidence to carry on with my life, to carry on with work, make decisions about your future. I know there's a support group here and there's someone who I can come and talk to whereas before I didn't. You thought you were alone, you thought you were the only person in the world, but you're not.' (Ray)

It is not simply the type of services provided that makes user-controlled organisations more appreciated. The fact that disabled people were clearly in control in running the organisation made a deep impression on newcomers and was widely described as a source of considerable satisfaction and pride. User-controlled agencies were regarded as much more aware of, and sensitive to, the barriers facing disabled people and, consequently, were more responsive to their individual needs. A man with physical impairments and experience of the 'mental health' system put it this way:

'When I was on my own without a PA or somebody I could exchange information or confidences with.… Well I would have either become a basket case or, to be honest with you, a suicidal case, because the effect of being long-term ill only gets worse. Psychologically the [CIL] gives the individual a sense of identity and a sense of which place to go for help. So it certainly is a lifeline in that respect.' (Peter)

The formal and informal peer support individual service users received from other disabled people active in the organisations studied was a key factor in combating the social isolation that many disabled people encounter. Having the opportunity to meet other disabled people either formally, for example, in PA employers' support groups, or informally in general meetings, social occasions, and during drop-in sessions was considered to be an immense benefit by the overwhelming majority of the people we talked to.

Notably, just under half (33) of the 76 user participants in the *Creating Independent Futures* study lived alone, while a further six stayed in residential or 'group' homes. The remainder lived with their family, partner or friends. The following statements typify the views of the majority of respondents:

'I've been a member of [the local CIL] for about three years now. I come to a lot of their meetings and found them most interesting. I look forward to meetings where a group of us get together and discuss our various incapacities in various ways … physical … mental.… We find it really interesting having a chat and playing games.' (Clive)

'All the disabled people here respect one another and we don't ask one another what our disabilities are unless you want to tell people yourself. And there's no person who thinks they're better than the other.' (Megan)

'I think as long as they have a variety of disabled people, then you all learn from one another.' (Sian)

Furthermore, membership of a multi-impairment organisation has important positive outcomes in terms of disability awareness:

> 'As far as I am concerned, [coming to the CIL] has taught me an awful lot because I've had a physical disability since I was six years old. I've had juvenile arthritis and I've always been involved with physical disability organisations. I was on the management committee of [the organisation] for several years and various other things but I didn't know much about people with learning difficulties, people with mental health problems, even people with sensory impairments, I'm afraid to say. So it has made me an awful lot more aware of other sorts of problems people face.' (Belinda)

Nonetheless, this participant also acknowledged that meetings which draw on multiple-impairment groups can sometimes pose problems both for organisers and participants:

> 'It can be quite difficult sometimes, because some people ... people with mental health problems get quite cross about things and might make a scene or something. But I think it's really good that we all come together sometimes and learn to listen to each other people's problems.' (Belinda)

The high level of satisfaction among participants with the services offered by user-led organisations is hardly a surprise, but important nonetheless. It was rooted in the priority attached to enhanced user choice and control, and peer support to lead less dependent lives. It was significant that this view was expressed by individuals with a very different range of impairments.

Wants and aspirations

Of course, user-controlled services, in common with all welfare provision, must operate within a variety of external (as well as internal) constraints. How far is this reflected in the perception of the relative 'failings' of user-controlled service provision compared with their stated objectives?

One widely referenced criticism was over the lack of information about the benefits of user-controlled services, and the organisations offering them among the general public and specifically disabled people:

> 'I certainly think they could improve by making more people aware that the place is here, Even now, I don't see this place advertised. People like myself, who become disabled, you don't know who to turn to … I think they should present themselves a bit better than they do.' (Ray)

Several people said that they had only heard about user-controlled services by 'chance' or 'luck', often because of their involvement with other more conventional services:

> 'Well I go to a day centre twice a week which is how I got into [the CIL] because one of the [disabled] women at the centre became involved in a clerical way and she invited some of the [day centre] clients, that are still there, to go to meetings and things.' (Linda)

Indeed, three participants had contacted their local user-controlled organisation after learning about it via their publicity leaflets. Surprisingly, only four participants had become aware of local user-controlled services through their involvement with other local impairment/disability groups.

> 'The [organisation] is very unknown and that bothers me. Even in the disabled world I find most people have never heard of it.' (Ceri)

It was a very real concern for some participants that CILs were not attracting younger disabled people with ideas and enthusiasm that were so necessary to keep the movement active:

> 'I know a lot of the people who've been involved, some of them have been involved for a long time … there's new people involved too. As long as they can continue to attract new people, I think that's the key to the success of the organisation. They need to bring new people into the organisation and engage them with the issues that need to be looked at. That means

keeping it relevant.… You won't engage young people if your organisation gets staid and middle class and middle of the road. You need to be fairly cutting edge … for them more than any other disability group on the area.' (Margaret)

A related issue is the difficulties associated with covering a large geographical area, particularly given the poor provision of accessible transport around the country. Several of the case study organisations have responsibility for very large areas, with much of it rural. While these organisations have tried to address this problem by developing telephone and computer-based options as well as operating from several locations, nevertheless, some people will still confront barriers when seeking to access support:

'[The CIL] is now a big organisation but if you live on the outskirts of [the area served] you can't get as involved as when you live close to this place. I come from the edge of [the area] so I feel [the organisation] could benefit if it could stretch out. You feel very much that you're on your own; you haven't got an organisation. I come down willingly because I feel that maybe I will learn something and perhaps can say something that someone else might find helpful. But it's a long way to come and very costly.' (Millie)

Some participants were unhappy about the accessibility of the buildings used by organisations. Comments include their geographical location, lack of accessible public transport, inaccessible or inappropriate buildings, including, in some cases difficulties with physical access once inside the building. The lack of control of user-led organisations in these areas was recognised, but the lack of access remained a contentious issue, with higher expectations of disability organisations.

Several participants commented on the inefficiency or ineffectiveness of specific aspects of user-controlled provision. These concerns mainly centred on administrative issues and issues surrounding the employment of only disabled staff. In practice, staff shortages are an all too common feature of user-controlled provision (see Chapter Six). This can easily impact on the continuity and effectiveness of service provision, as the following statements illustrate:

'I said could you get any help for me with gardening and things like that, because I'm a single parent now. I've got no one. I've got no one around the house to do these things. She said leave it with me and then no one ever came. I think she passed it on to someone. I don't know who it was that dealt with it, some sort of voluntary organisation that sent people out to help disabled people. But I've never heard anything.' (Lesley)

'I have written three letters to the [organisation] manager and to the [Independent Living) coordinator, all of which remain unanswered. That should not be acceptable.' (Ian)

'It can sometimes be a bit slow to respond, with the risk that a fairly minor problem can escalate before it is dealt with. Staff shortages and sick leave seem to present a lot of problems. The [organisation] is known for being a good employer but somewhere along the line this translates into a lot of staff being on [often long-term] sick leave. The problem seems to be a lack of contingency arrangements, so that remaining staff have to pick up the slack or things don't get dealt with.' (Liz)

Many respondents linked these problems to the innovatory nature of the services offered. While such explanations may help to enhance a sense of collective involvement they also tend to gloss over any difficulties encountered and thus contribute to feelings of insecurity that many people feel about the future of user-led provision.

The overwhelming majority of the participants in the *Creating Independent Futures* study were very aware of the precarious nature of their organisation's funding, particularly in comparison with service provision that is not under the direction of disabled users. They also appreciated the difficulties this creates for the continuity of services and staff retention:

'They are understaffed, no question ... [one member of staff] is in huge demand ... for the payroll, so you would ring ... but in the back of your mind you know that there's already a queue of people waiting to speak to her ... wanting for her to come out to their house.' (Anne)

'Very recently a lot of staff changes have taken place which makes it hard to have consistency.' (Ruth)

'In the area of service provision the only improvement would be to expand the range of services and this could only be done with extra funding.' (Les)

There was a broad consensus that investment should be made available for an expansion of provision offered by CIL-type organisations. In addition to the independent living category of services, these ranged from conventional services like occupational therapy through to swimming lessons and social activities such as discos. However, there was a firm opposition to any suggestion that CILs resurrect the much-criticised notion of the 'day centre'.

Further questions were raised about user-controlled services and their relationship with conventional professional groups like, for example, occupational therapists, and their professional associations, as well as mainstream service providers such as health authorities, local authority social services departments, and voluntary agencies run by non-disabled professionals. Most user-controlled organisations are linked in various ways to traditional service providers such as local authorities. However, participants were extremely critical of any suggestion that there might be a dilution in the control exercised by disabled people over CILs, or in their participation in service development and delivery. They also felt that those involved in the organisation and delivery of services should represent a range of impairments and that no one impairment group should dominate.

Nevertheless, it was recognised that the experience of disability alone was insufficient to equip disabled people with the knowledge and skills necessary to develop and run the increasingly complex array of services required by the disabled population as a whole:

'I do think disabled people should be involved in running services but they need to know what they are talking about. They should be given appropriate training. They should be suitable for the job, not just disabled.' (Bethan)

An associated related issue concerns the role of disabled staff. Some people maintained that it was very important for disability services to be run and controlled exclusively by disabled people. For this group, everyone involved should have experienced disability. Others argued that non–disabled people may be included but only when they can provide the type of expertise and support that would otherwise not be available.

Besides this, participants expressed differing views on the relationship between user-led services and other forms of provision. Some people argued strongly that CILs and other user-controlled initiatives should be independent of mainstream agencies and service providers, but other disabled participants were much more positive about links with statutory agencies. They argued that user-controlled services had a lot to gain from sharing information, support and so forth. A similar divergence in opinion characterised the approach to advocacy and campaigning activities, and what form, if any, these might take.

Review

Overall, disabled people criticised mainstream (statutory and voluntary) services for failing to address adequately the support needs of a diverse disabled population. Specific targets ranged from the professional domination of the assessment process, and particularly the opposition to self-assessment, the unreliability and lack of flexibility in services, through to their restricted aims. Access to services seemed determined largely by the availability of funding rather than by individual need.

In response to such shortcomings, disabled people have increasingly sought to promote user-led organisations. Although lacking the resources to provide a fully comprehensive service, CIL-type agencies are regarded as substantially more receptive to disabled people's needs. A key factor is their emphasis on user control and involvement of users in service design and delivery. Even so, there was a widespread feeling that it has been difficult to break down the entrenched impairment-specific focus of support services.

Accessing user-led services was inhibited by the relative lack of knowledge of the existence or aims of user-led organisations. Once involved, service users were impressed by the far greater choice and control over service provision, a feature particularly emphasised by those in receipt of direct payments, and other support, as with information and further training schemes, for living more ordinary lives in the community. However, despite these much higher levels of satisfaction among disabled people using user-led services, concerns were expressed about various aspects of such provision – from the accessibility of premises to the lack of resources. On this evidence, the development of user–controlled services is an important development within the matrix of services for disabled people. However, as the expectations of user–controlled services intensify, there is a question mark against how user–led organisations do and should respond.

The next task, in Chapter Eight, is to examine the role and impact of political campaigning on user–led organisations.

EIGHT

Politics and campaigning

Introduction

The unprecedented politicisation of disability by disabled activists and groups in Britain was fuelled by the philosophy of independent living and the social model of disability. Political campaigning has been an important factor in the government decision to introduce major legislation such as the 1995 Disability Discrimination Act and the 1996 Community Care (Direct Payments) Act. Despite their shortcomings, these have enhanced both disabled people's claim to citizenship rights and their participation in disability-related services. It is also necessary to consider how the changing politics of disability have impacted on Britain's network of user-controlled organisations and Centres for Independent/Integrated/Inclusive Living (CILs).

   This chapter will examine the conflicts and dilemmas for user-controlled organisations that arise from their dual roles of service provider and political advocate for disabled people's rights. Two main questions are posed: first, how far have disabled people's organisations maintained their traditional role in political campaigning and advocacy? Second, how far, and in what ways, has their campaigning role been constrained by the demands of being a service provider within an organisational and policy environment that is liable to prove hostile to overt political engagement. The discussion examines: first, the range of campaigning activities, from local to international levels, engaged in by user-led organisations; second, the aims and tactics of campaigning; third, the range and character of 'consciousness-raising' activities; and finally, the impact of campaigning on the relationships with funding bodies.

Politics: the local viewpoint

The politicisation of disability in the 1960s and 1970s generated both an ideological and a practical solution to the problem of disabled people's exclusion from everyday life in the development of the philosophy of independent living, and self-help organisations (Oliver and Zarb, 1989; Charlton, 1998). The growth of user-controlled provider organisations such as CILs signalled a further phase in collective political action. This was illustrated in the political action in support of direct payments:

> 'People in the scheme campaigned quite hard in terms of lobbying politicians, going to meetings, going to politicians and harassing them in order to establish and maintain the scheme … within an organisation of disabled people with a funding base to enable them to deliver a quality service.
>
> So it's not been a situation where we've had a director and a chair of social services who've said yes this is great, whatever you want you can have it. I think it's pretty much been driven by disabled people and we've worked hard to find allies to support us … and to make it clear both to senior politicians and to local politicians that it [the CIL] is what people wanted and if necessary they are prepared to fight for it.' (Andy)

However, there has been a significant question mark in the literature on social protest movements about the capacity of campaigning groups to maintain their radical edge once their ideas and policies are incorporated into the mainstream political agenda. As DeJong (1983) suggested in respect of the growth of the Independent Living Movement in the US, its political trajectory followed a 'natural history' of social protest movements (see Chapter Three). With the beginnings of acceptance of the grievances and policy recommendations, disabled people's groups began to seek influence increasingly within traditional government institutions and processes. This change in political direction has been reinforced by the gathering acceptance of disabled people's human and civil rights and the promotion of user involvement in service delivery by politicians and policy makers. This led some disability activists to argue that as more and more disabled individuals and agencies become embroiled in the complexities of traditional politics on the one hand and service development and delivery on the other that their priorities change and their radicalism in terms of both political aspirations and activities diminishes (Charlton, 1998; GMCDP, 2000).

A further dimension to user-controlled initiatives is that they seek not only to generate collective involvement in formal political institutions and activism, it is also about self-empowerment, political engagement and struggle for citizenship rights (Barton, 2001). From this perspective, organisational participation in wider political activities is crucially interwoven with the design and delivery of services designed to enable disabled individuals achieve greater autonomy and independence.

The responses to the *Creating Independent Futures* survey indicate a general concern to promote the implementation of the principles of independent living and the social model of disability and to challenge the mainstream service environment that continues to be dominated by individualistic perspectives. Seventy-three per cent of the organisations responding to our survey claim to campaign actively on disability issues. The main topics range widely: from disability rights, service cuts, charging for services through to environmental access. Over a quarter of groups (28%) organise activities on impairment-specific issues addressing the particular problems encountered by, for example, people with the label of 'learning difficulties' or people with 'mental health' problems. Thirteen per cent reported that they support campaigns to highlight specific barriers associated with gender, 'race'/ethnicity and sexuality. Far less, 10%, campaigned on 'carers' issues, and this tended to be related to personal assistance services and support rather than more traditional 'carers' concerns. In part this is explained by the higher profile given by politicians and policy makers to the perspectives of 'carers' in 'caring for' disabled family members (Morris, 1993a).

As illustrated in Table 8.1, most organisations are involved in active campaigning at the local level, but the number declines significantly when considering regional/national/international levels. There is a further tendency for campaigning to vary according to the type of issue. Thus, there is greater engagement in broad 'disability rights' campaigns at 'higher' levels, with regional and national action particularly evident among organisations in Wales and Scotland. Very few local agencies are involved in political activities at either the European or the international level.

Involvement in political campaigns can take a number of forms. Some agencies such as the Centre for Inclusive Living in Glasgow (CILiG), Lothian Centre for Integrated Living (LCIL) and West of England Centre

Table 8.1: Campaigning activity – at different levels (%)

	Local	Regional	National	European	International
Disability rights issues	73	42	53	9	6
Impairment-specific issues	28	10	9	1	n/a
Carers issues	10	n/a	n/a	n/a	n/a
Other, eg gender, sexuality, ethnicity	13	7	7	1	1

Source: Barnes et al (2000, p 25)

for Inclusive Living (WECIL) present themselves primarily as service providers. Others, notably, Cardiff and Vale Coalition of Disabled People (CVCDP), Greenwich Association of Disabled People's Centre for Independent Living (GAD) and Derbyshire Coalition for Inclusive Living (DCIL) – formerly Derbyshire Centre for Integrated Living – argue for a twin focus, while Disability Action North East (DANE) and Surrey Users Network (SUN) operate more exclusively as campaigning organisations.

The picture is complicated because some service provider organisations have close ties to separate local campaigning groups and agencies. For instance, the Lothian Coalition of Disabled People (LCDP) began operations in 1991 to campaign on disability issues in Edinburgh and Lothian. It was formed the same year as LCIL by leading members of LCIL and occupied offices in the same building until its demise in April 2004. The formation of the Coalition was considered necessary in order to avoid jeopardising the LCIL's emerging relationship with the local authority and its social services department. However, the withdrawal of funding from the local authority and dwindling support from local disabled people led to the Coalition's demise.

In some cases, disabled activists have established both a local campaigning group and (typically afterwards) a user-controlled service provider organisation. This happened in Derbyshire and in the West of England, where WECIL was formed by local disabled people many of whom were members of the West of England Coalition of Disabled People (WECODP). In such instances, the creation of the two user-led organisations is pre-eminently a pragmatic strategy rather than a reflection of distinct ideological positions. Indeed, the two organisations have overlapping membership and often share resources and political goals:

> 'We've always been separate from the Coalition but … we've done a lot of things together, and we're involved with a lot of things together and we work – we're kind of interdependent if you like. They're not totally campaigning because they have an information service that we use as well, and it's meant that we haven't had to develop a separate or bigger information service because the Coalition's grapevine has got that. They also spawned "Ideal Training", which is Disability Equality Training (DET). So again we use Ideal Training [schemes] and our disability equality trainers as well.' (Margaret)

'[The Coalition] is an overt campaigning organisation. Like, we wouldn't launch a campaign on a particular issue as that's the Coalition's job. But, we [the CIL] would always make sure that we're in situations where decisions were being made. So campaigning with a small 'c' we do all the time. We're forever talking to social services about their policies and practices and we talk to the Education Department about inclusive education, and to [Employment Agencies] about disabled people and employment. So we're always there banging on. And we do write to MPs [Members of Parliament] over particular issues. We invite local MPs to our AGM [Annual General Meeting] and lobby them too.' (Rebecca)

Campaigning issues and activities

In areas where overt disability activism has not flourished, the task of political engagement and support has fallen to the local user-controlled organisation. This has frequently entailed the provision of accommodation and transport, formal and informal lobbying of local politicians and policy makers. A notable example is the 'Scottish Personal Assistance Employers Network' (SPAEN, 2004), a campaigning organisation of and for personal assistance users initiated and developed by CILiG, LCIL and the National Centre for Independent Living (NCIL).

Some participants argued that a user-controlled service provider with a positive working relationship with its local authority can become a valuable resource for local politicians and policy makers. From that perspective, high-profile political campaigning may prove counterproductive:

'I think we have a disproportionate effect.... I think we're respected because we haven't done traditional campaigning in terms of Direct Action on the streets and all that.... Because we haven't done that, if somebody wants some feedback they will come to us, expecting to get an intelligent and constructive response. We're getting consulted quite a lot.' (Evan)

This suggests that some draw a distinction between political activity with a large 'P' and a small 'p'. Others denied that a service provider role was incompatible with political campaigning. The CVCDP, GAD and DCIL offer three such examples. CVCDP began as a small but active group campaigning for disability rights and independent living services for personal assistance users. It is now an established service provider in Cardiff and the Vale of Glamorgan but it has retained a wide-ranging political agenda. This was clearly indicated by its statement of objectives presented to the local authority's Policy and Audit Review Committee in July 2000:

i.   the development of the Disabled People's Movement through membership of the Cardiff and Vale Coalition of Disabled People; its activities and publications etc;
ii. increasing the power and influence of disabled people in public life;
iii. campaigning for civil rights legislation;
iv. influencing commercial and public bodies;
v.   maintaining and developing an independent living scheme for disabled people;
vi. the development of a disability and resource centre to provide information for disabled people on their rights and entitlements;
vii. the development of a training programme on disability to empower disabled people and educate staff in public and commercial bodies (Policy Review and Audit Scrutiny Committee, 2000, p 2).

Among its catalogue of services, GAD offers 'Campaigns for Disabled People's Rights' (GAD, 2003), while since March 2000 disability activism and user-controlled service provision in Derbyshire has been formally combined within one county-wide organisation – the 'Derbyshire Coalition for Inclusive Living'. Indeed, the choice of name is a symbolic reaffirmation of its members' political aspirations.

> In Derbyshire a Coalition was formed by disabled people to represent their interests directly. Social understanding of disability was promoted by campaigns, advocacy, and dialogue with public service authorities. (DCIL, 2003, p 1)

Other user-led agencies see their primary role as advocacy and campaigning. SUN and DANE provide obvious examples. Thus, SUN was established solely to represent service users' interests within the Surrey area:

> 'We're a campaigning organisation. We do offer support and training but also we do what I call empowerment. Particularly, support for small organisations that are having problems keeping

going, and we will put someone in like R... to support and work with them. Human rights, charging, anything that effects people directly – disadvantaged people – that's what we do. And we will campaign on what the members specifically tell us.' (Colin)

Similarly, DANE came into existence to challenge disabled people's social exclusion and denial of their citizenship rights.

> Formed in June 1992, Disability Action North East (DANE) is a political network of disabled people and our allies. DANE believes the source of disabled people's problems is not our bodies, minds, or intellect, but society. Disability is a social oppression. (DANE, 2004a, unpaged)

Moreover, all the organisations are members of the British Council of Disabled People (BCODP). This national link is reinforced by the overlap in involvement with some individuals engaged in the organisation and delivery of local disability services and politics as well as participating at the national, and sometimes international, levels. Additionally, some local groups network with similar organisations in other parts of the world in order to share experiences. In 1998, for example, DCIL hosted a training week for 10 Russian visitors. Individuals from DCIL and their Young Disabled People's Project have in turn attended events in Moscow. The exchange of ideas covered peer support, advocacy, community development and direct political action involving a demonstration highlighting the inaccessibility of Moscow's underground railway (DCIL, 2000, pp 2-3).

Direct action

From the outset, the Disabled People's Movement has been willing to employ a variety of tactics in its political campaigns. These have ranged from conventional lobbying and pressure group activity to more direct activities such as public demonstrations, marches and sit-ins. Nevertheless, user-controlled service providers have often been uneasy about engaging in direct political action. The reasons range widely and include an impact on their charitable status, relations with local authorities, funding arrangements, and the attitudes of service users and members.

When the fieldwork for the *Creating Independent Futures* study was being undertaken, it was perfectly legal for charitable organisations to campaign openly 'for the rights of people with disabilities and the elderly' and on 'equal opportunities matters' (Charity Commission, 2004, p 9), although they were:

> restricted in the extent to which they can engage in political activities by the legal rules applying to charities. (Charity Commission, 2004, p 5)

The interpretation of these rules was far from agreed, but many user-controlled service agencies have a charitable status. This led to considerable fears that failure to comply with these rules would result in a loss of revenue for the organisation. More generally, there is a degree of ambiguity about the role of charities and political engagement:

> Campaigning by charities to mobilise public opinion to influence government policy can arouse strong feelings. On the one hand, many people think that charities should be allowed and indeed have a duty, to campaign freely to change public policy on any issue if it is relevant to their work and if they have direct experience to offer. On the other hand, some argue that such campaigning is a misuse of charity funds, a misdirection of charities and a misuse of the fiscal concessions from which charities benefit. (Charity Commission, 1999, p 12)

In addition, many user-led organisations are linked through a variety of funding arrangements to various statutory bodies such as local authority social services departments, and National Health Service (NHS) Trusts. This can act as a constraint on local user group political action, and explains why some organisations, such as DANE, have fought hard to avoid becoming reliant on funding from such agencies. The dilemma for local groups is exacerbated because the interests of their members are directly or indirectly affected by policies emerging from local and health authorities – such as possible charges for day, domiciliary and respite 'care' and other non-residential services.

Research by Age Concern England shows that the amount people who are charged for services that they use varies significantly. Many people who rely on 'home care' saw the costs rise during 2003-04, some by as much as £234 per week. Only a third of local authorities provide transitional support grants to help deal with these increases. With most authorities charging by the hour, it is those who need the highest levels of support that are paying the most. Furthermore, disability benefits are often counted as income and therefore 'clawed back through charges: amounting to a tax on disability' (Independently, 2004, p 6). Consequently, many user-led organisations have been active in the campaign against charging for services, working together with national organisations such as NCIL and BCODP. This included lobbying local directors of social services.

Moreover, the shift from core funding to short-term service-level agreements has had a significant impact on user-controlled organisations' campaigning activities:

> 'You can imagine how social services would feel if we were to campaign all the time and that was all that we ever did. You campaign by putting your point across when you consult and that's good campaigning practice. If we were to go out on the street waving a banner saying this ought to be changed, you would find it very hard to justify that because your funding restrictions are such that it's not what you use your money for.... Ten or fifteen years ago organisations could solely exist as campaigning organisations; that doesn't exist anymore. You actually have to produce a service. Campaigning organisations are funded from other sources of funding, not through local authority money anymore. It's going to continue getting worse.' (Andrew)

Many local user-controlled service providers simply do not have the financial and human resources to organise and finance a significant level of campaigning. For instance, to organise a public meeting for disabled people with various impairments from diverse ethnic backgrounds requires the production and distribution of information in several formats and languages, the acquisition of an appropriate and accessible venue, the organisation of accessible transport, and the employment of personal assistants (PAs) and interpreters. In other cases, the users' organisation had no established tradition of activist campaigning, but recognised that this was an aspect of their role that required action. As one chairperson commented, 'We do want to have our voice heard in ... [the region] because it isn't at the moment' (Joel). Yet without a tradition of political campaigning, the organisation decided that the best course of action was to organise a two-day course on disability advocacy in order to raise political awareness among its members.

From a local authority standpoint, those with the responsibility of liaising with a user-controlled organisation argued that they were not so bothered about political activism as by the financial constraints of closely regulated budgets. As one senior administrator in a large urban authority explained:

> 'Those tensions will always be around but what I don't want to do with [the organisation] is say "look, we fund you, you must do what we say". But rather say to them, you must understand our position, we have to account for public money, we'll get behind in our annual budget if we don't.' (Katy)

A further consideration for user groups is that political control of the local authority has fluctuated in ways that make planning services uncertain. While some local authorities are relatively tolerant towards overt campaigning by local groups that they fund, others are not. Even then, local authority reaction is liable to vary depending on the subject of the campaign. A user-generated campaign for 'jargon-free' language illustrates the point well as, once implemented, it received substantial support from local bodies.

> 'The jargon, the way they put it ... is disempowering. They send you letters, and you have no idea what all this rubbish is about, and it frightens you, instead of having a straight letter in plain English. So I got up at the Annual General Meeting and said I think we ought to run a plain English, jargon-free, gobbledegook-free campaign. It was accepted by the board and we funded it. We've actually run about a dozen days, which were taken by social services, health services and loads of voluntary groups. They've been fully booked. We have a workshop where we explain how to produce newsletters in plain English and we also support the social services and health services, and they'll send us their leaflets before they print them for us to check over if we understand them.' (Colin)

Empowerment and consciousness raising

While there has been an extraordinary increase in disability activism in Britain over the last half century it is important to remember that the majority of people with accredited impairments have not been party to the criticism of a medicalised, or individual, approach to disability. Others have more explicitly distanced themselves from an overt disabled identity and/or are not members of an organisation of disabled people.

However, there is considerable empirical evidence to support the view that disability is an equal opportunities issue, and that discrimination against people with accredited impairments (Barnes, 1991) remains prevalent throughout British society (Christie with Mensah-Coker, 1999; Miller et al, 2004; PMSU, 2004). This includes a traditional belief that the term 'disabled' signifies social and psychological inadequacy and dependence. Hence, coming to terms with the social, material and psychological consequences of impairment, whether congenital or acquired, is a traumatic experience for many people.

The 'stigma', 'internal oppression', or 'psycho-emotional' dimensions of disability have been widely associated with low self-esteem, limited self-confidence, and a significant withdrawal from everyday social interaction (Wilson, 2003). Turning this around, so as to bring about the empowerment of disabled people, is a complex and difficult process. It is not a once-for-all event or without changes in direction. Empowerment is the outcome of everyday experience and action that leads to critical reflection on common-sense knowledge and traditional explanations (Worrell, 1988; Campbell and Oliver, 1996). The ethos of user-led services is geared to the empowerment of service users; however, it does not necessarily lead to further political engagement. This should not be surprising given that, historically, Britain has been more of a 'passive' rather than a 'participatory' democracy (Beresford and Campbell, 1994), and that people with accredited impairment/s encounter considerable environmental and cultural barriers engaging in conventional political activity (Barnes and Mercer, 2001).

Hence, user-controlled organisations have actively sought to generate political awareness among disabled people and their allies, most notably through Disability/Distress Equality Training (DET) and peer support and advocacy services. Unlike orthodox, professionally led 'Disability Awareness' courses that tend to be impairment specific and explain discrimination solely in terms of negative public attitudes, DET has its roots in the social model of disability and disabled people's struggle for equal opportunities and social justice. Its purpose is to redirect attention from disability as personal tragedy to social oppression. It emphasises the environmental and cultural barriers that disabled people encounter and the links with other oppressed groups (Gillespie-Sells and Campbell, 1991; Swain and Lawrence, 1994). It is often argued by disability activists that DET has played a significant role in raising awareness of disability and the political consciousness of disabled people (Oliver and Barnes, 1998).

Indeed, over two thirds of the organisations that responded to the *Creating Independent Futures* survey and all nine case study organisations offer DET. For many groups developing and delivering these courses for both service users and local and health authority staff is one of their main activities. A key element of the thinking behind the development of DET is that courses are delivered by disabled people themselves. With this in mind, many organisations run 'Training for Trainers' courses such as those pioneered by the London Boroughs Disability Resource Team (LBDRT) in the early 1990s (Gillespie-Sells and Campbell, 1991). Such activities often generate a valuable source of income both for the organisation and for individual trainers:

> 'One of the aspects of our mission statements is to train as many service providers as we possibly can in Disability Equality/ Awareness Training, user equality and empowerment. And we get money from the social services to train all their new staff. It's always been about the users doing training; so you build up people with a much more positive approach with the confidence and skills to do the training themselves and then move on.' (John)

Peer support and advocacy services are a key feature of user-controlled provision. Within the context of disability, advocacy usually refers to the situation where a person or group is 'pressing their case with influential others about situations which either effect them directly or, and more usually, trying to prevent changes that will leave them worse off' (Brandon, 1995, p 1). These can take a variety of forms such as training courses, workshops, community development work, and formal advocacy services. For example, in addition to their 'Rights and Responsibilities of Being a (Personal Assistant) Employer' and DET programme, LCIL hosts a series of events designed to generate self-advocacy, esteem and confidence. Workshop titles for 2004–05 included 'Self-advocacy', 'I'm OK (Self-esteem)', 'An Introduction to Being Assertive', 'Dealing with Niceness' and 'Managing Conflict' (LCIL, 2004).

Other groups organise similar workshops and events in different locations such as disability resource centres, day centres and residential homes. By openly supporting not only disabled service users but 'carers' and their families, SUN has opted for an inclusive approach. One of its main activities is organising focus groups across the county of Surrey, sometimes in conjunction with other local groups such as the Surrey Association of Disabled People. Some of these events are impairment specific, for people with 'learning difficulties' or 'mental health' systems users and survivors, for example. According to one of their group facilitators this is the 'main way that users engage with us about their particular services and issues' (Sandy). These meetings provide SUN with a first-hand insight into user concerns and in so doing enable it to develop a coherent policy that accurately reflects its members' interests.

Similar events can also be used to generate self-advocacy:

> 'We do training for users, for example, how to say no. Under the DLA [Disabled Living Allowance] if you're in high care they send a doctor around to interrogate you. So we train people how to deal with that situation, and how an advocate works. For instance, it's very hard to get up in a room, as I found when I was in business, to do a presentation in front of other people. Now when you're in a wheelchair or have to stand up there on crutches; it's doubly bad so you need peer support.
>
> ... We have a chap called J... he goes round and trains people how he talks and explains to them. And we have a film showing him going to places, inaccessible places. It shows him going to the social services building, where he can't get in. And it shows him kicking the doors in, to show how disempowered he is. He wants to talk to social services but he can't get into the building. That's how we do it, accessibility and all that sort of thing.' (Kevin)

Advocacy services are also wide-ranging. WECIL has developed the 'Disabled Mothers' Advocacy Project' (DMAP) and the 'Care Management Advocacy Project' (CMAP). The former comprised an individual advocacy service and a support group for disabled mothers. This support group provided a highly regarded forum for disabled mothers to meet together to discuss common issues and share information. Unfortunately due to limited funding the project was ended in March 2003. The CMAP scheme is specifically designed for people going through the 'Care Management' assessment process at any level. It aims to help disabled individuals work out what services they might need and who should provide them. The service is for all disabled adults living in Bristol (WECIL, 2003). Since its inception in 1995, there has been a continuing increase in the use of the service, rising to 134 requests in 2002-03, and:

> the range and number of enquiries continues to show that Advocacy is needed on a wide variety of issues which effect disabled people's lives including health, housing and benefits. (WECIL, 2003, p 12)

The demand for this type of support also means that local provider agencies may find themselves working with other advocacy agencies that provide similar services for specific impairment groups.

> 'We have a particularly active People First in [the local area] so we do a lot of work with people [with learning difficulties]. We also have a MIND advocacy, so a lot of people are going to them. And we would certainly support that because we want a diversity of provision so people have choice, so it would be silly of us not to welcome competition.... However, what we find ... is that people don't fit easily into those categories, so there are quite a few people who we work with who also experience emotional or mental distress as well as possibly other impairments. So yes I think that one way or another they are pretty well represented.' (Lana)

It is notable too that local user-controlled organisations that engage in this type of activity sometimes run the risk of souring their relations with local authority staff, as suggested by a social worker in the North of England:

> 'We [social services] have to assess the person's ability to manage direct payments, and we don't think that person has demonstrated that they are capable of managing it. Now [the local CIL] are supporting them because everybody should have the right to direct payments. So we're coming from our rightful places if

you like. There just needs to be a dialogue about it. They need to hear that we can't always say yes. We need to hear that they have the right to support the individual and that won't always be comfortable.' (Kath)

Other consciousness-raising activities might include seminars, conferences, and supporting disability arts (see discussion later). In addition to the dominant service issue activities and concerns, particularly personal assistance and direct payments, there is also an established tradition within the Disabled People's Movement of service provider organisations directed by users hosting meetings on political topics such as disability discrimination and human rights. For example, since 2002 Greater London Action on Disability (GLAD), a London-wide user-controlled service provider organisation has held various conferences with titles as diverse as 'Disability Rights Commission Consultation', 'Disabled Women Hold Up the Sky', 'Inclusion Not Ignorance', 'Transport Conference', all held in 2002, and in 2003, 'The Social Model of Disability: Is it Inclusive?', and 'Black and Ethnic Minority Mental Health User Groups and User Involvement' (GLAD, 2004).

A further dimension in the politicisation of disabled people in recent years has been the emergence of disability culture and art. This grew out of the interventions of disabled artists and performers and explores issues around disability, often drawing on social model debates and the affirmation of impairment as a symbol of difference rather than shame, and the assertion of the significance and value of a 'disabled' identity and lifestyle. This can mean anything from openly exploring the experiences of impairment and disability, to the role of prostheses or other artificial aids (Barnes and Mercer, 2001).

Since the 1970s, disquiet over the prevalence of disablist imagery in popular culture and the arts among the disabled community has prompted the development of a positive alternative, now known as the Disability Arts Movement:

Arts practice should also be viewed as much as a tool for change as attending meetings about orange badge provision.... Only by ensuring an integrated role for disability arts and culture in the struggle can we develop the vision to challenge narrow thinking, elitism and dependency on others for our emancipation. To encourage the growth of a disability culture is no less than to begin the radical task of transforming ourselves from passive and dependent beings into active and creative agents for social change. (Morrison and Finkelstein, 1992, pp 11-12)

The production of a wealth of examples of disability arts including photographs, paintings, sculpture, novels, poetry, plays, music and performance art (Arts Council, 2003) has achieved a growing recognition among disabled people across Britain. Newsletters and magazines produced by user-led groups have contributed, along with events publicising the work of disabled artists. For example, in their long-standing campaign against genetic research, DANE hosted a national conference entitled 'Hands Off Our Genes'. Besides presentations and workshops the conference included a 'Celebration of Diversity Exhibition', with photographs and writings focusing on the links between eugenics, genetics and Nazi Germany's euthanasia programme. In addition, there was a cartoon board by Claire Lewis featuring the activities of the characters 'Di Versity' and 'Hugh Genics', and a series of comedy sketches by the 'Grin and Bear It' Independent Theatre Group (DANE, 2004b).

Don't upset the applecart

It was also certainly felt by some participants, both officers and users, in user-controlled organisations that there were instances where some campaigns have triggered considerable hostility from local officials. One research participant gave the example of an incident following a demonstration in which members of their organisation had taken part. The protest was directed against the outcome of a local authority community 'care' assessment that had recommended 'residential care' for a disabled person who wished to remain in their own home with appropriate support:

'A week after that happened I was called to meet one of the managers of social services and had an "informal" conversation. It was to say that three people [from our organisation] were part of the rescue [demonstration], and somebody from the social services had spotted this. And I think people were asking, including the vice chair ... "well if this carries on, this could affect your grant". So that was a warning.' (Jennie)

Another chief executive of a user service provider recalled a similar incident that occurred following a demonstration by disabled people against the local authority's proposed charging policy. However, in this case, the ensuing tensions came from local councillors rather than local authority staff who seemed, unofficially, in support of the protest:

> 'There is definitely a tension. Not so much with social service workers – I can remember with the charging policy protest we had people haranguing us and the director came up to me and said:"As far as I'm concerned this is absolutely the correct thing for you to do; it's part of the democratic process". But the elected members of the council weren't very happy and they wonder why are we putting money into this organisation who then tell us how crap we are.' (Steve)

It is also important, but perhaps not unsurprising, to note that some professionals participating in the *Creating Independent Futures* study viewed the campaigning activities of disabled people's organisations as undermining their traditional role as experts on disability policy and services. For instance, one social worker stated:

> 'We don't want to use user-led organisations to raise issues, we should be doing it ourselves.' (James)

A further consideration that may inhibit some organisations from becoming involved in direct political action is that throughout the 1990s there was a steady but substantial growth in campaigning organisations at both the national and local levels. Moreover in addition to user-controlled organisations and groups such as disabled people's Direct Action Network (DAN), People First, run by people with learning difficulties, and Shaping Our Lives, a broadly based service user organisation, all of whom organise nationally and locally, many traditional provider organisations are now moving into the political arena. For example, Scope, formerly known as the 'Spastics Society', recently announced its intention to move centre-stage into disability politics:

> Campaign networks have been formed and are being developed that allow disabled people to shape Scope's campaigning priorities and activities. Scope's strategic and corporate priorities will

increasingly be shaped by the key issues and barriers faced by disabled people. (Hurst and Mainwearing, 2004, p 13)

Nonetheless, the user participants in the *Creating Independent Futures* study demonstrated considerable variation in their attitudes towards different forms of political engagement. The vast majority were very supportive of 'conventional' lobbying tactics such as consultation exercises and engaging in dialogue with local authority social services departments, health authorities and trusts. They were equally supportive of the links that local user provider groups had with other national campaigning agencies such as the BCODP.

However, there were considerable worries among service users that involvement in overt political campaigning might cause difficulties in the relationships with local authorities and other funding agencies and, as a consequence, put the future development of locally based user-controlled services at risk. Many felt that this 'was not a risk that was worth taking' (Christopher). Some participants went so far as to argue that user-led service providers should not participate in any sort of political campaigning. The main reason offered was that such organisations were already over-stretched and that campaigning would only undermine their ability to provide effective disability services.

> 'I don't think we should be seen as a militant group. If people can see you, the general public, they may see you as being militant. If you use the [organisation] and it goes through a normal channel for protest, it's not seen as a political animal, and people won't be deterred from using [its] services. In any walk of life the only way to alter things is to persuade the people in power; and no matter how militant you are it's not going to get you anywhere.' (Cyril)

However, while in favour of conventional lobbying, a significant minority was vehemently opposed to direct action. Some felt that it was demeaning and that it would antagonise public opinion and erode their support.

> 'I think it [direct action] can. It gives the public the wrong perception. A few months ago people from [another local campaigning group were] all going down to Parliament. And they show you on television, all these cripples getting on buses

with wheelchairs. I thought that was demeaning. We could do without it. I think disabled people should be valued for who they are, not for their problems.' (Sharon)

'I'm totally against people who do obstructive campaigning. I don't believe in direct action. We don't want to antagonise Mr and Mrs Joe Public because we need them for support.' (Daniel)

It is also the case that some people who are interested in getting involved in direct political action were deterred by the activities of some campaigning groups. The following statement from a woman with a recently acquired impairment and therefore new to disability issues illustrates this point:

'I tried to get involved but I said I couldn't have an opinion on certain issues I know nothing about. They said they'd contact me about attending some training days, but I never heard from them again. I also felt that they only wanted people who felt angry and oppressed. So now I'm angry because a disability group rejected me because I wasn't angry enough. They were pretty scary people and had a style that probably matched the inquisition.' (Beth)

In contrast, a small minority of disabled participants favoured involvement in direct political action on disability issues and had been actively involved in public demonstrations and marches themselves; and they were extremely positive about their participation. Even so, they acknowledged that organisations that routinely engaged in overt political activity ran a considerable risk that they would be penalised by their funding agencies:

'I think the justification for not campaigning is that the [organisation] cannot rock the boat in case it puts funding at risk. It's a serious consideration, but as a movement we cannot afford to take this line because every improvement we've achieved has been precisely because people have taken risks … but if [the organisation] is seen as too acquiescent then its powers can be eroded very easily by funders and other authorities. Take away campaigning and a social model approach, and haven't we just got another social services department in disguise?' (Helen)

Although committed to political action, some disabled participants argued that local user-controlled service providers must strive to reflect the views of all the disabled people in their area. Given that many disabled people did not share their radical approach, this should act as a constraint when deciding on an organisation's political activities:

> 'Not all disabled people are members of [the organisation] and we do have to take on board some of that.… I think we've got to be sensitive to the fact that it's not just members that we need to be looking at; it's the spectrum of disabled people in [the local area] really.' (Fred)

The perceived decline in enthusiasm for overt political action (at least by those active in the movement since the 1970s and 1980s) was explained in terms of a combination of 'campaign fatigue', and a deterioration in their impairment:

> 'I used to be really keen but as I've got older and the [impairment] has got worse, I just haven't the energy. I think a lot of people feel like that. It's not that they don't want to [get involved], it's just that they don't feel able.' (Ben)

> 'Life's short and you want to enjoy it. Why should you have to go out 365 days a year campaigning when you could be enjoying yourself? And every time you go out there it's a battle; it is, and it's a battle just to exist.' (Ray)

Review

Most if not all user-led service provider organisations regard political campaigning as central to their aims and objectives although this was interpreted in different ways. A proactive campaigning style was evident at many of the case study locations: this was seen as an integral aspect of the organisation's work and inseparable from its role as a representative organisation of disabled people and not incompatible with its role as a service provider. It included taking part in national protest action such as those against charging for services as well as specifically local issues. Other organisations placed a greater emphasis on a 'behind the scenes' approach at least in terms of seeking to influence local council committees or equivalent groups.

A wide range of campaigning methods was employed, from the production of newsletters and other publicity and information material to more direct action. There was a degree of overlap in membership with more overtly 'direct action' groups such as DAN. A significant minority of user-led organisations sought alliances with other groups, such as local minority ethnic group organisations and more broadly based community groups.

All of the participating organisations were conscious of the potential negative consequences of their campaigning activity, however minor, on their relationship with their funding agencies and particularly the local authority. Although none of the organisations have reached the stage where funding has been threatened by local authority hostility to their activities, all user-controlled agencies viewed this as a distinct possibility. This view was further echoed by the local authority representatives.

In the following chapter, discussion centres on how the politicisation of disability by user-led organisations has impacted on recent policies on health and 'social care' for disabled people.

NINE

Policy change or retrenchment?

Introduction

We now draw together the main themes raised in previous chapters concerning the implementation of a social model approach to service provision for disabled people. Attention centres on the practical implications of developing user-controlled services.

Throughout its history the Disabled People's Movement has campaigned for recognition of the right of disabled people not to be forced into routine and significant dependence on non-disabled people. The political goal has been a society that facilitates and supports an independent lifestyle. In this struggle, user-controlled organisations have been accorded a crucial role.

The discussion in this chapter will concentrate on three main areas: first, the links between user-led organisations and traditional statutory and voluntary sector service providers, and how far and in what ways possibilities are being exploited for services supportive of independent living and social inclusion. A second section reviews attempts to counter the entrenched dominance of professionals in disabled people's lives, and the potential for alternative ways of delivering services. One such suggestion has been to create a new 'profession allied to the community', with practitioners adhering to a social model approach. A further possibility, strongly promoted by New Labour, is the development of meaningful partnerships between key stakeholders and service providers and disabled people's organisations. Finally, we review recent New Labour proposals for a significant shift in health and 'social care' policy that accords a major role to independent living-type support services, including user-controlled organisations.

Dependence, independence or inclusion?

As human beings:

> We rely on each other in a multitude of ways from the provision
> of the essentials of food, water and shelter to the complexities
> of feelings of self esteem. (Parker, 1993, p 11)

However, such interdependence is widely overshadowed in Western industrial societies by the idea that individuals should be self-sufficient or independent. This notion gained considerable impetus during the social and intellectual upheavals of the late 18th and early 19th centuries. Yet, there has been a resurgence of such thinking in the final quarter of the 20th century associated with a neo-liberal ideology that identified the rising costs of state welfare systems and their negative impact on self-help, individualism and entrepreneurial initiative as a major threat to economic growth and success. This has had an evident impact on both New Right and New Labour government policies,

Although the Disabled People's Movement has tried hard to develop user-controlled services that are separate from orthodox professionally led provision, findings from the *Creating Independent Futures* project show that this has been a very uneven struggle. Hence, the majority of disabled people remain reliant on statutory and voluntary agencies across both the local and national levels. This is most obviously the case with respect to funding support. In particular, the limited and mostly short-term nature of financial support available to user-controlled services has acted as a severe constraint on the level and range of service provision. While large service contracts allow organisations more breathing space in which to work up grant applications and tenders for service contracts, organisations with only limited and short-term income are far less able to devote the required time and resources to service planning and development.

> 'We have such a lot of vision about what we want to do, where we want to go. It feels like we're always dealing with crisis after crisis, but we never get to really deal with something properly, or we do, we start it off and it goes really well, but it's lucky if it does really well. I find it really hard working from crisis after crisis and not be able to say, "OK well we've got that out of the way, let's move forward now". It just feels like we're on a rocky boat that's going up and down all the time.' (Terri)

Furthermore, with many Centre for Independent/Integrated/Inclusive Living (CIL)-type organisations tied to local statutory agencies such as local authority social services departments, the incentive to generate income by charging for particular services such as Disability/Distress Equality Training (DET) is reduced. With an annual review of local authority budgets,

organisations that generate more income than anticipated run the risk of
a reduction in their future funding:

> 'Obviously they're going to have their mechanisms for ensuring
> that they get value for money. But at the end of the day we
> generate X pounds of surplus, and we want to do this or that or
> the other with it.... We should be able to do that. We think that
> they wouldn't claw it back now, particularly if we can make an
> argument for doing something specific with it. But if we just
> hang on to it for reserves, which I think would be a good thing
> as we have no reserves ... we may have problems.
>
> A lot of it depends on relationships between us and the council
> and these change. Both the key people [in the local authority],
> the finance person has left and J... [social services administrator]
> is leaving – they're restructuring social work yet again. So we're
> going to have to forge new relationships with people ... some of
> these fundamental things are based on relationships rather than
> on explicit ... contractual arrangements or policies.' (Evan)

The fragility of inter-organisational relationships, particularly within the
current economic context creates particular difficulties:

> 'It's the "Best Value" philosophy. Recently when I met the
> Director of Social Services and we were talking about [another
> locally based organisation], and he said to me: "Well, it's so many
> thousands of pounds a year for your service; we could buy it
> somewhere else cheaper. So if it's accessible and cheaper I will.
> So if somebody down the road, not necessarily a disabled people's
> organisation, decides to set up a welfare rights service, and they
> welcome disabled people as well, we could use them because it's
> cheaper".
>
> ... What we've done over the years is given away a lot of
> knowledge, a lot of experience, a lot of skills.... Our direct
> payments, for example, we gave [another organisation] a lot of
> information and resources, and they undercut us by 50% and
> won the contract. What do you do?' (Jennie)

The loss of valuable service contracts is a major anxiety. Moreover,
competition has been fuelled by increased government interest in

promoting user choice and control, particularly in the case of direct payments. At both the national and local levels, organisations of and for disabled people are bidding against each other for service contracts. While direct payments support services are a core activity of CIL-type services, only 25% of English local authorities have support facilities that claim to be 'user led'. The remainder (61%) use charities such as the Shaw Trust, for example, in-house provision, or have subcontracted the service to other local authority social services departments (14%) (Jolly, 2005). Part of the reason for this is that many organisations run and controlled by users do not have the financial resources to cope with a much increased demand. Such organisations operate on a shoe-string budget, have considerable difficulty in recruiting and retaining skilled staff, and rely heavily on voluntary help (see Chapter Six).

As confirmation of the interdependence between user-controlled services and traditional provision – as between disabled and non-disabled people – a number of user-controlled groups have decided to replace the traditional 'independent' description in their organisation's name with the term 'integrated' or, more often, 'inclusive' living. Indeed, the socio-political interpretation of disability advocates an inclusive approach to impairment, and the Disabled People's Movement is committed to the struggle for a meaningful and inclusive participatory society that respects and celebrates difference (Barton, 2001):

> 'To me integrated and independent living is about all of us together. It doesn't matter if you're disabled or not disabled.' (Chris)

Other participants emphasised that user-led organisations should not become 'disability ghettos' and thus reproduce the type of segregation so evident elsewhere in society:

> 'You cannot say this is run by disabled people purely for disabled people, I think you've got to involve able-bodied people as well, you've got to bring everybody along with it.... If you exclude able-bodied people you're going to alienate them.' (Ray)

Needless to say, such a broad-based approach can present considerable dilemmas for user-controlled organisations.

Furthermore, user-led organisations have tried to respond positively to the diversity of need within the disabled population and dispense with the impairment-specific focus of traditional approaches to service delivery. Despite this, entrenched barriers remain:

> 'As a client group I suppose children's disability is a key area. They are one client group that we don't do as much for, although it's not through not wanting to ... and my own knowledge is that that they wouldn't necessarily want to become part of us. But I know that they are very protective of their own organisation because of the difficulties of confidentiality.' (Jake)

> 'I think we have quite a difficulty in representing the sort of people stuck in residential homes, people that have communication difficulties, deaf and blind people. There's an ongoing thing with Alzheimer's Disease Society who want us to represent more people. We say: "Well, no one's actually found a way to do it".' (Larah)

The difficulties of operating an inclusive approach to service delivery have been further exacerbated by recent government initiatives to extend access to direct payments to service users:

> Many Councils believe they have a duty to offer direct payments. They don't. They have a duty to make direct payments. That's what the law now says.... The assumption should be that the only times when care should be delivered, in my view, other than by a direct payment is when the individual themselves has made a personal and positive choice to receive the care directly and not via a direct payment. (Stephen Ladyman, cited in NCIL, 2003, p 2)

The experience of the Centre for Inclusive Living in Glasgow (CILiG) illustrates this point. In 2004 CILiG secured the contract with Glasgow Social Work Department to provide support services for disabled people and other service users receiving direct payments. Hitherto, the emphasis had been on an indirect payments scheme, which was effectively frozen in 1996 and supported only 100 disabled people. Apart from a relatively small pilot project supporting around 15 applicants introduced in 2000, no new direct payments were issued in Glasgow until 2004. Although CILiG had been operational since 1996 the contract took 12 months to secure. This may be explained by budgetary constraints in the Social Work Department and the lack of bridging finance from the Scottish Executive. Alternatively, others:

> point rather to an entrenched political and organisational culture fundamentally committed to public sector provision and inherently unenthusiastic about the prospect of giving up power and control to service users. (D'Aboville, 2006, p 146)

The commissioning process and the need to be accountable to service users raise complex issues for CIL-type organisations. As direct payments are rolled out to a wider range of 'community care' service users such as asylum seekers or people fleeing domestic violence, the impact on disabled service users is uncertain. Most significantly, the role of support organisations with respect to the specific goal of enhancing independent living for disabled people may be under threat:

> [CILiG's] current position is that it will provide a service to a wider range of direct payment recipients and encourage participation through a stakeholders' forum, but it will not compromise disabled people's ultimate control over the organisation. Should this arrangement no longer be sustainable, for instance if the number of non-disabled people service users were to grow dramatically, then [CILiG] would work toward assisting those service users to establish their own support systems. (D'Aboville, 2006, p 147)

While the campaign for direct payments remains central to disabled people's struggle to achieve a more independent lifestyle, with more choice and control of their lives, the pattern of implementation has been the subject of continuing debate. A widespread concern is that local authorities and professionals have been less impressed by the philosophy behind such schemes and have viewed them simply as a different way of delivering much the same set of health and social services. There has also been a suspicion that direct payments are being used to further a neo-liberal agenda and cut back on and privatise the public sector provision of health and 'social care' services. In other words, they are viewed as instrumental in promoting the interests of individual 'consumers' rather than with the collective empowerment of disabled people.

While the budgetary constraints on direct payments have been severely criticised by organisations of disabled people, the growth in the number of disabled people receiving direct payments has continued. Furthermore, disabled activists have drawn a clear line between the New Right's view of citizenship, which stresses the restriction of state action as a way of advancing individual freedom and responsibility, and their advocacy of a more interventionist state. For disabled people's organisations, the aim is to dismantle 'disabling barriers' and generate a higher profile for the public sector in facilitating independent living support needs.

Equally, policies to encourage more choice in social welfare services will not by themselves bring about social inclusion. They must also be reinforced by a much greater emphasis on human rights and equal citizenship. Choice between different services must not be detached from issues of their quality and appropriateness in giving a new meaning to disabled people's everyday lives. Hence, the level of resources devoted to promoting social inclusion is crucial.

Another dilemma around inclusion for organisations under the direction of users is whether to employ non-disabled staff. From the outset the Disabled People's Movement has welcomed non-disabled people as allies and supporters. Additionally, some user-controlled agencies, such as the Derbyshire Coalition for Inclusive Living (DCIL), previously known as the Derbyshire Centre for Integrated Living (see Chapter Five), have operated an inclusive employment policy although other user-led organisations have always favoured recruiting only disabled people to staff positions.

Nevertheless, this policy has been difficult to sustain. An embedded set of barriers against disabled people in education and paid employment is exacerbated by the difficulties experienced by user-controlled organisations in maintaining their service role. There has also been an increasing tendency for the statutory and voluntary sectors to poach disabled staff from user-led organisations. This is fuelled by the relatively greater job security and higher wages that most traditional service providers can offer compared to CIL-type organisations.

Professional dominance and new styles of working

Government literature and policy statements have increasingly taken issue with the traditional top-down approach to welfare services. This has extended to a growing critique of the professional dominance of service provision and the way in which this has acted as an effective barrier to reform measures in general and to the continuing individual dependence of disabled people and other service users on the health and social welfare system. This criticism from government has overlapped with enduring criticism from disabled service users that public sector welfare structures effectively encourage professionals to use 'coercion, domination, persuasion and manipulation to structure the lives to whom they provide services' (Abberley, 2004, p 239).

Moreover, most of the social welfare workforce comprises professions and other occupations that, in varying degrees, have been allied to traditional individualistic medical or deficit explanations for disability (D'Aboville, 1991). These views characterise welfare services in both the statutory and voluntary sectors. As a consequence, staff, regardless of their status within these agencies:

> are not so much 'following orders' as reproducing for others, as truth and common sense, a set of values and norms they have internalised from their own exposure to the cultures and structures of the institution. (Hughes and Ferguson, 2000, p 127)

Professional practice has therefore been strongly criticised by the Disabled People's Movement as both oppressive and dependency creating. Nonetheless, as discussed in Chapter Seven, users often acknowledged the complexity of the professional's role and the policy and financial constraints under which they have to operate. Moreover, evidence suggests that these pressures contribute to disproportionate levels of long-term 'sick leave' and high levels of staff turnover among 'health care' workers employed by local authorities (Bevans, 2005).

However, this did not detract from research participants' resolve that disabled people should be involved, at every level, in the development of support services, including professional intervention, for disabled people. The following statements represent the general consensus among respondents that disabled people have the first-hand personal experience of disability and therefore 'know best' what a disabled service user wants:

'We have a better insight into what we actually need.' (Chris)

'The people who ran my old care firm were fit and fine and
they'd no idea what it was like to be disabled at all. The people
at the Coalition know what it is like to be disabled.' (Dave)

The inclusion of disabled people at all levels of the organisation was felt to
be an empowering experience and contrasted with agencies dominated
by non-disabled professionals:

'In a non-user-led environment with no peer support … you
realise what you are missing. It's all social services workers with
social services voices and it's quite disempowering.' (Mel)

The central issue here is that professionalism is generally associated with
'disabling practices' and non-disabled staff (Oliver and Sapey, 1999; Swain
et al, 2003; Abberley, 2004). This is obviously reinforced by the acute
shortage of disabled professionals across the main sectors and levels of the
'disability business'. This is a clear indication of the barriers to paid
employment that exist throughout the contemporary labour market for
people with accredited impairments, including those designated as the
'caring' professions.

   Physiotherapy is a case in point. Since at least the 19th century a small
number of visually impaired people have worked as physiotherapists.
Physiotherapy had its roots in tactile massage: a skill where a visual
impairment is not necessarily a marked disadvantage. Yet, through the 20th
century, physiotherapy developed a more complex knowledge base, stressed
formal educational qualifications, and became more hospital based.
Physiotherapists now use a great deal of electrical equipment, work in
intensive care units with people who have had major surgery, serious
accidents and/or neurological damage, as well as in rehabilitation and long-
stay units. In addition, they have to cope with an increasing amount of
paperwork, as well as navigate busy wards where the environment constantly
changes. This has made it increasingly more difficult for practitioners with
a visual impairment to practise, and corresponding recruitment barriers
have similarly been imposed on potential applicants with an impairment.
In 1994, there were only 516 visually impaired physiotherapists
(approximately 2%) of the total number of the Chartered Society's register

and many of these were retired, working in private practice or overseas (French, 2001).

More typically, those born with an accredited impairment are often socialised into a dependency role and are disadvantaged educationally. Consequently they are likely to experience difficulties acquiring the necessary qualifications for entry into one of the 'caring' professions. Conversely, the overwhelming majority of disabled people have acquired conditions and will have often already developed a career in other fields.

While most research participants, both users and staff, felt that it was very important for user-controlled services to be run and staffed by disabled people, it was recognised that the experience of disability alone was insufficient to equip a person with an impairment with the knowledge and skills necessary to develop and run the increasingly complex array of support services needed by the disabled users:

> 'Because of discrimination ... there's a lack of disabled people with certain skills that we need in order to make things work.... Currently within [the CIL] we find it very difficult to recruit people to posts ... I think if it came to a point where we are going to say that we had to shut up shop because we couldn't recruit disabled people [and] we wouldn't recruit non-disabled people, I think that would be a terrible position.' (Andrew)

Consequently, most disabled users accepted that non-disabled people could be involved in CIL-type organisations provided that they have the level of expertise and support not otherwise available, and that effective control of the organisations and delivery of services remains with the user membership.

Of course, disabled people who have undertaken a particular form of professional education and training may hold radically different views on disability issues. Thus physiotherapists, both disabled and non-disabled, will probably agree, for example, that lower limb exercise is essential for people with physical impairments who have difficulty walking in order to prevent muscle wastage and excessive weight gain. One highly critical response from disabled people has been to ask the question: 'What's so wonderful about walking?' (Oliver, 1993), with the clear implication that professional energies would be best directed elsewhere.

Another radical suggestion has been for the development of a different form of professional education and training. For example, Vic Finkelstein, a vigorous critic of the 'professions allied to medicine', has argued that disabled people's organisations should strive to develop a new form of professional located in the social model of disability. He refers to this new occupational grouping as a 'Profession Allied to the Community' and 'the disabled people's trade union'. Such workers would provide a sustainable and accessible critique of the limitations of the 'cure' or 'care' ideologies that pervade conventional approaches to community-based support for disabled people, and most significantly, create innovative and 'systematic forms of help' based on a social barriers approach to disability as an effective alternative to orthodox approaches (Finkelstein, 1999b, p 23).

Although there is some support for this idea within the Disabled People's Movement (Rae, 2005) and among disabled academics (Swain and French, 2003), an appropriate education and training programme has yet to be devised. It is also questionable whether the population of disabled service users as a whole would understand or welcome such a development as 'liberating'. Equally important, there is the very real danger that the creation of another disability-related occupation would come to represent nothing more than just another group of professional 'experts' jostling for a role within the lives of people with accredited impairments.

Partnerships

A feature of the New Labour modernisation reforms has been its emphasis on greater 'collaboration' and the promotion of much closer working relationships and partnerships between and with organisations and agencies in the health and 'social care' field. This ambition extends to the involvement of the range of organisations representing disabled people (DH, 2005a). It also incorporates a wider discourse around such terms as 'joined-up' government, 'integrated delivery' and 'seamless' services, which are all seemingly part of a project to create a 'partnership culture' (Balloch and Taylor, 2001). This relates to wider debates about changes in the state and state governance, and some commentators have suggested that this turn to market-based policies is fracturing established hierarchies between state, welfare institutions and civil society (Clarke, 2004).

However, what New Labour means by 'partnerships' is far from clear, even if their intended role in facilitating more collaboration is more transparent (Glendinning et al, 2002). The partnerships can take a wide variety of different forms but revolve around 'a joint working relationship where the partners:

- are otherwise independent bodies;
- agree to co-operate to achieve a common goal ...;
- create a new organisational structure or process to achieve this goal ...;
- plan and implement a joint programme ...;
- share relevant information; and
- pool risks and rewards.' (Audit Commission, 1998, p 8)

Such 'partnerships' may involve relationships between different elements (public, private and voluntary) of the mixed economy of welfare, echoing a long tradition going back at least to the 1601 Poor Law (see Chapter Two). Indeed, in the post-1945 welfare state, the status of the 'partnership' between the health and 'social care' services has been the subject of continuing debate and reform proposals. More recently, the quest for better policy coordination has been likened to an administrative Holy Grail (Peters, 1998).

Different models of partnership have been identified, each with its own rationale. For example, a 'synergy' or 'added value' model seeks to maximise the additional value of combining organisations with their own particular assets or features. In contrast, a 'transformation' model highlights how partners bring different capacities to influence the form and direction of the partnership (Powell and Glendinning, 2002, p 5). In the case of possible 'partnerships' between disabled people's organisations and either statutory bodies or other voluntary organisations, the 'synergy' approach has relevance where there is a shortage of financial and human resources, just as the 'transformation' model is relevant to situations where organisations have very different priorities and interests.

In practice, the overwhelming majority of CIL-type organisations are linked in some degree to other forms of provision in both the statutory and voluntary sectors. Yet, in practice, the notion of 'partnership' alarms some staff and users, who argue strongly that user-led organisations should maintain their distance. There is an evident suspicion that entering into a 'partnership' with a New Labour government pursuing its political project of modernisation is a two-edged sword. It allows some increased autonomy to user-led organisations but this is contained and regulated by continuing central regulation and surveillance and crucial funding controls.

An associated fear is that non-disabled professionals will take over or 'colonise' disabled people's initiatives or that traditional service providers might deter disabled people from becoming involved:

'Sometimes you have social workers or members of the council sitting in at the meetings. I've often found it's so easy for them to take over the meeting.' (Myfanwy)

'I personally think it should be more independent because I think if you start talking about social services or charities, I'm not being awful but it puts people off. They'll just say: "I've had social services before, I don't want them again".' (Jennie)

A specific illustration of the tension, if not conflict, is the social work role in the assessment of service need. A single, shared assessment has been broadly accepted by disabled people, although in practice cooperation has been nullified by the use of a health or medical model template. What looks as a partnership to service providers is viewed as an instance of colonisation by professionals and administrators that threatens a return to traditional 'welfarism' rather than support for independent living (Gillinson et al, 2005). In other words, in this example, talk of partnership is only possible if there is a fundamental shift in the mainstream approach to the provision of 'social care'. This requires a transformation in the approach taken by professionals as well as a much enhanced role for user-led organisations.

Others took a more resigned or pragmatic approach:

'Complete independence [for CILs] would be nice in theory, but it's impossible isn't it, where do you get your funding from?' (Ray)

'I think that independence would be ideal but probably the way funding is going at the moment, and how people get the money, would make it quite difficult to make it completely independent, separate.' (Richard)

Indeed, for those people involved with organisations that had chosen not to opt for charitable status, it was felt that local authority funding was the lesser of two evils, the alternative being charity money:

'The financial support [from the local authority] would have to be there, how would they exist unless by voluntary contributions? And then you become a charity.' (Anne)

For those individuals who are strongly involved in user-controlled services there was a general awareness of the tensions that can arise when user-controlled organisations develop what is regarded as too 'cosy' a relationship with local authorities. This was especially evident among those involved in organisations threatened by cuts in funding:

> 'I think that tension is always there. There is a lot of anger because there was a feeling that we were trying to build up a partnership with the borough and then they cut the funding to some vital services so there's a lot of resentment and anger and we cannot really trust them.' (Sheila)

In contrast, several user participants were more positive about links with statutory and voluntary agencies. They argued that services controlled and run by users had a lot to gain from working in tandem with other organisations, such as social services departments and health authorities:

> 'They certainly need advice and things from people like health authorities.' (Lesley)

> 'The organisation should have a link to the council for things such as advice, information, equality issues.' (James)

Notwithstanding these differences, participants agreed that user-controlled initiatives must be provided with the appropriate resources to initiate and develop services for disabled people. Several people had experience of other forms of user involvement initiated by professional-led service providers, but these were dismissed as tokenistic and generally inappropriate.

Same old services: SOS or something else?

Over recent years, there has been growing criticism of mainstream services and a readiness to explore services for disabled people that have shed their service or professional domination. One move with considerable support among policy makers has been towards the greater 'personalisation' of 'social care' services. This might take a number of different forms:

> Firstly ... providing people with a more customer-friendly interface for existing services....
>
> Second ... giving users more say in navigating their way through services once they have got access to them.... Public service professionals should take more account of users....
>
> Third ... giving service users more control over how money is spent ... more power to make their own decisions....
>
> Fourth ... users are not just consumers but co-designers and co-producers of a service....
>
> Fifth, personalization could mean self-organisation ... the professionals are designing environments, networks and platforms through which people can together devise their own solutions. (Leadbetter, 2004, pp 21-4)

Government thinking surrounding services for disabled people has moved increasingly in the direction of such 'personalisation' so as to introduce a more user-centred and comprehensive approach commensurate with a social model of disability. Probably the most significant 'official' statement of this position is elaborated in the *Improving the Life Chances of Disabled People* document produced by the Prime Minister's Strategy Unit (PMSU, 2005). Drawing on extensive research and consultation with a variety of stakeholders including disabled people and disabled representatives of organisations directed by users, the report sets out an impressive agenda in order to fulfil the following aim:

> By 2025 disabled people in Britain should have full opportunities and choices to improve their quality of life and will be respected and included as vital members of society. (PMSU, 2005, p 4)

To realise this goal, 'practical' measures are advanced to enable disabled people achieve 'independent living'; improve support systems for families with disabled children; facilitate a smooth transition into adulthood for disabled young people; and improve support and incentives for disabled workers for getting and staying in employment (PMSU, 2005, p 4). This government commitment to 'delivering a better future for disabled people' and supporting 'disabled people in living independently' was reiterated by the Prime Minister at the official launch of the new Office for Disability Issues in December 2005 (DWP, 2005a).

At the core of this strategy lies the promotion of independent living, which, following the Disability Rights Commission (DRC, 2002a, 2002b), is defined as:

> all disabled people having the same choice, control and freedom
> as any other citizen – at home, at work and as members of the
> community. (PMSU, 2005, p 58)

Under such proposals, individual choice and control would move to centre stage in planning and delivering services, and materialise as 'individualised budgets'. These offer a new way of dealing with the continual criticism of the inefficiency and confusion of the present system, which contains an often bewildering fragmentation of service provision across many different departments and agencies, across both the national and local authority levels.

The suggestion is that individualised budgets would facilitate independent living by bringing together the various sources of support. This budget would be based on assessed need, and the individual service user would then decide how to use the money allocated. This might be drawn as a cash payment, following the example of direct payments schemes, or it might be taken in the form of an agreed service equivalent, or alternatively as a mixture of services and cash payment.

Additionally, and in response to the criticism that the range of support needs covered by existing systems is often interpreted much too narrowly as 'personal care', there would be a considerable widening of the range of eligible service support. The areas identified extend beyond 'personal care' to cover personal assistance, advocacy service and the purchase of aids and equipment. They include family responsibilities, education and training, paid employment, transport, and wider involvement in the community and leisure activities. Given the stated intention to ensure that the cost implications of these changes are 'neutral', the possibly 'heroic assumption' is made that sufficient funding will be available by drawing on current finances. This comprises very many different sources, such as 'community care' budgets, social services expenditure on equipment and adaptations, Independent Living Funds, and Access to Work (Morris, 2005). Overall, the government anticipates that this form of personalisation of service support will provide a significant enhancement to user choice in terms of the level and character of support received, and thus the goal of 'independent living'.

Significantly in this regard, the PMSU maintains that Centres for

Independent Living (CILs) – it does not differentiate between 'independent', 'integrated' and 'inclusive' living – should be at the heart of these policy developments.

> By 2010 each locality (defined as that area covered by a Council with social services responsibilities) should have a user led organisation modelled on existing Centres for Independent Living. (PMSU, 2005, p 76)

However, the responsibility for implementing this particular recommendation rests primarily with the Department of Health (DH). Its Green Paper – *Independence, Well-Being and Choice: Our Vision for the Future of Social Care for Adults in England* (DH, 2005a) provides an insight into how it understands its responsibilities. It accepts:

> the principle that everyone in society has a positive contribution to make to that society and that they should have a right to control their own lives. (DH, 2005a, p 9)

Yet, beyond the endorsement of the use of direct payments and individual budgets as a means of delivering support, there are relatively few innovative policy suggestions. The Green Paper is replete with the language of 'care' rather than rights and there is no mention whatsoever of a social model analysis of disability nor, indeed, a definition of independent living.

'Care' is a multi-faceted concept with an ambiguous set of meanings. In its most typical usage, 'care' indicates concern and consideration for others and being 'cared for' is viewed as fundamental to the human experience. Alternatively, as stressed in Chapter Two, the concept of 'care' has negative meanings for many disabled people. It is integral to the individual approach to 'disability' and legitimises professional dominance of disabled people's everyday lives.

Additionally, most 'informal care' is supplied by women on an unpaid basis, in their role within the family or as friends. Moreover, most of those employed in providing 'personal care' are female. Such patterns have attracted considerable criticism from feminists that health and 'social care' policies have exploited women's labour and time. Furthermore, disabled feminists have pointed out that non-disabled feminists have ignored or denied disabled women's contribution as 'carers' (Morris, 1991, 1993a). Yet, overall, disabled people regard 'care' as the opposite of what they want from government policy or service providers and also that it misrepresents what people need to live independently and as equal citizens in the community:

> 'I'd say we don't want to be cared for at all. I would say that we want to be facilitated, supported and empowered.... Care to me has connotations of custody and lack of control and looking after somebody who is getting sick and getting worse.... Caring and care in the community is about control – maintaining us in a certain position – and it's about seeing disabled people as people with individual problems. It's not empowering at all.' (Campbell, cited in Williams, 1993, p 94)

Moreover, although the PMSU document sets out its definitions of illness, impairment and disability, along broadly social model lines, it is inconsistent in the way it uses these terms. Despite this, it is adamant that the culture of 'care' is a barrier to equality and citizenship for disabled people:

> One of the most significant barriers to enabling disabled people to be full citizens is the culture of care and dependency within health and social care structures. Associated with this 'culture of care' is a failure to see expenditure on independent living as a form of economic and social investment. Instead of meeting disabled people's additional requirements to enable them to improve their life chances, resources are used in a way that maintain and create dependency. (PMSU, 2005, p 60)

The Green Paper states that, at the local level, directors of adult social services will be expected to work with a range of partners including primary health care trusts, the private and voluntary sectors. Services will be delivered by a trained workforce or by informal 'carers' with appropriate support. Yet, although the role of the voluntary and community sectors is highlighted as an 'integral part of the social care workforce' (DH, 2005a, p 68), there is no mention of CILs or strategies to facilitate their proposed support role. There is a similar lack of detail on how service contracts will be awarded to service provider organisations led, managed and controlled by disabled people or other services users.

These omissions undermine the stated emphasis in government documents on support for 'independent living' (see Chapter Two). Many local and national non–user-led organisations have now adopted the terminology of independent living. For its part, there is no consensus within the Disabled People's Movement about what constitutes a CIL. This has generated considerable unease that, with the PMSU report's general endorsement of the concept, organisations not led, managed or controlled by disabled people will find it relatively easy to adopt the phrase in order to secure funding. This has prompted one organisation controlled and run by disabled people to suggest that:

> Existing disabled people's organisations could lead in the development of a national system of accreditation to confirm what constitutes a CIL, for example, run by disabled people themselves who promote a social model. This would not be about the standard of advice or services, as the Community Legal Service already have a national quality mark that such organisations can apply for, and at different levels. Neither would this just be about direct payments, but about all aspects of independent living. (Breakthrough UK, 2005, p 8)

The emphasis on the use of voluntary services and help is equally perplexing and is not commensurate with the notion of independence, equality of opportunity, nor equal citizenship. Service providers cannot plan and deliver effective and reliable support for service users if they are reliant on a voluntary workforce:

> There is some concern that the vision in the Green Paper relies heavily on the idea that support for disabled people will continue to be given mostly on a voluntary basis. While we recognise the importance to society of family and friendship networks, there are many examples, which show that supporting a disabled friend, or member of a family creates enormous stress on these relationships. (NCIL, 2005, unpaged)

A related issue concerns the emphasis placed within the Green Paper on people with 'high support needs' and the management of risk in order to ensure that users receive the support and protection needed to ensure their own well-being and the safety of society, and 'to "protect" care assessors and care workers from blame when accidents occur' (DH, 2005a, p 29). Even so, the 'entitlement to independent living' has not been extended into 'a right to not be forced to move into residential care' (Morris, 2005, p 18). Instead, the Green Paper suggests a 'right to request' that service providers take into account individual circumstances and preferences as well as 'the financial, organisational and legal implications of both the status quo and alternative options' (DH, 2005a, p 32).

The assumptions within these statements tend to undermine any meaningful notion of choice and control. This is clearly illustrated by the suggestion that the key role in the 'social care' assessment process is to made by a designated professional who may be called a 'person-centred planning facilitator', 'care manager', 'care navigator' or 'care broker' (DH, 2005a, p 36).

> Talking about protecting society from risk, does not seem to be the language of recognising the unique and valuable role, which every individual has to play in our community. There is plenty of evidence that disabled people with so called higher support needs can and do take on full and equal parts at all levels in our society. For us the issue is simply a matter of making sure that the right support is available and being provided. (NCIL, 2005, unpaged)

Crucially both the PMSU document and the Green Paper contend that improving the life chances of disabled people and ensuring their independence, well-being and choice can be achieved without additional funding. The government maintains that the gradual reallocation of existing resources will be sufficient to bring about the proposed changes within government departments guided by a new 'slim' strategic unit: the Office of Disability Issues. This will be accountable to several government departments, most notably the DH, the Department for Work and Pensions, the Department for Education and Skills, the Office of the Deputy Prime Minister, and the Department for Transport (PMSU, 2005, p 183).

With many competing pressures and priorities, resource allocation at the national level is often complex and problematic. However, if resources are to be used effectively then budget allocations must be made with a clear understanding of their impact and desired effect. Of specific concern is the DH assertion that the overall effect of the Green Paper proposals should be 'cost-neutral for local authorities', although it agreed to 'look closely at the cost implications for individual local authorities' of any detailed proposals (DH, 2005a, p 42).

Given that there is a wealth of evidence that local authority support for locally based user-controlled service provider organisations and independent living-type services, such as direct payments, has been patchy and unenthusiastic, disabled people are entitled to be pessimistic about what these proposals for independent living will yield.

Review

Current government thinking displays an increasing readiness to acknowledge the 'failings' of mainstream services. The validity of disabled people's complaint that they were fitted into existing services is now widely accepted. The government has responded positively to demands to shift the policy emphasis to 'personalising' services to individual need, and promoting independent lives in the community. Additionally, there has been a parallel recognition that the social exclusion generally of disabled people needs to be addressed as a political priority. Proposals have been made to enhance the life chances of disabled people over the next 20 years, which acknowledge that increased choice and control in disabled people's everyday lives depends not only on the provision of personal assistance but on the removal of disabling social and environmental barriers such as exist in family life, education, paid employment and leisure.

Needless to say, these are still only proposals, and their translation into specific policies and practices may yet contain some unwelcome surprises for disabled people. Moreover, those planning and delivering the traditional system of service provision will need further persuasion. Concerns range from a lack of appreciation of the main thrust of the social model of disability and the philosophy of independent living, continuing professional reluctance to build a more equal relationship with disabled people in planning and delivering support services, and the general difficulties of moving a complex system of health and 'social care' in new directions, not least if the necessary funding and other resources are not available.

Drawing on these insights the concluding chapter will highlight key policy issues and implications for politicians, policy makers and practitioners concerned with the future development of services for disabled people and their families.

TEN

Future directions

Introduction

Since the middle of the 20th century, there has been a gradual but intensifying politicisation of disability by disabled people and their organisations, with an evident impact on government social welfare policies. The economic, political and cultural upheavals of the 1960s coupled with the harsh realities of traditional exclusionary policies for people with accredited impairments provided a fertile breeding ground for radical new ways of thinking about disability. These include the concept of independent living, the re-interpretation of disability as social oppression, the social model of disability, and the demand for choice and control of disability-related services.

Subsequent trends in the political climate and the ensuing escalating marketisation of social welfare precipitated the slow but significant shift of these ideas from the margins to the mainstream. Over the last decades this is clearly reflected in the UK with the introduction of the 1995 Disability Discrimination Act, the 1996 Community Care (Direct Payments) Act and subsequent amendments, and the Prime Minister's Strategy Unit (PMSU) document *Improving the Life Chances of Disabled People* with its unequivocal endorsement of independent living, a socio-political understanding of disability, individualised budgets and 'Centres for Independent Living' (CILs) (PMSU, 2005). However, this formulation offers no recognition of distinctions now made by disabled people between 'independent', 'integrated' and 'inclusive' living (see Chapter Five). Furthermore, while there is a general consensus within the Disabled People's Movement on the desirability of these ideas, the implementation of government policies presents a significant challenge for disabled activists and their organisations.

This concluding chapter will draw together some salient policy implications for politicians, policy makers and professionals concerned with the further development of independent living for disabled people and user involvement in services for this increasingly large and diverse section of the UK population.

Key themes and issues

Both the philosophy of independent living and the social model of disability warrant an holistic analysis of disabled people's individual and collective disadvantage in order to provide a just solution to their social exclusion.

The definition of disabled people involves three elements:

> (i) the presence of an impairment (ii) the experience of externally imposed restrictions and (iii) self identification as a disabled person. (Oliver, 1996b, p 5)

However, the definition of impairment is contentious. Since the early 1980s the international Disabled People's Movement has regarded impairment as raising issues of bio-psychosocial functioning whether physical, sensory or cognitive. Although often linked to congenital conditions the overwhelming majority of disabled people acquire their impairments later in life through disease, illness, accidents or violence, and the incidence of impairment increases significantly with age. Recent official figures suggest that there are 11 million disabled adults and 770,000 disabled children in the UK (ONS, 2004). Nevertheless, the reported incidence of physical impairment is decreasing, while the numbers of people with 'mental illness and behavioural disorders' are increasing (PMSU, 2005, p 20).

Notwithstanding the diversity of the disabled population, how people respond to impairment, whether congenital or acquired, is determined by a range of factors including the type and severity of the condition, socio-economic resources, ethnicity, age, gender and much more besides. Consequently, not all people with accredited impairments experience environmental and social barriers as 'externally imposed restrictions' or will necessarily self-identify as a 'disabled person'.

In general terms, the term 'disabled', when applied to a person or group of people, is still very much associated with the traditional 'personal tragedy' understanding of disability. From this perspective, disabled people are set apart from 'the ordinary' and liable to be considered 'unfortunate, useless, different, oppressed and sick' (Hunt, 1966, p 146). Moreover, in a society organised mainly around the liberal utilitarian values of individuality and self-reliance, to identify as 'disabled' may be construed as an acknowledgement of undesirable difference. Indeed, where the absence of other socially sanctioned identities is frequently denied, the 'cripple role' (Shakespeare, 1996, p 100) may carry the semblance of 'security' but, in practice, location within the 'deserving poor' carries few 'rewards'. For example, people with accredited impairments experience higher levels of unemployment and underemployment and are far 'more likely to live in *poverty* – the income of disabled people is, on average, less than half of that earned by non disabled people' (PMSU, 2005, p 6, emphasis in original).

Furthermore:

> since the emergence of the Disabled People's Movement, particularly in Britain, the word 'disabled' before 'people' or 'person' has come to signify identification with this collective political identity. (Oliver and Barnes, 1998, p 18)

But, in practice, the number of people with accredited impairments who self-identify in this way is relatively small in comparison to the disabled population as a whole, or as it is recorded in national surveys (Barnes et al, 1999; PMSU, 2004). This can be explained with reference to various factors, both structural and personal. For the most part, to be defined as a disabled person carries little social, economic or political advantage – quite the opposite in many contexts.

On top of this, the diversity of late capitalist society has encouraged 'multiple' or 'simultaneous' oppressions' (Thomas, 1999; Vernon, 1999). Consequently for many disabled people impairment and disability are mediated by a range of other social factors such as age, gender, ethnicity and social class. Equally important, although the Disabled People's Movement has tried to represent all sections of the disabled population, it is open to criticism for its failure to address the concerns of impairment-specific groups such as people labelled with 'learning difficulties' or 'mental health systems users and survivors' (Beresford and Wallcraft, 1997; Lee, 2002). Additionally, CIL–type organisations have endeavoured to provide a comprehensive and inclusive service for disabled people and their families but without obvious success. This may be explained in large part by the chronic shortage of resources, both financial and human, and a lack of investment by government and other agencies concerned with disability issues at both the national and local levels. But the lack of appropriate action by user-led or controlled organisations must also be taken into account.

These considerations raise important questions for the future of the UK's Disabled People's Movement and user-controlled organisations striving to provide a comprehensive service commensurate with the notion of independent living and the social model of disability.

Independent living: beyond 'social care'

Recent government policy statements have endorsed the principle of independent living. However, strong doubts remain as to their interpretation of the practical implications of this philosophy with reference to community-based support or 'social care' services and the role of CIL-type initiatives. These reservations are re-enforced further when considering the wider aspects of the independent living agenda (Gillinson et al, 2005). To reiterate, from a Disabled People's Movement perspective, independent living is founded on two basic assumptions:

- Human beings, regardless of the nature, complexity and/or severity of impairment, are of equal worth, and have the right to participate in all areas of mainstream community life.
- Whatever the character and severity of an impairment, individuals should be empowered to make choices and exercise control in their everyday lives (Bracking, 1993; Morris, 1993a, 2004; Charlton, 1998).

Equal worth: right to life and childhood 'disability'

With reference to the issue of 'equal worth', while the PMSU report adopts a social model account of 'disability', which is defined as: 'the disadvantage experienced by an individual ... resulting from barriers to independent living or educational employment or other opportunities, that impact on people with impairments or ill health' (PMSU, 2005, p 5), there is no attempt to address the concerns of disabled people and their organisations regarding selective abortion for unborn children with accredited impairments and euthanasia practices for people with 'terminal illness'.

Again, mainstreaming in the *Improving the Life Chances of Disabled People* report is linked to support for families with disabled children, the transition to adulthood for young disabled people, and help and incentives for disabled people to secure and stay in employment (PMSU, 2005). In recognition that disabled children are more likely to live in poverty than non-disabled children, the government contends that families with a disabled child should have access to individualised budgets in order to access 'ordinary lives' through effective support in mainstream settings. This support is to be provided by a 'key worker' whose functions include information, communication and 'care' coordination. Educational information and support is to be provided by a special educational needs coordinator. Yet, there is no clear statement that inclusive provision should be the norm either in nursery, pre-school or school placements. Concern has been expressed that 'specialist' alternatives may be considered if everyone involved with the child agrees that inclusive provision is inappropriate (Breakthrough UK, 2005, p 13).

As the majority of disabled children have non-disabled parents with little knowledge of disability issues (Oliver and Barnes, 1998), it is important to address their fears and concerns. It is equally important to recognise that several factors contribute to disabled young people's prolonged dependence on their families. These include the absorption of disability and child-related benefits into the familial budget, parental over-protection, unemployment and underemployment, lack of peer contact, and the cumulative emotional and psychological implications of social exclusion known variously as 'felt stigma' or 'internal oppression' (Barnes and Mercer, 2003).

Acknowledging that the transition to adulthood is a particularly difficult period for disabled young people, the government maintains that, in due course, the introduction of individualised budgets and person-centred planning will facilitate a smoother transition from children's to adult services. Nonetheless there is potential conflict here as parental or 'carers' views on support and independence do not always correspond to those of their disabled offspring. In the meantime the PMSU document states that:

> many disabled teenagers, especially those with learning difficulties, could benefit from children's services well beyond the current age cut offs for these services. To address this children's services … should move to include all disabled people up to the age of 25, and should support disabled young people living at home or moving in to independent living. (PMSU, 2005, p 12)

Such a policy effectively perpetuates the infantilisation of young disabled people and tends to sidestep the widespread view that for young people generally the key to adult status is securing paid employment, hence the emphasis placed by the National Employment Panel (NEP), an employer-led organisation that advises the government on labour market policies and performance, on increasing the 'number of disabled learners studying towards all levels of training and qualifications' and making employment training mandatory in post-16 educational needs provision (NEP, 2005, p 37).

Work and employment

In most industrialised countries paid work is a key signifier of class, status and power. This means that people on the margins of the labour market encounter a variety of economic, political and social deprivations. This form of distributive injustice is widely experienced by disabled people throughout the 'developed' world (Marin et al, 2004; PMSU, 2004). The latest figures for the UK suggest that 50% of disabled people are 'economically inactive' – neither working nor actively seeking work – compared with 15% of non-disabled people. Although unemployment among people labelled with 'learning difficulties' and/or designated 'mental illnesses' is especially high, 'for all impairment types labour market disadvantage is substantial' (NEP, 2005, pp 15-16).

Moreover, there are disproportionate numbers of disabled people in less skilled, lower-paid jobs with fewer promotion prospects, and an over-representation in specific occupations or congregated in sheltered workshops. Disabled people are particularly under-represented in the professions and management jobs, where there are higher earnings, job security and opportunities for promotion. Conversely, disabled people are over-represented in low-skilled, poorly paid, less secure jobs. Disabled men working full time earned on average 25% less than their non-disabled counterparts while the wages of disabled women were only two thirds those of disabled men (Burchardt, 2000).

Most of the employment section of the *Improving the Life Chances of Disabled People* report is given over to 'improving' the disabled person. This is illustrated by comments on the 'problem of unemployment', a policy focus dedicated to enhancing the individual's job readiness, and is commensurate with a long-standing government commitment to reduce the numbers of disabled people on state welfare. For example:

> There are situations where benefit dependency is ingrained in the community or family culture. (PMSU, 2005, p 139)

This approach is further endorsed by the emphasis on the role of general practitioners and occupational health therapists as providers of help and advice on 'fitness for work'. While this approach may have some value, it has not been able to significantly reduce unemployment among disabled people, and ultimately confirms the established orthodoxy that disabled people are unable to work due to personal deficits (Roulstone, 2002).

Hitherto, official and sociological analyses of work and disability have failed to address in sufficient depth or breadth the various social and environmental barriers that confront disabled people in the labour market. As a consequence many writers from within a disability studies perspective drawing upon the insights of the philosophy of independent living and the social model of disability have argued for a reconfiguration of the meaning of work in order to remove the stigma associated with unpaid labour (Barnes and Mercer, 2005).

Physical environment

Notwithstanding that the PMSU report acknowledges the structural barriers to disabled people's access to independent living generally and the labour market in particular, including transport, housing and the built environment, it is weak on implementation. With regard to transport barriers, despite successive legislation the UK's public transport infrastructure is largely inaccessible to large sections of the disabled population. Where transport barriers exist, local authorities are 'encouraged' to use the Department for Transport's *Accessibility Planning Guidance* document (DfT, 2004) to address the travel experiences of disabled people. This should be addressed within 'independent living assessments' and individualised budgets 'for example, where someone needs 'mobility training' or confidence building to use public transport' (PMSU, 2005, p 84).

Disabled people when compared to non-disabled contemporaries do not have equal access to housing; this is especially so for people who use wheelchairs, whether in the public or private sector. This is not taken fully into account in the report. There is evidence that the adoption of accessible or 'Lifetime Homes' standards for new-build housing is both popular with householders and financially cost-effective (Rowe, 1990; Cobbold, 1997). Also as part of *The London Plan: Spatial Development Strategy for Greater London* (GLA, 2004), all new homes are to be built to Lifetime Homes standards, whether constructed by local authorities, registered social landlords or private developers. The government has yet to make such a policy mandatory across the UK. Again, the combination of inadequate community-based support and the scarcity of accessible housing mean that many disabled people have no choice but to live in residential homes. Most disabled people, especially those with high support needs, are fearful of being forced into 'residential care' (Breakthrough UK, 2005; NCIL, 2005), which is viewed as the antithesis of independent living.

Moreover, there is little meaningful discussion of the problems disabled people encounter with regard to the built environment generally in recent government literature, particularly the PMSU report. This is important as although there has been some significant improvement over the last decade or so, disabled people still encounter considerable difficulty gaining equal access to public buildings and amenities. This is due to the extensive use of the terms 'reasonable', 'practical' and 'impractical' throughout UK legislation and policy statements that serve to effectively undermine any concerted moves to eradicate this form of structural inequality. For example, in a statement for service providers the Department for Work and Pensions stated:

> It's all about doing what is practical in your individual situation and making use of what resources you have. You will not be required to make changes that are impractical or beyond your financial means. (DWP, 2005a, unpaged)

Consequentially numerous permutations can emerge that allow businesses and service providers to be relieved of their obligation to make substantial improvements to both their services and their properties. Legislation is loosely associated with Part M of the Building Regulations, first introduced in 1985, and periodically amended to accommodate changes in the law. However, as there is no specific 'rulebook':

> Enforcement and compliance is, therefore, left to building inspectors and consultants which in turn leaves questions of rigour and consistency open to debate. (Prideaux, 2005, p 35)

Implementation

Despite these concerns the government's appetite for the development of independent living is evidenced further by an ambitious and impressive list of proposals for a phased programme of target setting and policy reviews and the devolution of responsibility for implementation to government departments. Lead responsibility will rest with the Minister for Disabled People and the newly formed Office of Disability Issues (ODI). This is now officially designated as the 'champion for disabled people' by providing a cross-government focus for improved collaboration between ministers, officials and departments and 'improving outcomes and securing equal opportunities for disabled individuals and families' (DWP, 2005b, unpaged). The ODI is also charged with facilitating the 'involvement of disabled people themselves' (PMSU, 2005, p 183). This is to be achieved by the development of 'user involvement protocols' and the establishment of a:

> National Forum for Organisations of Disabled People, chaired by the Minister [for Disabled People] through which disabled people can meet and contribute to policy development. (PMSU, 2005, p 186)

This is complemented by the setting up of an Independent Living Task Force (PMSU, 2005, p 192).

While there is a great deal of emphasis in the PMSU report on the importance of disabled people's involvement in these policy developments, it is not really clear how this involvement is to be enacted. Certainly the ODI is to be staffed by people who have been seconded from other government departments but there is no mention in the PMSU document of the need for them to have experience of impairment or knowledge of disability issues. Such concerns are compounded by the fact that government departments have a poor record in the employment of disabled people – in 2005 this stood at only 4% of the workforce (Kotecha, 2005). A more effective approach would be to ensure that people with an awareness of disability and independent living issues are integrated fully into government departments at all levels, nationally, regionally and locally.

The National Forum will be chaired by the Minister for Disabled People but apart from the reference to organisations 'of' disabled people there is no clear indication of who will be included in the Forum's membership. The issue is clouded further by the statement that:

> There must be a sustained effort to build up the capacity of organisations *representing* disabled people and their ability to work together and with other partners. Government contracts have

the potential to assist this process. (PMSU, 2005, p 186, emphasis added)

As mentioned in previous chapters, over recent years the boundaries between organisations 'of' and 'for' disabled people have become increasingly blurred. Although several of the latter have now apparently joined campaigns for disabled people's rights and laid claim to the notion of independent living, their commitment to user accountability and meaningful involvement is open to question. This is reflected by the fact that, in concert with government departments, their record on employing disabled workers is consistently poor, especially in positions of authority (Oliver and Barnes, 1998; Calvi, 2003).

What is more, the rationale behind the government's intention to set up a national forum for organisations of disabled people is seriously open to question given that there are two well-established national autonomous bodies that already fulfil this role: namely, the British Council of Disabled People, established in 1981, and the National Centre for Independent Living (NCIL) (see Chapter Three).

Equally worrying is the assertion that no extra funding is to be made available for the implementation of these proposals. The financial implications of eradicating exclusion and implementing independent living policies and practices cannot be overlooked. There is almost universal agreement that the economic consequences of social exclusion are no longer acceptable and that a thorough cost-benefit analysis of independent living is likely to show that in the long term these can be considerably reduced if not eliminated altogether. Even so, it is naive to assume that the introduction of policies to facilitate meaningful independent living for disabled people can proceed without substantial investment by central government.

Independent living in an inclusive society

To facilitate greater user involvement in the development and delivery of services, people have to feel empowered. But empowerment cannot be imposed from above, it must be organic in that people must want to empower themselves. With limited resources, severe under-investment and varying degrees of opposition from traditional service providers, the Disabled People's Movement and its member organisations have, by example, had a major impact on the way social services and support are delivered. In so doing they have empowered thousands of disabled people across the UK. If this process is to continue it is essential that appropriate funding be made available to local organisations led, managed and controlled by disabled people, particularly in the process of delivery and the infrastructure of direct payments, and freed of local authority regulation and control. This is fundamental to independent living and should be managed and delivered by an overarching representative body of disabled people (Barnes, 2004; Breakthrough UK, 2005).

Given the recent history and devolution of government in the UK, separate agencies should be established in England, Scotland, Northern Ireland and Wales. Sufficient resources should be made available to ensure that these structures are able to develop and support national networks of user-led initiatives that are sensitive and responsive to impairment, ethnic and cultural diversity within the disabled population at the local level.

Much of the rhetoric surrounding independent living revolves around enhancing individual 'choice' in provision. However, the main self-determination issue for disabled people is not simply about service delivery mechanisms, but about whether levels of resources are sufficient to deliver the required services. All too often funding at the local level is insufficient to enable people to access the services needed to live independently. This must be rectified if meaningful independent living is to become a reality. Additionally, any significant shift in service delivery should include a radical reappraisal of the role of professionals and social support workers. As part of this change in approach, user-controlled organisations should be actively involved in professional development and training (NCIL, 2005).

Besides, the concept of independent living encompasses the full range of human experience and rights. As a consequence it poses a direct challenge to contemporary capitalist societies such as the UK, and more globally. This is because people with designated impairments will always experience varying degrees of economic, political and social disadvantage in societies organised around the core capitalist values of economic rationality, the profit motive, and individualism. Indeed, to achieve a lifestyle comparable to their peers, disabled people need far more than user-led services. To attain independent living disabled people need equal access to mainstream schools, jobs, transport, houses, public buildings, leisure, and so on, or 'all the things that non-disabled people take for granted' (Bracking, 1993, p 14).

Given the limited ambition of recent government initiatives in this regard, little significant progress will be made without further changes. It must be recognised that these will have significant resource implications, as effective barrier removal cannot be achieved 'on the cheap'. These short-term costs must be offset against the long-term gains of a barrier-free environment in which socially created dependence is considerably reduced if not eliminated altogether. While such a policy may fly in the face of recent economic and political trends, it is important to remember that the notion of a fully inclusive and equitable capitalism is unrealistic. Yet, it is apparent that the level and forms of social exclusion have in some (but not all) areas diminished slightly over recent years, although a clear social division remains. The limited progress of disabled people in a relatively 'affluent' country such as the UK must, however, be set against a far less certain improvement in social inclusion for disabled people in relatively 'poorer' countries.

Review

The information collected as part of the *Creating Independent Futures* study suggests that the recent impetus towards greater user involvement in the development and delivery of services controlled and run by disabled people cannot be sustained without significant policy changes at the national and local levels. This will involve a radical re-think on the part of everyone involved in the development and delivery of services for disabled people, in terms of what can and cannot be realistically achieved by user-led organisations within the current socio-political climate.

References

Note: References marked ★ are also available at: www.leeds.ac.uk/disability-studies/archiveuk/index.html

Abberley, P. (1987) 'The concept of oppression and the development of a social theory of disability'. *Disability, Handicap and Society*, 2 (1), 5-19.

Abberley, P. (1992) 'Counting us out: a discussion of the OPCS disability surveys'. *Disability, Handicap and Society*, 7 (2), 139-56.

Abberley, P. (1995) 'Disabling ideology in health and welfare: the case of occupational therapy'. *Disability and Society*, 10 (2), 221-32.

Abberley, P. (2004) 'A critique of professional support and intervention', in J. Swain, S. French, C. Barnes and C. Thomas (eds) *Disabling Barriers: Enabling Environments* (2nd edn). London: Sage Publications, 239-44.

Albrecht, G.L. (1992) *The Disability Business*. London: Sage Publications.

Armstrong, D. (1983) *Political Anatomy of the Body: Medical Knowledge in Britain in the Twentieth Century*. Cambridge: Cambridge University Press.

Arts Council (2003) *Celebrating Disability Arts*. London: Arts Council.

Audit Commission (1986) *Making a Reality of Community Care*. London: Audit Commission.

Audit Commission (1998) *A Fruitful Partnership: Effective Partnership Working*. London: Audit Commission.

Audit Commission (2002) *Tracking the Changes in Social Services in England: Joint Review Team Sixth Annual Report 2001/2*. Wetherby: Audit Commission.

Back, L. and Solomos, J. (1993) 'Doing research, writing politics, the dilemmas of political intervention in research on racism'. *Economy and Society*, 22 (2), 178-99.

Balloch, S. and Taylor, M. (2001) 'Introduction', in S. Balloch and M. Taylor (eds) *Partnership Working: Policy and Practice*. Bristol: The Policy Press, 1-14.

Barker, I. and Peck, E. (1987) *Power in Strange Places*. London: Good Practices in Mental Health.

Barnes, C. (1991) *Disabled People in Britain and Discrimination: A Case for Anti-Discrimination Legislation*. London: Hurst and Co. in association with the British Council of Organisations of Disabled People.★

Barnes, C. (1992) 'Qualitative research: valuable or irrelevant?' *Disability, Handicap and Society*, 7 (2), 115-24.

Barnes, C. (ed) (1993) *Making Our Own Choices: Independent Living and Personal Assistance*. Belper: British Council of Organisations of Disabled People and Ryburn Press.★

Barnes, C. (1995) *From National to Local: An Evaluation of the Effectiveness of National Disablement Information Providers Services to Local Disablement Information Providers*. Derby: The British Council of Organisations of Disabled People.★

Barnes, C. (1997) *Older People's Perceptions of Direct Payments and Self Operated Support Systems*. Derby: The British Council of Disabled People and Help the Aged.

Barnes, C. (2003) 'What a difference a decade makes: reflections on doing "emancipatory" disability research'. *Disability and Society*, 18 (1), 3-17.

Barnes, C. (2004) 'Independent living, politics and implications'. Invited presentation at the Social Care Institute for Excellence (SCIE) National Conference on Independent Living, Kensington Tara Hotel, London, 22 November.★

Barnes, C. and Mercer, G. (eds) (1997a) *Doing Disability Research*. Leeds: The Disability Press.★

Barnes, C. and Mercer, G. (1997b) 'Breaking the mould? An introduction to doing disability research'. In C. Barnes and G. Mercer (eds) *Doing Disability Research*. Leeds: The Disability Press, 1-14.★

Barnes, C. and Mercer, G. (2001) 'The politics of disability and the struggle for change', in L. Barton (ed) *Disability, Politics and the Struggle for Change*. London: David Fulton Publishers, 11-23.

Barnes, C. and Mercer, G. (2003) *Disability*. Cambridge: Polity Press.

Barnes, C. and Mercer, G. (2005) 'Disability, work and welfare: challenging the social exclusion of disabled people'. *Work, Employment and Society*, 19 (5), 527-45.

Barnes, C. and Oliver, M. (1995) 'Disability rights: rhetoric and reality in the UK'. *Disability and Society*, 10 (1), 111-16.

Barnes, C., McCarthy, M. and Comerford, S. (eds) (1995) *Assessment, Accountability and Independent Living: Confirmation and Clarification of a Disability Led Perspective*. Unpublished report of Conference held at Coombe Abbey, Coventry, 23–24 May.

Barnes, C., Mercer, G. and Shakespeare, T. (1999) *Exploring Disability*. Cambridge: Polity Press.

Barnes, C., Mercer, G. and Morgan, H. (2000) *Creating Independent Futures: An Evaluation of Services Led by Disabled People. Stage One Report*. Leeds: The Disability Press.★

Barnes, C., Morgan, H. and Mercer, G. (2001) *Creating Independent Futures: An Evaluation of Services Led by Disabled People. Stage Three Report*. Leeds: The Disability Press.★

Barnes, C., Mercer, G. and Morgan, H. (2002) *Creating Independent Futures: Conference Report*. Leeds: The Disability Press.★

Barnes, M. and Wistow, G. (1994a) 'Learning to hear voices: listening to users of mental health services'. *Journal of Mental Health*, 3 (5), 525-40.

Barnes, M. and Wistow, G. (1994b) 'Achieving a strategy for user involvement in community care'. *Health and Social Care in the Community*, 2 (6), 347-56.

Barton, L. (2001) *Disability Politics and the Struggle for Change*. London: David Fulton.

BCODP (British Council of Disabled People) (2001) Personal communication.

Begum, N. (1993) 'Independent living, personal assistance and disabled black people', in C. Barnes (ed) *Making Our Own Choices: Independent Living and Personal Assistance*. Belper: British Council of Organisations of Disabled People and Ryburn Press, 51-54.★

Begum, N. (1994) 'Mirror, mirror on the wall', in N. Begum, M. Hill and A. Stevens (eds) *Reflections: Views of Black Disabled People on their Lives and Community Care*. London: Central Council for Education and Training in Social Work, 17-36.

Begum, N. and Gillespie-Sells, K. (1994) *Towards Managing User-Led Services*. London: REU (Race Equality Unit).

Beresford, P. (1993) 'A programme for change: current issues in user involvement and empowerment', in P. Beresford and T. Harding (eds) *A Challenge to Change: Practical Experience of Building User-Led Services*. London: National Institute for Social Work, 9-29.

Beresford, P. (2000) 'Service users' knowledges and social work theory: conflict or collaboration?' *British Journal of Social Work*, 30 (4), 489-503.

Beresford, P. (2004) 'Treatment at the hands of professionals', in J. Swain, S. French, C. Barnes and C. Thomas (eds) *Disabling Barriers: Enabling Environments* (2nd edn), London: Sage Publications, 245-50.

Beresford, P. and Campbell, J. (1994) 'Disabled people, service users, user involvement and representation'. *Disability and Society*, 9 (3), 315-25.

Beresford, P. and Croft, S. (1993) *Citizen Involvement: A Practical guide for Change*. Basingstoke: Macmillan.

Beresford, P. and Wallcraft, J. (1997) 'Psychiatric system survivors and emancipatory research: issues, overlaps and differences', in C. Barnes and G. Mercer (eds) *Doing Disability Research*. Leeds: The Disability Press, 67–87.★

Beresford, P., Croft, S., Evans, C. and Harding, T. (1997) 'Quality in personal social services: the developing role of user involvement in the UK', in A. Evers, R. Haverinen, K. Leichsenting and G. Wistow (eds) *Developing Quality in Personal Social Services*. Aldershot: Ashgate, 63–81.

Bevans, L. (2005) 'Poll reveals high level of long-term sickness among social services staff'. *Community Care*, 14–20 April, 6.

Bewley, C. and Glendinning, C. (1994) *Involving Disabled People in Community Care Planning*. York: Joseph Rowntree Foundation.

Blaxter, M. (1976) *The Meaning of Disability*, London: Heinemann.

Borsay, A. (2005) *Disability and Social Policy in Britain since 1750: A History of Exclusion*. Basingstoke: Palgrave Macmillan.

Bott, S. and Rust, A. (1997) 'Involving physically disabled users in service planning and delivery: Shropshire as a case study'. *Research, Policy and Planning*, 15 (2), 38–42.

Bowl, R. (1996) 'Legislating for user involvement in the UK: mental health services and the National Health Service and Community Care Act 1990'. *International Journal of Social Psychiatry*, 42 (3), 165–80.

Bracking, S. (1993) 'Independent living: a brief overview', in C. Barnes (ed) *Making Our Own Choices: Independent Living and Personal Assistance*. Belper: British Council of Organisations of Disabled People and Ryburn Press, 14–15.★

Brandon, D. (1995) *Advocacy: Power to People with Disabilities*. Birmingham: Venture Press.

Braye, S. (2000) 'Participation and involvement in social care: an overview', in H. Kemshall and R. Littlechild (eds) *User Involvement and Participation in Social Care*. London: Jessica Kingsley Publishers, 9–28.

Braye, S. and Preston-Shoot, M. (1995) *Empowering Practice in Social Care*. Buckingham: Open University Press.

Breakthrough UK (2005) *A Response to the Prime Minister's Strategy Unit Report Improving the Life Chances of Disabled People*. Manchester: Breakthrough UK.★

Brechin, A., Liddiard, P. and Swain, J. (eds) (1981) *Handicap in a Social World*. Milton Keynes: Hodder and Stoughton in association with The Open University.

Brisenden, S. (1986) 'Independent living and the medical model of disability'. *Disability, Handicap and Society*, 1(2), 173-8.

Brisenden, S. (1989) 'A charter for personal care', in Disablement Income Group (DIG), *Progress London*. No 16, London: DIG.

Bristow, A. (1981) *Crossroads Care Attendant Schemes*. Rugby: Association of Crossroads Care Attendant Schemes.

Brown, H. and Smith, H. (eds) (1992) *Normalisation: A Reader for the Nineties*. London: Tavistock.

Burchardt, T. (2000) *Enduring Economic Exclusion: Disabled People, Income and Work*. York: Joseph Rowntree Foundation.

Bury, M. (1996) 'Defining and researching disability: challenges and responses', in C. Barnes and G. Mercer (eds) *Exploring the Divide: Illness and Disability*. Leeds: The Disability Press, 17-38.★

Bury, M. (1997) *Health and Ilness in a Changing Society*. London: Routledge.

Calvi, N. (2003) 'Can charities change'. *Disability Now*, May, 17. London: Scope.

Campbell, J. and Oliver, M. (1996) *Disability Politics: Understanding our Past, Changing our Future*. London: Routledge.

Campbell, P. (1996) 'The history of the user movement in the United Kingdom', in T. Heller, J. Reynolds, R. Gomm, R. Muston and S. Pattison (eds) *Mental Health Matters*. Basingstoke: Macmillan, 218-25.

Carson, G. and Speirs, J. (2004) 'Developing a user-led project: creating employment opportunities for disabled people within the housing sector', in C. Barnes and G. Mercer (eds) *Disability Policy and Practice: Applying the Social Model*. Leeds: The Disability Press, 35-50.

Carter, J. (1981) *Day Services for Adults: Somewhere to Go*. London: George Allen and Unwin.

Centre for Independent Living (1982) 'Independent living: the right to choose', in M. Eisenberg, C. Griggins and R. Duval (eds) *Disabled People as Second-Class Citizens*. New York: Springer Publishing Company, 247-60.

Chamberlain, J. (1988) *On our Own*. London: MIND.

Chappell, A.L. (1992) 'Towards a sociological critique of the normalisation principle', *Disability, Handicap and Society*, 7 (1), 35-51.

Chappell, A.L. (2000) 'Emergence of participatory methodology in learning difficulty research: understanding the context'. *British Journal of Learning Disabilities*, 28 (1), 38-43.

Charity Commission (1999) *CC9 Political Campaigning by Charities*. September. London: Charities Commission.

Charity Commission (2004) *CC9 Campaigning and Political Activities by Charities*. London: Charities Commission.

Charlton, J.I. (1998) *Nothing About Us Without Us: Disability Oppression and Empowerment*. Berkeley, CA: University of California Press.

Christie, I. with Mensah-Coker, G. (1999) *An Inclusive Future? Disability, Social Change and Opportunities for Greater Inclusion by 2010*. London: Demos.

CILiG (Centre for Independent Living in Glasgow) (2004) *Centre for Independent Living in Glasgow: Annual Review 2003*. Glasgow: Glasgow Centre for Independent Living.

Clarke, J. (2004) *Changing Welfare Changing States: New Directions in Social Policy*. London: Sage Publications.

Clarke, J. and Newman, J. (1997) *The Managerial State: Power, Politics and Ideology in the Remaking of Social Welfare*. London: Sage Publications.

Cobbold, C. (1997) *A Cost benefit Analysis of Lifetime Homes*. York: Joseph Rowntree Foundation.

Cocks, E. and Cockham, J. (1995) 'The participatory research paradigm and intellectual disability'. *Mental Handicap Research*, 8 (1), 25-37.

Coleridge, P. (1993) *Disability, Liberation and Development*. Oxford: Oxfam Publications.

Cook, D. (2002) 'Consultation, for a change?: Engaging users and communities in the policy process'. *Social Policy and Administration*, 36 (5), 516-31.

Corker, M. (1995) 'Mental health services and counselling – are they the same?' *Deafness*, 11 (3), 9-15.

Corker, M. (1999) 'New disability discourse, the principle of optimization and social change', in M. Corker and S. French (eds) *Disability Discourse*. Buckingham: Open University Press, 192-209.

Cousins, C. (1987) *Controlling Social Welfare*. Brighton: Wheatsheaf Books.

Crewe, N. and Zola, I.K. (1983) 'Preface', in N. Crewe and I.K. Zola (eds) *Independent Living for Physically Disabled People*. San Francisco, CA: Jossey-Bass, ix-xvi.

Crowther, A. (1981) *The Workhouse System, 1834–1929: The History of an English Social Institution*. London: Methuen.

D'Aboville, E. (1991) 'Social work in an organisation of disabled people', in M. Oliver (ed) *Social Work: Disabled People and Disabling Environments.* London: Jessica Kingsley Publishers, 64-85.

D'Aboville, E. (2006) 'Implementing direct payments: a support organisation perspective', in J. Leece and J. Bornat (eds) *Developments in Direct Payments.* Bristol: The Policy Press, 145-8.

DANE (Disability Action North East) (2004a) *DANE: Breaking the Social Barriers that Disabled Us.* (Publicity Leaflet). Newcastle Upon Tyne: DANE.

DANE (2004b) *Hands Off Our Genes: Disabled People's Conference; 24th January 2004, Mea House, Newcastle Upon Tyne, Information Pack.* Newcastle Upon Tyne: DANE.

Daunton, M.J. (1996) 'Payment and participation: welfare and state formation in Britain, 1900-1951', *Past and Present*, 150, 169-218.

Davies, C. (2002) *Changing Society: A Personal History of Scope (formerly The Spastics Society) 1952-2002.* London: Scope.

Davis, A., Ellis, K. and Rummery, K. (1997) *Access to Assessment: Perspectives of Practitioners, Disabled People and Carers.* Bristol: The Policy Press.

Davis, J.M. (2000) 'Disability studies as ethnographic research and text: research strategies and roles for promoting change?', *Disability and Society*, 15 (2), 191-206.

Davis, K. (1981) '28-38 Grove Road: accommodation and care in a community setting', in A. Brechin, P. Liddiard and J. Swain (eds) *Handicap in a Social World.* Sevenoaks: Hodder and Stoughton in association with The Open University, 322-7.

Davis, K. (1990) *A Social Barriers Model of Disability: Theory into Practice.* Derby: Derbyshire Coalition of Disabled People.★

Davis, K. (1993) 'The crafting of good clients', in J. Swain, V. Finkelstein, S. French and M. Oliver (eds) *Disabling Barriers: Enabling Environments.* London: Sage Publications in association with The Open University, 197-200.

Davis, K. and Mullender, A. (1993) *Ten Turbulent Years: A Review of the Work of the Derbyshire Coalition of Disabled People.* Nottingham: University of Nottingham Centre for Social Action.

Davis, L. (1995) *Enforcing Normalcy: Disability, Deafness, and the Body.* London and New York: Verso.

DCIL (Derbyshire Centre for Inclusive Living) (2000) *The Russia Project: DAN and DCIL in Moscow.* Derby: DCIL, www.dcil.org.uk/about (accessed 5/02/04).

DCIL (2003) *Derbyshire Coalition for Inclusion Living:What DCIL is*. Derby: DCIL, www.dcil.org.uk/about (accessed 5/02/04).

DeJong, G. (1979) 'Independent living: from social movement to analytic paradigm'. *Archives of Physical Medicine Rehabilitation*, 60, 435–46.

DeJong, G. (1981) 'The movement for independent living: origins, ideology and implications for disability research', in A. Brechin, P. Liddiard and J.Swain (eds) *Handicap in a Social World*. Sevenoaks: Hodder and Stoughton in association with The Open University Press, 239-48.

DeJong, G. (1983) 'Defining and implementing the independent living concept', in N. Crewe and I. Zola (eds) *Independent Living for Physically Disabled People*. London: Jossey-Bass, 4-27.

DeJong, G. (1988) 'The challenge of middle age in the independent living movement'. *Disability Studies Quarterly*, Summer. Available at: www.independentliving.org/toolsforpower/tools3c.html

DfT (Department for Transport) (2004) *Accessibility Planning Guidance: Full Guidance*. London: DfT.

DH (Department of Health) (1989) *Caring for People*. London: HMSO.

DH (1991) *Care Management and Assessment: Managers Guide*. London: HMSO.

DH (1994) *A Framework for Local Community Care Charters in England: Consultation Document*. London: DH.

DH (1998) *Modernising Social Services: Promoting Independence, Improving Protection, Raising Standards*. London: DH.

DH (2000) *A Quality Strategy for Social Care*. London: DH.

DH (2005a) *Independence, Well-being and Choice: Our vision for the Future of Social Care for Adults in England*. London: DH.

DH (2005b) *Direct Payments and Health*. London: DH, www.dh.gov.uk/ PolicyAndGuidance/OrganisationPolicy/FinanceAndPlanning/ DirectPayments/fs/en (accessed 17/05/05).

DH (2005c) *Community Care Statistics 2003-04: Referrals, Assessments and Packages of Care, England – National Summary*. London: DH, www.dh.gov.uk/PublicationsAndStatistics/Publications/ PublicationsStatistics/PublicationsStatisticsArticle/fs/ en?CONTENT_ID=4098062&chk=tO1%2Byw (accessed 17/05/05).

Disabled Living Centres Council (2004) Disabled Living Centres Council Homepage, www.lboro.ac.uk/info/usabilitynet/dlcc.html (accessed 25/02/04).

Dominelli, L. (1998) 'Anti-oppressive practice in context', in R. Adams, L. Dominelli and M. Payne (eds) *Social Work: Themes, Issues and Critical Debates*. London: Macmillan, 3-22.

Drake, R. (1994) 'The exclusion of disabled people from positions of power in British voluntary organisations'. *Disability and Society*, 9 (4), 461-80.

Drake, R. (1996) 'A critique of the role of the traditional charities', in L. Barton (ed) *Disability and Society: Emerging Issues and Insights*. Harlow: Longman, 147-66.

Drake, R. (1999) *Understanding Disability Policies*. Basingstoke: Macmillan.

Drake, R. (2001) 'Welfare states and disabled people', in G. Albrecht, K. Seelman and M. Bury (eds) *Handbook of Disability Studies*. London: Sage Publications, 412-29.

DRC (Disability Rights Commission) (2002a) *Independent Living and the DRC Vision*. January. London: DRC.

DRC (2002b) *Policy Statement on Social Care and Independent Living*. London: DRC.

DSS (Department of Social Security) (1998) *A New Contract for Welfare: Support for Disabled People*. London: DSS.

DWP (Department for Work and Pensions) (2005a) 'New Office for Disability Issues launched today brings disabled people to the heart of government'. *News Release*, 1 December. London: DWP.

DWP (2005b) *Service Providers and the DDA: What does the Disability Discrimination Act Mean for Service Providers*. London: DWP, www.dwp.gov.uk/employers/dda/providers.asp (accessed 26/07/05).

Edwards, A. (2002) 'What is knowledge in social care?' *MCC: Building Knowledge for Integrated Care*, 10 (1), 13-16.

Ellis, K. (2000) 'User involvement, community care and disability research', in H. Kemshall and R. Littlechild (eds) *User Involvement and Participation in Social Care*. London: Jessica Kingsley Publishers, 215-32.

Ellis, K. and Rummery, K. (2000) 'Politics into practice: the production of a disabled person's guide to accessing community care assessments', in H. Kemshall and R. Littlechild (eds) *User Involvement and Participation in Social Care*. London: Jessica Kingsley Publishers, 97-110.

ENIL (European Network of Independent Living) (1989) *Independent Living*. Strasbourg: ENIL.

Evans, C., Carmichael, A. and members of the Direct Payments Best Value Project Group of Wiltshire & Swindon Users' Network (2002) *Users' Best Value: A Guide to Good Practice in User Involvement*. York: Joseph Rowntree Foundation.

Evans, J. (1993) 'The role of Centres for Independent/Integrated Living and networks of disabled people', in C. Barnes (ed) *Making Our Own Choices: Independent Living and Personal Assistance*. Belper: British Council of Organisations of Disabled People and Ryburn Press, 59-63.★

Exworthy, M. and Halford, S. (1999) 'Professionals and managers in a changing public sector: conflict, compromise and collaboration?', in M. Exworthy and S. Halford (eds) *Professionals and the New Manageralism in the Public Sector*. Buckingham: Open University Press, 1-17.

Fagan, T. and Lee, P. (1997) 'New social movements and social policy: a case study of the disability movement', in M. Lavalette and A. Pratt (eds) *Social Policy: A Conceptual and Theoretical Introduction*. London: Sage Publications, 140-60.

Fido, J. (1977) 'The charity organization and social casework in London, 1869-1900', in A.P. Donajgrodski (ed) *Social Control in Nineteenth Century Britain*. London: Croom Helm, 207-30.

Fiedler, B. (1988) *Living Options Lottery: Housing and Support Services for People with Severe Physical Disabilities*. London: Prince of Wales Advisory Group on Disability.

Finkelstein, V. (1980) *Attitudes and Disabled People*. New York: World Rehabilitation Fund.★

Finkelstein, V. (1998) 'The biodynamics of disablement'. Paper presented at the Disability and Rehabilitation Workshop in Harare, Zimbabwe, 29 June.★

Finkelstein, V. (1999a) 'Doing disability research.' *Disability and Society*, 14 (6), 859-67.

Finkelstein, V. (1999b) 'A profession allied to the community: the disabled people's trade union', in E. Stone (ed) *Disability and Development: Learning from Action and Research on Disability in the Majority World*. Leeds: The Disability Press, 21-4.

Fletcher, S. (1995) *Evaluating Community Care: A guide to Evaluations led by Disabled People*. London: The King's Fund.

Flynn, R. (1999) 'Managerialism, professionalism and quasi-markets', in M. Exworthy and S. Halford (eds) *Professionals and the New Managerialism in the Public Sector*. Buckingham: Open University Press, 18-36.

French, S. (ed) (1994) *On Equal Terms: Working with Disabled People*. Oxford: Butterworth Heinemann.

French, S. (2001) *Disabled People and Employment: A Study of the Working Lives of Visually Impaired Physiotherapists*. Aldershot: Ashgate.

GAD (Greenwich Association of Disabled People) (2003) *GAD – CIL Annual General Report 2002-2003*. London: GAD.

Gillespie-Sells, K. and Campbell, J. (1991) *Disability Equality Training: Trainers Guide*. London: Central Council for Education and Training in Social Work and the London Boroughs Disability Resource Team.★

Gillinson, S., Green, H. and Miller, P. (2005) *Independent Living: The Right to be Equal Citizens*. London: Demos.

GLA (Greater London Authority) (2004) *The London Plan: Spatial Development Strategy for Greater London*. London: GLA.

GLAD (Greater London Action on Disability) (2000) *Reclaiming the Social Model: Conference Report*. London: GLAD.

GLAD (2004) *GLAD Conference Report Summaries*, www.glad.org.uk/services/report-summaries/index (accessed 7/06/04).

Glasby, J. and Littlechild, R. (2002) *Social Work and Direct Payments*. Bristol: The Policy Press.

Glaser, B. and Strauss, A. (1967) *The Discovery of Grounded Theory*. New York: Aldine.

Gleeson, B. (1999) *Geographies of Disability*. London: Routledge.

Glendinning, C. (2006) 'Direct payments and health', in J. Leece and J. Bornat (eds) *Developments in Direct Payments*. Bristol: The Policy Press, 253-68.

Glendinning, C., Halliwell, S., Jacobs, S., Rummery, K. and Tyrer, J. (2000) *Buying Independence: Using Direct Payments to Integrate Health and Social Services*. Bristol: The Policy Press.

Glendinning, C., Powell, M. and Rummery, K. (eds) (2002) *Partnerships, New Labour and the Governance of Welfare*. Bristol: The Policy Press.

GMCDP (Greater Manchester Coalition of Disabled People) (1995) *Information Bulletin Manchester*. August. Manchester: GMCDP.

GMCDP (2000) 'Where have all the activists gone?' *Coalition*, August, Part 1 and October, Part 2. Manchester: GMCDP.

Goffman, E. (1961) *Asylums: Essays on the Social Situation of Mental Patients and Other Inmates*. New York: Doubleday.

Goffman, E. (1963) *Stigma: Some Notes on the Management of Spoiled Identity*. New Jersey: Prentice Hall.

Goodinge, S. (2000) *A Jigsaw of Services: Inspection of Services to Support Disabled Adults in their Parenting Role*. London: Department of Health, Social Services Inspectorate.

Goodley, D. and Moore, M. (2000) 'Doing disability research: activist lives and the academy'. *Disability and Society*, 15 (6), 861-82.

Gouldner, A. (1965) *Applied Sociology: Opportunities and Problems*. New York: Free Press.

Gouldner, A. (1971) *The Coming Crisis of Western Sociology*. London: Heinemann.

Griffiths, R. (1988) *Community Care: Agenda for Action*. London: HMSO.

Guba, E.G. and Lincoln, Y.S. (1994) 'Competing paradigms in qualitative research', in N.K. Denzin and Y.S. Lincoln (eds) *The Handbook of Qualitative Research*. Thousand Oaks: Sage Publications, 105-17.

Habermas, J. (1981) 'New social movements'. *Telos*, 49 (Fall), 33-7.

Hahn, H. (1987) 'Civil rights for disabled Americans: the foundation of a political agenda', in A. Gartner and T. Joe (eds) *Images of the Disabled, Disabling Images*. New York: Praeger, 181-203.

Harding, S. (1987) 'Introduction: is there a feminist method?', in S. Harding (ed) *Feminism and Methodology: Social Science Issues*. Milton Keynes: Open University Press, 1-14.

Harris, A., Cox, E. and Smith, C. (1971) *Handicapped and Impaired in Great Britain Volume 1*. London: HMSO.

Hasler, F. (2003) Personal communication.

Hasler, F., Campbell, J. and Zarb, G. (1999) *Direct Routes to Independence*. London: Policy Studies Institute.

Hirschman, A. (1970) *Exit, Voice and Loyalty: Responses to Decline in Firms, Organisations and States*. Cambridge, MA: Harvard University Press.

Hitchcock, T., King, P. and Sharpe, P. (1997) 'Introduction: chronicling poverty – the voices and strategies of the English poor, 1640-1840', in T. Hitchcock, P. King, and P. Sharpe (eds) *Chronicling Poverty: The Voices and Strategies of the English Poor, 1640-1840*. Basingstoke: Macmillan, 1-18.

Hudson, B. (1999) 'Dismantling the Berlin Wall: developments at the health–social care interface', in H. Dean and R. Woods (eds) *Social Policy Review 11*. Luton: Social Policy Association, 187-204.

Hughes, G. and Ferguson, R. (eds) (2000) *Ordering Lives: Family, Work and Welfare*. London: Open University/Routledge.

Hugman, R. (1991) *Power in Caring Professions*. London: Macmillan.

Humphries, S. and Gordon, P. (1992) *Out of Sight: The Experience of Disability 1900-1950*. London: Northcote House.

Hunt, P. (1966) 'A critical condition', in P. Hunt (ed) *Stigma: The Experience of Disability*. London: Geoffrey Chapman, 145-59.★

Hunt, P. (1981) 'Settling accounts with the parasite people: a critique of *A Life Apart* by E.J. Miller and G.V. Gwynne'. *Disability Challenge*, 1, 37–50.★

Hurst, R. and Mainwearing, T. (2004) 'Foreword', in P. Miller, S. Parker and S. Gillinson (2004) *Disablism: How to Tackle the Last Prejudice*. London: Demos.

Imrie, R.F. and Wells, P.E. (1993) 'Disablism, planning and the built environment'. *Environment and Planning C: Government and Policy*, 11 (2), 213-31.

Independently (2004) 'Age Concern's Campaign for Free Personal Care', *Independently*, May/June, 6-7, London: National Centre for Independent Living.

Innes, J. (1994) 'The domestic face of the fiscal–military state', in L. Stone (ed) *An Imperial State at War: Britain from 1689 to 1815*. London: Routledge, 97-108.

Jolly, D. (2005) 'Disabled people and direct payments, a comparative study: draft working paper'. Unpublished. Leeds: Centre for Disability Studies, University of Leeds.

Jones, K. (1972) *A History of Mental Health Services*. London: Routledge and Kegan Paul.

Kelly, L., Burton, S. and Regan, L. (1994) 'Researching women's lives or studying women's oppression? Reflections on what constitutes feminist research', in M. Maynard and J. Purvis (eds) *Researching Women's Lives from a Feminist Perspective*. London: Taylor and Francis, 27-48.

Kestenbaum, A. (1993) *Making Community Care a Reality*. Nottingham: Independent Living Fund.

Kestenbaum, A. (1996) *Independent Living: A Review*. York: Joseph Rowntree Foundation.

Kotecha, P. (2005) 'Woefully low'. *Disability Now*. London: Scope, April, 4.

Lakey, J. (1994) *Caring about Independence: Disabled People and the Independent Living Fund*. London: Policy Studies Institute.

Langan, M. and Clarke, J. (1993) 'The British welfare state: foundation and modernisation', in A. Cochrane and J. Clarke (eds) *Comparing Welfare States: Britain in International Context*. London: Sage Publications, 19-48.

Lather, P. (1991) *Getting Smart: Feminist Research and Pedagogy with/in the Postmodern*. New York: Routledge.

LCIL (Lothian Centre for Integrated Living) (2002) *Lothian Centre for Independent Living: Annual Report 2001–2002*. Edinburgh: LCIL.

LCIL (2004) *Learning Opportunities Booklet 2004–05*. Edinburgh: LCIL.

Leadbetter, C. (2004) *Personalisation through Participation*. London: Demos.

Lee, P. (2002) 'Shooting for the moon: politics and disability at the beginning of the twenty first century', in C. Barnes, M. Oliver and L. Barton (eds) *Disability Studies Today*. Cambridge: Polity Press.

Lenny, J. (1993) 'Do disabled people need counselling?', in J. Swain, V. Finkelstein, S. French and M. Oliver (eds) *Disabling Barriers: Enabling Environments*. London: Sage Publications, 233-40.

Lewis, J. (1995) 'Family provision of health and welfare in the mixed economy of care'. *Social History of Medicine*, 8 (1), 1-16.

Lewis, J. (1996) 'The boundary between voluntary and social service in the late nineteenth and early twentieth centuries'. *Historical Journal*, 39 (1), 155-77.

Lincoln, Y.S. and Guba, E.G. (2000) 'Paradigmatic controversies, contradictions, and emerging confluences', in N.K. Denzin and Y.S. Lincoln (eds) *The Handbook of Qualitative Research* (2nd edn). Thousand Oaks: Sage Publications, 163-88.

Lindow, V. and Morris, J. (1995) *Service User Involvement: Synthesis of Findings and Experience in the Field of Community Care*. York: Joseph Rowntree Foundation.

Lister, R. (1998) 'From equality to social inclusion: New Labour and the welfare state'. *Critical Social Policy*, 18 (2), 215-25.

Lloyd, M., Preston-Shoot, M., Temple, B. and Wuu, R. (1996) 'Whose project is it anyway? Sharing and shaping the research and development agenda'. *Disability and Society*, 11 (3), 301-15.

Lovelock, R. and Powell, J. with Craggs, S. (1995) *Shared Territory: Assessing the Social Support Needs of Visually Impaired People*. York: Joseph Rowntree Foundation.

Luckhurst, L. (2005) *Wider Options: Report of a Research Project into Intensive Support Schemes for Direct Payments*. London: National Centre for Independent Living.

March, J., Steingold, B., Justice, S. and Mitchell, P. (1997) 'Follow the Yellow Brick Road! People with learning difficulties as co-researchers'. *British Journal of Learning Difficulties*, 25, 77-80.

Marin, B., Prinz, C. and Queisser, M. (eds) (2004) *Transforming Disability Welfare Policies: Towards Work and Equal Opportunities*. Aldershot: Ashgate.

Marshall, T.H. (1950) *Citizenship and Social Class*. Cambridge: Cambridge University Press.

Martin, J. and White, A. (1988) *OPCS Surveys of Disability in Great Britain: Report 2 – The Financial Circumstances of Disabled Adults Living in Private Households.* London: HMSO.

Martin, J., Meltzer, H. and Elliot, D. (1988) *OPCS Surveys of Disability in Great Britain: Report 1 – The Prevalence of Disability among Adults.* London: HMSO.

Martin, J., White, A. and Meltzer, H. (1989) *OPCS Surveys of Disability in Great Britain: Report 4 – Disabled Adults: Services, Transport and Employment.* London: HMSO.

Martin, J.P. (1985) *Hospitals in Trouble.* Oxford: Blackwell.

Martinez, K. (2003) 'Independent Living in the U.S. & Canada', www.independentliving.org/docs6/martinez2003.html (accessed 4/05/04).

Mason, P. (1990) 'The place of Le Court residents in the history of the disability movement'. Unpublished paper.★

Matthew, S. (2001) *Research Project into User Groups and Empowerment.* London: Mental Health Foundation.

Maynard, M. (1994) 'Methods, practice and epistemology: the debate about feminism and research', in M. Maynard and J. Purvis (eds) *Researching Women's Lives from a Feminist Perspective.* London: Taylor and Francis, 10-26.

Maynard-Campbell, S. and Maynard-Lupton, A. (2000) *Bureaucratic Barriers to Normal Day to Day Activity.* Derby: Muscle Power.★

Melucci, A. (1980) 'The symbolic challenge of contemporary movements'. *Social Research*, 52 (4), 789-816.

Mercer, G. (2002) 'Emancipatory disability research', in C. Barnes, M. Oliver and L. Barton (eds) *Disability Studies Today.* Cambridge: Polity Press, 228-49.

Mies, M. (1983) 'Towards a methodology for feminist research', in G. Bowles and R.D. Klein (eds) *Theories of Women's Studies.* London: Routledge and Kegan Paul, 117-39.

Miller, C. (2001) *An Investigation into Auricular Acupuncture.* London: Mental Health Foundation.

Miller, E.J. and Gwynne, G.V. (1972) *A Life Apart.* London: Tavistock.

Miller, P., Parker, S. and Gillinson, S. (2004) *Disablism: How to Tackle the Last Prejudice.* London: Demos.

Ministry of Health (1948) *National Assistance Act, 1948, Circular 87/48.* 7 June. London: HMSO.

Ministry of Health (1950) *Report of the Ministry of Health for the year ended 31 March 1949.* Cmd 7910. London: HMSO.

Moore, M., Beazley, S. and Maelzer, J. (1998) *Researching Disability Issues.* Buckingham: Open University Press.

Moore, N. (1995) *Access to Information: A Survey of the Provision of Disability Information.* London: Policy Studies Institute.

Morgan, H., Barnes, C. and Mercer, G. (2001) *Creating Independent Futures: An Evaluation of Services Led by Disabled People. Stage Two Report.* Leeds: The Disability Press.★

Morris, J. (1991) *Pride Against Prejudice: Transforming Attitudes to Disability.* London: The Women's Press.

Morris, J. (1992) 'Personal and political: a feminist perspective in researching physical disability'. *Disability, Handicap and Society*, 7 (2), 157-66.

Morris, J. (1993a) *Independent Lives? Community Care and Disabled People.* Basingstoke: Macmillan.

Morris, J. (1993b) *Community Care or Independent Living?* York: Joseph Rowntree Foundation.

Morris, J. (1994) *The Shape of Things to Come? User Led Social Services.* Social Services Policy Forum Paper No 3. London: National Institute for Social Work.

Morris, J. (1998) 'The personal social services: identifying the problem', in A. O'Neil and D. Statham (eds) *Shaping Futures: Rights, Welfare and Social Services.* London: National Institute for Social Work/Joseph Rowntree Foundation, 63-67.

Morris, J. (2004) 'Independent living and community care: a disempowering framework'. *Disability and Society*, 19 (5), 427-42.

Morris, J. (2005) 'Independent living: the role of evidence and ideology in the development of government policy'. Unpublished paper.★

Morris, P. (1969) *Put Away: A Sociological Study of Institutions for the Mentally Retarded.* London: Routledge and Kegan Paul.

Morrison, E. and Finkelstein, V. (1992) 'Culture as struggle: access to power', in S. Lees (ed) *Disability Arts and Culture Papers.* London: Shape, 14-22.★

Mottingly, R. (2002) *Supporting People with Multiple Impairments.* York: York Publishing Services.

NCIL (National Centre for Independent Living) (1999) *Personal Assistance Support Schemes Directory.* London: NCIL.

NCIL (2003) 'A Toast to NCIL'. *Personal Assistance Users Newsletter.* London: NCIL, November/December, 2.

NCIL (2005) *Independence, Well-being and Choice: Draft Summary of NCIL Response to the Green Paper on Social Care in England.* London: NCIL (also available at: www.ncil.org.uk/Green_paperres.asp).

NCSC (National Care Standards Commission) (2003) *National Care Standards Commisson: About Us.* www.carestandards.org.uk/about+us/ default (accessed 18/06/03).

Needham, C. (2003) *Citizen-consumers: New Labour's Marketplace Democracy.* London: Catalyst.

NEP (National Employment Panel) (2005) *Able to Work – Report of the National Employment Panel's Employers' Working Group on Disability.* London: NEP.

Nicholls, V. (2001) 'Foreword', in S. Matthew, *Research Project into User Groups and Empowerment.* London: Mental Health Foundation, 3-4.

Oakley, A. (2000) *Experiments in Knowing: Gender and Method in the Social Sciences.* Cambridge: Polity Press.

Oldman, C. and Quilgars, D. (1999) 'The last resort? Revisiting ideas about older people's living arrangements'. *Ageing and Society,* 19 (4), 363-84.

Oliver, M. (1981) 'A new model of the social work role in relation to disability', in J. Campling (ed) *The Handicapped Person: A New Perspective for Social Workers.* London: RADAR, 19-32.

Oliver, M. (1983) *Social Work with Disabled People.* Basingstoke: Macmillan.

Oliver, M. (1986) 'Social policy and disability: some theoretical issues'. *Disability, Handicap and Society,* 1(1), 5-18.

Oliver, M. (1990) *The Politics of Disablement.* Basingstoke: Macmillan.★

Oliver, M. (1992) 'Changing the social relations of research production?' *Disability, Handicap and Society,* 7 (2), 101-14.

Oliver, M. (1993) 'What's so wonderful about walking?' *Inaugural Professorial Lecture.* Greenwich: University of Greenwich, 9 February.★

Oliver, M. (1996a) 'A sociology of disability or a disablist sociology?', in L. Barton (ed) *Disability and Society: Emerging Issues and Insights.* Harlow: Longman, 18-42.

Oliver, M. (1996b) *Understanding Disability: From Theory to Practice.* Basingstoke: Macmillan.

Oliver, M. (1997) 'Emancipatory research: realistic goal or impossible dream', in C. Barnes and G. Mercer (eds) *Doing Disability Research.* Leeds: The Disability Press, 15-31.★

Oliver, M. and Barnes, C. (1997) 'All we are saying is give disabled researchers a chance'. *Disability and Society,* 12 (5), 811-13.

Oliver, M. and Barnes, C. (1998) *Social Policy and Disabled People: From Exclusion to Inclusion.* London: Longman.

Oliver, M. and Hasler, F. (1987) 'Disability and self-help: a case study of the Spinal Injuries Association'. *Disability, Handicap and Society,* 2 (2), 113-25.

Oliver, M. and Sapey, B. (1999) *Social Work with Disabled People* (2nd edn). Basingstoke: Macmillan.

Oliver, M. and Zarb, G. (1989) 'The politics of disability: a new approach'. *Disability, Handicap and Society*, 4 (3), 221–40.

Oliver, M. and Zarb, G. (1992) *Greenwich Personal Assistance Schemes: Second Year Evaluation*. London: Greenwich Association of Disabled People.★

Oliver, M., Zarb, G., Silver, J., Moore, M. and Salisbury, V. (1988) *Walking into Darkness: The Experience of Spinal Injury*. Basingstoke: Macmillan.

ONS (Office of National Statistics) (2004) *Living in Britain: Results from the 2002 General Household Survey*. London: ONS, 139-62.

Pagel, M. (1988) *On Our Own Behalf: An Introduction to the Self Organisation of Disabled People*. Manchester: Greater Manchester Coalition of Disabled People Publications.

Parker, G. (1993) *With this Body: Caring and Disability in Marriage*. Buckingham: Open University Press.

Peace, S., Kellaher, L. and Willcocks, D. (1997) *Re-evaluating Residential Care*. Buckingham: Open University Press.

Pearson, C. (2006) 'Direct payments in Scotland', in J. Leece and J. Bornat (eds) *Developments in Direct Payments*. Bristol: The Policy Press, 33-47.

Peck, E. and Barker, I. (1997) 'Users as partners in mental health – ten years of experience'. *Journal of Interprofessional Care*, 11 (3), 269-77.

Pelling, M. (1998) *The Common Lot: Sickness, Medical Occupations and the Urban Poor in Early Modern England*. Harlow: Addison Wesley Longman Limited.

People First (1994) *Outside Not Inside …Yet*. London: People First London Boroughs.

Peters, B.G. (1998) 'Managing horizontal government: the politics of co-ordination'. *Public Administration*, 76 (2), 295-311.

Pfeiffer, D. (2000) 'The devils are in the details: the ICIDH2 and the disability movement'. *Disability and Society*, 15 (7), 1079-82.

PMSU (Prime Minister's Strategy Unit) (2004) *Improving the Life Chances of Disabled People: Analytical Report*. London: Cabinet Office.

PMSU (2005) *Improving the Life Chances of Disabled People: Final Report*. London: Cabinet Office.

Pointon, A. (1999) 'Out of the closet: new images of disability in the civil rights campaign', in B. Franklin (ed) *Social Policy, the Media and Misrepresentation*. London: Routledge, 222-37.

Policy Review and Audit Scrutiny Committee (2000) *E-Democracy:Your City your Say*, www.Cardiff.gov.uk/government/English/council_papers/Policy_Review_Audit_S (accessed 24/05/04).

Porter, R. (1987) *Mind-Forg'd Manacles: A History of Madness in England from the Restoration to the Regency*. Harmondsworth: Penguin.

Powell, M. and Glendinning, C. (2002) 'Introduction', in C. Glendinning, M. Powell and K. Rummery (eds) *Partnerships, New Labour and the Governance of Welfare*. Bristol: The Policy Press, 1–14.

Prideaux, S. (2005) 'Good Practice for Providing Reasonable Access to the Physical Built Environment for Disabled People'. Unpublished paper. Leeds: Centre for Disability Studies, University of Leeds.

Rae, A. (1993) 'Independent Living, Personal Assistance and Disabled Women', in C. Barnes (ed) *Making Our Own Choices: Independent Living, Personal Assistance and Disabled People*. Derby: British Council of Organisations of Disabled People, 47–50.

Rae, A. (2005) 'A day of reckoning'. *Coalition*. Manchester: Manchester Coalition of Disabled People, 16–17.

Reason, P. (ed) (1988) *Human Inquiry in Action: Developments in New Paradigm Research*. London: Sage Publications.

Reason, P. (1994) 'Three approaches to participative inquiry', in N.K. Denzin and Y.S. Lincoln (eds) *The Handbook of Qualitative Research*. Thousand Oaks: Sage Publications, 324–9.

Reeve, D. (2000) 'Oppression within the counselling room', *Disability and Society*, 15 (4), 669–682.

Rhodes, R. (1999) 'Foreword', in D. Stoker (ed) *The New Management of British Local Governance*. Basingstoke: Macmillan, xii–xxvi.

Riddell, S., Pearson, C., Jolly, D., Barnes, C., Priestley, M. and Mercer, G. (2004) 'The development of direct payments in the UK: implications for social justice'. *Social Policy and Society*, 4 (1), 75–85.

Rioux, M. and Bach, M. (eds) (1994) *Disability Is Not Measles*. North York, Ontario: Roeher Institute.

Roberts, R. (1973) *The Classic Slum*. Harmondsworth: Pelican Books.

Robson, P., Locke, M. and Dawson, J. (1977) *Consumerism or Democracy: User Involvement in the Control of Voluntary Organisations*. Bristol: The Policy Press.

Rodgers, J. (1999) 'Trying to get it right: undertaking research involving people with learning difficulties'. *Disability and Society*, 14 (4), 421–33.

Ross, K. (1995) 'Speaking in tongues: involving users in day care services'. *British Journal of Social Work*, 25 (December), 791–804.

Roulstone, A. (2002) 'Disabling pasts: enabling futures? How does the changing nature of capitalism impact on the disabled worker and jobseeker?'. *Disability and Society*, 17 (6), 627–42.

Rowe, A. (ed) (1990) *Lifetime Homes: Flexible Housing for Successive Generations*. London: Helen Hamlyn Foundation.

Rummery, K. (2002) *Disability, Citizenship and Community Care: A case for Welfare Rights?* Aldershot: Ashgate.

Ryan, J. with Thomas, F. (1980) *The Politics of Mental Handicap*. Harmondsworth: Penguin.

Sainsbury, S. (1973) *Measuring Disability*, Occasional Papers on Social Administration, No 54. London: Bell.

Sample, P.L. (1996) 'Beginnings: participatory action research and adults with developmental disabilities'. *Disability and Society*, 11 (3), 317–22.

Sanderson, I. (1999) 'Participation or democratic renewal: from instrumental rationality to communicative rationality'. *Policy & Politics*, 27 (3), 325–42.

Scott, A. (1990) *Ideology and New Social Movements*. London: Unwin Hyman.

Scull, A. (1979) *Museums of Madness: The Social Organization of Madness in Nineteenth Century England*. London: Allen Lane.

Seebohm Report (1968) *Report of the Committee on Local Authority and Allied Personal Services*. Cmnd 3703. London: HMSO.

Shakespeare, T. (1993) 'Disabled people's self-organisation: a new social movement?' *Disability, Handicap and Society*, 8 (3), 249–63.

Shakespeare, T. (1996) Disability, identity and difference, in C. Barnes and G. Mercer (eds) *Exploring the Divide: Illness and Disability*. Leeds: The Disability Press, 94–113.★

Shakespeare, T. and Watson, N. (2002) 'The social model of disability: an outmoded ideology'. *Research in Social Science and Disability*, 2, 9–28.★

Shakespeare, T., Gillespie-Sells, K. and Davies, D. (1996) *The Sexual Politics of Disability: Untold Desires*. London: Cassell.★

Shapiro, J.P. (1993) *No Pity: People with Disabilities Forging a New Civil Rights Movement*. New York: Times Books.

Shaw, I. (1999) *Qualitative Evaluation*. London: Sage Publications.

Shearer, A. (1981) *Disability, Whose Handicap?* Oxford: Blackwell.

SIA (Spinal Injuries Association) (1981) *People with Spinal Chord Injury: Treatment and Care*. London: SIA.

SIA (2004) *Spinal Injuries Association: Homepage*. London: Spinal Injuries Association, www.the-sia.org.uk/home

Silverman, D. (1998) 'Research and social theory', in C. Seale (ed) *Researching Society and Culture*. London: Sage Publications, 97–110.

Silverman, D. (2001) *Interpreting Qualitative Data* (2nd edn). London: Sage Publications, 97–110.

Simkins, J. and Tickner, V. (1978) *Whose Benefit?* London: Economic Intelligence Unit Ltd.

SPAEN (Scottish Personal Assistance Employers Network) (2004) www.spaen.co.uk/home.htm (accessed 24/05/04).

SSI (Social Services Inspectorate) (1991) *Getting the Message Across: A Guide to Developing and Communicating Policies, Principles and Procedures on Assessment.* London: HMSO.

Stainton, T. and Boyce, S. (2002) *An Evaluation of the Cardiff and Vale Independent Living Scheme and the Implementation of Direct Payments.* Cardiff: The Wales Office of Research and Development.

Stalker, K. (1998) 'Some ethical and methodological issues in research with people with learning difficulties'. *Disability and Society*, 13 (1), 5–19.

Stalker, K., Barron, S., Riddell, S. and Wilkinson, H. (1999) 'Models of disability: the relationship between theory and practice in non-statutory organisations'. *Critical Social Policy*, 19 (1), 5–29.

Stone, D.A. (1985) *The Disabled State.* Basingstoke: Macmillan.

Stone, E. and Priestley, M. (1996) 'Parasites, pawns and partners: disability research and the role of non-disabled researchers'. *British Journal of Sociology*, 47 (4), 699–716.

Swain, J. (1995) 'Constructing participatory research: in principle and in practice', in P. Clough and L. Barton (eds) *Making Difficulties: Research and the Construction of Special Educational Needs.* London: Paul Chapman Publishing Ltd, 75–93.

Swain, J. and French, S. (2003) 'Practice: are professionals parasites?', in J. Swain, S. French and C. Cameron (eds) *Controversial Issues in a Disabling Society.* Buckingham: Open University Press, 131–41.

Swain, J. and Lawrence, P. (1994) 'Learning about disability or challenging understanding', in S. French (ed) *On Equal Terms: Working with Disabled People.* Oxford: Butterworth-Heinemann, 87–102.

Swain, J., French, S. and Cameron, C. (eds) (2003) *Controversial Issues in a Disabling Society.* Buckingham: Open University Press.

Thomas, C. (1999) *Female Forms: Experiencing and Understanding Disability.* Buckingham: Open University Press.

Thomas, D. (1982) *The Experience of Handicap.* London: Methuen.

Thompson, N. (1997) *Promoting Equality: Challenging Discrimination and Oppression in the Human Services.* London: Macmillan.

Topliss, E. and Gould, B. (1981) *A Charter for the Disabled*. Oxford: Basil Blackwell and Martin Robertson.

Touraine, A. (1981) *The Voice and the Eye: An Analysis of Social Movements*. Cambridge: Cambridge University Press.

Townsend, P. (1962) *The Last Refuge*. London: Routledge and Kegan Paul.

Townsend, P. (1979) *Poverty in the United Kingdom*. Harmondsworth: Penguin.

Turner, B. (1987) *Medical Power and Social Knowledge*. London: Sage Publications.

Turner, M. (1998) *Shaping our Lives: Project Report*. London: National Institute for Social Work.

Turner, M. (2003) *Shaping our Lives: From Outset to Outcome*. London: Shaping Our Lives.

Turner, M., Brough, P. and Findlay-Williams, R.B. (2003) *Our Voice in our Future: Service Users Debate the Future of the Welfare State*. York: Joseph Rowntree Foundation.

UN (United Nations) (1985) *Declaration of the Rights of Disabled Persons*. New York: UN.

UN (1993) *Standard Rules on the Equalization of Opportunities for Persons with Disabilities*. New York: UN.

UPIAS (Union of the Physically Impaired Against Segregation) (1976) *Fundamental Principles of Disability*. London: UPIAS.★

Vasey, S. (1992) 'A response to Liz Crow'. *Coalition*, September, 42-4.

Vernon, A. (1997) 'Reflexivity: the dilemmas of researching from the inside', in C. Barnes and G. Mercer (eds) *Doing Disability Research*. Leeds: The Disability Press, 158-76.★

Vernon, A. (1999) 'The dialectics of multiple identities and the disabled people's movement'. *Disability and Society*, 14 (3), 385-98.

Walmsley, J. and Johnson, K. (2003) *Inclusive Research with People with Learning Difficulties: Past, Present and Futures*. London: Jessica Kingsley Publishers.

Walton, J.K. (1980) 'Lunacy in the Industrial Revolution'. *Journal of Social History*, 13 (1), 1-22.

Ward, L. (1997) 'Funding for change: translating emancipatory disability research from theory to practice', in C. Barnes and G. Mercer (eds) *Doing Disability Research*. Leeds: The Disability Press, 32-48.★

Wates, M. (1997) *Disabled Parents: Dispelling the Myths*. Cambridge: National Childbirth Trust Publishing in association with Radcliffe Medical Press.

WECIL (West of England Centre for Inclusive Living) (2003) *Annual General Report 2002/2003*. Bristol: WECIL.

Weller, D.J. and Miller, P.M. (1977) 'Emotional reactions of patients, family and staff in acute care period of spinal cord injury: Part 1'. *Social Work in Health Care*, 4, (2), 369-77.

WHO (World Health Organization) (1980) *International Classification of Impairments, Disabilities and Handicaps*. Geneva: WHO.

WHO (1999) *International Classification of Functioning and Disability, Beta-2 Draft, Short Version*. Geneva: WHO.

WHO (2005) *ICF Introduction*. Geneva: WHO, www.who.int/ classifications/icf/en (accessed 10/11/05).

Williams, F. (1992) 'Somewhere over the rainbow: universality and diversity in social policy', in N. Manning and R. Page (eds) *Social Policy Review 4*. Canterbury: Social Policy Association, 200-19.

Williams, F. (1993) 'Anthology: care', in J. Bornat, C. Pereira, D. Pilgrim and F. Williams (eds) *Community Care: A Reader*. London: Macmillan, 81-95.

Williams, K. (1981) *From Pauperism to Poverty*. London: Routledge and Kegan Paul.

Williams, V., Simons, K. and Swindon People First Research Team (2005) 'More researching together: the role of nondisabled researchers in working with People First members'. *British Journal of Learning Disabilities*, 33 (1), 6-14.

Wilson, A. and Beresford, P. (2000) '"Anti-oppressive practice": emancipation or appropriation?' *British Journal of Social Work*, 30 (5), 55-73.

Wilson, S. (2003) *Disability, Counselling and Psychotherapy: Challenges and Opportunities*. London: Palgrave Macmillan.

Wistow, G. and Barnes, M. (1993) 'User involvement in community care: origins, purposes and applications'. *Public Administration*, 71, Autumn, 279-99.

Witcher, S., Stalker, K., Roadburg, M. and Jones, C. (2000) *Direct Payments: The Impact on Choice and Control for Disabled People*. Edinburgh: Scottish Executive Central Research Unit.

Worrell, B. (1988) *People First: Advice for Advisors*. Ontario, Canada: National People First Project.

Younghusband, E. (1978) *Social Work in Britain: 1950-1975: A follow-up Study*. London: George Allen and Unwin.

Zarb, G. (1992) 'On the road to Damascus: first steps towards changing the relations of research production'. *Disability, Handicap and Society*, 7(2), 125-38.

Zarb, G. (1997) 'Researching disabling barriers', in C. Barnes and G. Mercer (eds) *Doing Disability Research*. Leeds: The Disability Press, 49-66.★

Zarb, G. and Nadash, P. (1994) *Cashing in on Independence: Comparing the Costs and Benefits of Cash and Services*. Derby: British Council of Organisations of Disabled People.★

Index

A

Abberley, P. 3, 38, 42, 62, 121, 166, 167
Accessibility Planning Guidance (DfT) 187
accountability
  disability research 56
  user-led organisations 71, 86-91, 92
advocacy 148-50
Age Concern 105, 144-5
Albrecht, G.L. 19
Armstrong, D. 19
arts 151-2
Ashley, J. 17-18
assessment 135, 171
Audit Commission 41, 94, 170

B

Bach, M. 35, 53
Back, L. 54
Balloch, S. 169
Barker, I. 73, 94
Barnes, C. 2, 5, 6, 15, 29, 34, 43, 46, 47, 53, 56,
  59, 61, 62, 63, 67, 68, 74, 75, 90, 95, 116,
  117, 120, 147, 148, 151, 183, 185, 187, 190,
  191
Barnes, M. 72, 94
Barton, L. 138, 162
Begum, N. 39, 75
Beresford, P. 22, 33, 42, 55, 72, 73, 74, 75, 90,
  121, 147, 183,
Best Value 26, 93, 94, 161
Bevans, L. 166
Bewley, C. 73, 75
Blaxter, M. 19, 53
Blind Persons Act 1920 13
Borsay, A. 10, 11, 13
Bott, S. 74
Bowl, R. 73
Boyce, S. 124
Bracking, S. 184, 191
Brandon, D. 148
Braye, S. 73, 74
Breakthrough UK 177, 185, 188, 191
Brechin, A. 33
Brisenden, S. 19, 33, 39
Bristol 78
Bristow, A. 45
British Council of Disabled People (BCODP)
  4, 33, 82, 143, 190
  research 5, 46, 56, 62, 95
  terminology 6

  see also Creating Independent Futures
British Deaf Association 30, 104
Brown, H. 73
Burchardt, T. 186
Bury, M. 53, 90

C

Calvi, N. 190
campaigning *see* politics
Campbell, J. 3, 33, 37, 60, 75, 84, 90, 147, 148
Campbell, P. 76
capitalism 191, 192
Cardiff and Vale Coalition of Disabled People
  65, 78-9, 90
  politics and campaigning 140, 141-2
  service provision 98, 99
'care' 6, 40, 175-6
Care Standards Act 2000 26-7
'carers' 6, 18, 19, 25
Caring for People (DH) 24
Carson, G. 101
Carter, J. 17, 38
Centre for Inclusive Living in Glasgow 65, 79,
  87, 90
  direct payments 163-4
  politics and campaigning 139-40, 141
  service provision 99-100, 101, 102
Centres for Independent/Integrated/Inclusive
  Living (CILs) 4-5, 77-8, 121, 183
  direct payments 98
  New Labour policy 174-5, 177
  US 31-2
  see also Creating Independent Futures;
    Derbyshire Centre for Integrated Living;
    Hampshire Centre for Independent Living
Chamberlain, J. 57
Chappell, A.L. 59, 73
charitable status 144
Charities Acts 31
Charity Commission 144
Charlton, J.I. 3, 5, 32, 138, 184
charters 25
Cheshire Homes 16, 46, 51-2, 116
children 12-13, 15, 184-5
choice 123-4, 184, 191
Christie, I. 147
Chronically Sick and Disabled Persons Act
  1970 (CSDPA) 17-18, 38, 42, 47
CIL de Gwynedd (CILdG) 65, 80, 87, 89

service provision 99, 102

CILiG *see* Centre for Inclusive Living in Glasgow

citizenship 28, 37, 165

Clarke, J. 14, 23, 24, 25, 26, 169

Cobbold, C. 187

Cockham, J. 59

Cocks, E. 59

Coleridge, P. 3

Commission for Social Care Inspection 27

community care 18, 24

Community Care (Direct Payments) Act 1996 24-5, 78, 95, 137, 181

consciousness raising 147-50

Conservative Party 3-4, 23-5, 28

consumerism 23, 44, 71, 72-3

control 71, 123-4, 184

Cook, D. 25

Corker, M. 55, 62, 128

counselling 44-5, 128

Cousins, C. 14

Coventry Independent Living Group 80

Craggs, S. 73

Creating Independent Futures 5, 63-8, 120, 192
accountability and user control 86-91
applying the social model of disability 82-6
dependence, independence or inclusion 160-5
empowerment and consciousness raising 148-52
growth of user-led services 76-82
partnerships 171-2
politics and campaigning 139-46, 152-7
professional dominance 166-7, 168
resources 106-13
service monitoring or control 102-6
service patterns 97-102
service users' views 122-36

Crewe, N. 33

critical social theory 53

Croft, S. 72

Crowther, A. 12

culture 34, 151-2

CVCDP *see* Cardiff and Vale Coalition of Disabled People

D

D'Aboville, E. 44, 164, 166

DANE *see* Disability Action North East

Daunton, M.J. 11

Davies, C. 16

Davis, A. 42

Davis, J.M. 61

Davis, K. 45-6, 47, 75, 77, 84, 95

Davis, L. 12

Davis, M. 45-6

Deaf people 55

DeJong, G. 31, 32, 138

democratic participation 72, 76

Department of Health (DH) 25, 74, 169, 178
Caring for People 24
direct payments 120, 121
Framework for Local Community Care Charters in England 25
Independence, Well-being and Choice 4, 175, 176, 177-8
Modernising Social Services 4, 26

Department of Transport 178, 187

Department for Work and Pensions (DWP) 173, 188, 189

Derbyshire 45-6, 47

Derbyshire Centre for Integrated Living (DCIL) 47-8, 77, 81, 84, 87, 89, 90, 95

Derbyshire Coalition of Disabled People (DCODP) 44, 47, 77-8

Derbyshire Coalition for Inclusive Living (DCIL) 65, 77-8, 82
inclusive employment policy 165
politics and campaigning 140, 141, 142, 143
service provision 98, 99, 100

DIAL (Disablement Information and Advice Line) 47, 82

direct action 143-6, 154-5, 157

Direct Action Network (DAN) 34

direct payments 3, 5, 24-5, 73, 95-7, 115
assessment 117
New Labour policy 26, 162, 163-5
political action 138
support schemes 98, 99-100
take up 120, 121
users' views 124-5

Direct Payments Technical Advisory Group 46, 95

disability 6
changing policy perspectives 22-7
historical perspectives on policy 9, 10-13
as personal tragedy 19-22
re-thinking 1, 2-5
and welfare state 13-18
see also social model of disability

Disability Action North East 65, 66, 80-1, 112
empowerment and consciousness raising 152
politics and campaigning 140, 142, 143, 144
service provision 98, 99

disability activism 1-2, 29, 30-1, 48-9
in Britain 33-5
critiques of traditional community services 38-43
Independent Living Movement 31-2
social model of disability 35-8
user-led services 43-8
see also politics; user-led organisations

Disability Arts Movement 151-2
Disability Discrimination Act 1995 26, 28,
   137, 181
disability research 5-6, 68-9
   conventional 51-4
   Creating Independent Futures 63-8
   methodology and methods 59-62
   social model perspective 54-9
Disability Rights Commission (DRC) 174
Disability/Distress Equality Training (DET)
   84, 97, 98, 101, 127, 147-8
Disabled Living Centres Council 100
disabled people 182-3
Disabled Peoples' International (DPI) 3, 82
Disabled People's Movement *see* disability
   activism
Disabled Persons (Employment) Act 1944 15
Disabled Persons (Services, Consultation and
   Representation) Act 1986 25, 41-2
Disablement Income Group (DIG) 33
Disablement Information and Advice Line
   UK (DIAL UK) 47, 82
Dominelli, L. 42
Drake, R. 2, 13, 15, 16, 17, 31, 37, 72
du Boisson, M. 33

E

Education Act 1944 15
Edwards, A. 74
Ellis, K. 42, 59
emancipatory disability research 51, 53-9,
   68-9
employment 100-1, 185-7
empowerment 147, 190-1
equal worth 184-6
European Network on Independent Living
   (ENIL) 48, 82
Evans, J. 16, 41, 46
Exworthy, M. 23

F

Fagan, T. 30
Ferguson, R. 166
Fido, J. 11
Fiedler, B. 40
Finkelstein, V. 22, 36, 55, 56, 57, 151-2, 168-9
Fletcher, S. 74
Flynn, R. 26
*Framework for Local Community Care Charters in
   England* (DH) 25
French, S. 42, 169
Friendly Societies 11
Fundamental Principles of Disability (UPIAS) 35
funding 106-9, 114, 133, 134, 144, 145, 157,
   160-1, 191

G

General Social Care Council (GSCC) 26
Gillespie-Sells, K. 75, 84, 148
Gillinson, S. 171, 184
Glasby, J. 24, 46, 75, 95, 121
Glaser, B. 65
Gleeson, B. 11
Glendinning, C. 26, 42, 73, 75, 121, 124, 169,
   170
Goffman, E. 17
Goodinge, S. 121
Goodley, D. 59
Gordon, P. 39
Gould, B. 18, 36
Gouldner, A. 54
Greater London Action on Disability (GLAD)
   77, 82, 151
Greater Manchester Coalition of Disabled
   People (GMCDP) 41, 138
Greenwich Association of Disabled People's
   Centre for Independent Living (GAD) 65,
   77
   politics and campaigning 140, 141, 142
   service provision 99, 100
Griffiths, R. 23
Grove Road integrated housing scheme 45-6
Guba, E.G. 60
Gwynne, G. 17, 52

H

Habermas, J. 30
Hahn, H. 34
Halford, S. 23
Hampshire Centre for Independent Living 46,
   77, 81
Hampshire Coalition of Disabled People 48
handicap 20
Harding, S. 59
Harris, A. 20, 21, 53
Hasler, F. 33, 44, 45, 77
Health and Social Care Act 2001 26, 121
Help the Aged 46, 95
Hirschman, A. 23
Hitchcock, T. 10
housing 101, 187-8
Hudson, B. 121
Hughes, G. 166
Hugman, R. 14, 39
Human Rights Act 1998 34
Humphries, S. 39
Hunt, P. 2, 39, 52, 182
Hurst, R. 153-4

I

impairment 21, 22, 182
  definitions 6, 20, 35, 36
Improving the Life Chances of Disabled People
  (PMSU) 4, 27, 173, 178, 181, 187, 189-90
  'care' 176
  Centres for Independent Living 174-5, 177
  employment 186
  equal worth 184
  user-led services 120
  young people 185
Imrie, R.F. 34
inclusion 27, 37, 71, 165, 192
Independence, Well-being and Choice (DH) 4, 175,
  176, 177-8
independent living 3-4, 49, 184
  in an inclusive society 190-2
  disability activism 29
  equal worth 184-6
  implementation 188-90
  New Labour policy 27, 173-4, 176, 181
  physical environment 187-8
  service support 93, 94-7
  seven needs 47-8, 93
  work and employment 186-7
Independent Living Fund (ILF) 41, 96, 116
Independent Living Movement (ILM) 3, 30,
  31-2
information 25, 44-5, 47, 98-9
  users' views 125-7
Innes, J. 11
International Classification of Functioning,
  Disability and Health (ICF) 22
International Classification of Impairments,
  Disabilities and Handicaps (ICIDH) 20-1, 22

J

Johnson, K. 59
Jolly, D. 162
Jones, K. 12
Joseph Rowntree Foundation 59

K

Kelly, L. 62
Kestenbaum, A. 41, 43
Kotecha, P 189

L

Labour Party *see* New Labour
Ladyman, S. 163
Lakey, J. 124
Langan, M. 14
Lather, P. 55

Lawrence, P. 148
LCIL *see* Lothian Centre for Integrated Living
Le Court Residential Cheshire Home 16, 46,
  51-2
Leadbetter, C. 173
Lee, P. 30, 183
Lenny, J. 128
Leonard Cheshire Foundation 116
Lewis, J. 13
Liberation Network 33
Lifetime Homes 187-8
Lincoln, Y.S. 60
Lindow, V. 75
Lister, R. 26
Littlechild, R. 24, 46, 75, 95, 121
Living Options Project 40
Lloyd, M. 57, 58, 59
local authorities
  community services 38, 103
  CSDPA 18, 47
  direct payments 24, 96-7, 120
  NHSCCA 25, 41
  residential care 15-16
  social model of disability 84-5
  and user-led organisations 74-5, 79-81, 87,
    91, 108, 109, 146, 172
London Boroughs Disability Resource team
  (LBDRT) 148
Lothian Centre for Integrated Living 65, 79,
  87, 90
  empowerment and consciousness raising
    148-9
  politics and campaigning 139-40, 141
  service monitoring or control 105
  service provision 99, 100
Lothian Coalition of Disabled People (LCDP)
  140
Lovelock, R. 73
Luckhurst, L. 121

M

Mainwearing, T. 153-4
March, J. 59
Marin, B. 186
Marshall, T.H. 14
Martin, J. 18, 20, 21, 53
Martin, J.P. 17
Martinez, K. 31
Mason, P. 52
Matthew, S. 58
Maynard, M. 55, 62
Maynard-Campbell, S. 42, 116
Maynard-Lupton, A. 42, 116
medical model of disability 1, 19-21, 22
Melucci, A. 30
MENCAP 116

Mensah-Coker, G. 147
Mental Deficiency Act 1913 12
Mental Health Act 1983 25
Mercer, G. 15, 59, 62, 63, 67, 74, 75, 147, 151,
    185, 187
Mies, M. 54
Miller, C. 58
Miller, E. 17, 52
Miller, P. 147
Miller, P.M. 22
MIND 31, 104-5, 150
Ministry of Health 15-16, 17, 18
minority ethnic groups 105-6
Modernising Social Services (DH) 4, 26
Moore, B. 33
Moore, J. 59
Moore, M. 57, 59
Moore, N. 47, 125
Morgan, H. 68
Morris, A. 17
Morris, J. 39, 40, 41, 42, 43, 44, 55, 59, 75, 76,
    94, 96, 139, 174, 175, 177-8, 184
Morris, P. 17
Morrison, E. 151-2
Mottingly, R. 42
Mullender, A. 47, 77, 95

N

Nadash, P. 46, 59, 62, 95, 96, 124
National Assistance Act 1948 15-16, 18, 24,
    47, 95
National Care Standards Council (NCSC) 27
National Centre for Independent Living
    (NCIL) 5, 63, 82, 141, 188, 190
    Green Paper 177, 178, 191
    see also Creating Independent Futures
National Employment Panel (NEP) 186
National Forum for Organisations of Disabled
    People 189, 190
National Health Service and Community
    Care Act 1990 (NHSCCA) 3-4, 23, 24, 25,
    41, 78, 79
National Health Service Reform and Health
    Care Professions Act 2002 26
National Insurance Act 1911 13
National League of the Blind and Disabled
    (NLBD) 30
Needham, C. 25
networking 81-2
New Labour 25-7, 28
    independent living 4, 184-90
    partnerships 159, 169-70
    support services 159, 172-9
New Right 23-5, 28
Newman, J. 14
Nicholls, V. 58

O

Oakley, A. 62
Office of the Deputy Prime Minister 178
Office for Disability Issues (ODI) 173, 178,
    189
Office for National Statistics (ONS) 20, 182
Office for Population Censuses and Surveys
    (OPCS) 20, 21, 53, 62
Oldman, C. 18
Oliver, M. 1, 2, 3, 19, 22, 30, 34, 39, 40, 42, 44,
    45, 47, 57, 58, 61, 62, 68, 75, 96, 138, 147,
    148, 167, 168, 185, 190
    disabled people 182, 183
    emancipatory disability research 51, 53, 54,
    60
    research gains 55, 56
    social model of disability 36, 37

P

Pagel, M. 30
Parker, G. 39, 159
partnerships 169-72
Peace, S. 17
Peck, E. 73, 94
peer support 98, 100, 128-9, 148
Pelling, M. 10
People First 59, 76, 104, 150, 153
personal assistants (PAs) 3, 5, 45, 95-6, 115
    support services 99-100
personal tragedy view of disability 1, 6, 19-22,
    31, 36, 182
personalisation 172-3, 179
Peters, B.G. 170
Pfeiffer, D. 22
physiotherapy 167-8
Pointon, A. 34
politics 137
    attitudes towards 152-6
    campaigning issues and activities 141-6
    empowerment and consciousness raising
    147-52
    local viewpoint 137-41
    see also disability activism
Poor Law Act 1601 10, 170
Poor Law Amendment Act 1834 10
Porter, R. 11
Powell, J. 73
Powell, M. 170
Preston-Shoot, M. 74
Prideaux, S. 188
Priestley, M. 62
Prime Minister's Strategy Unit (PMSU) 90,
    147, 182, 183, 186
    self-assessment 117

user-led services 120, 121
*see also Improving the Life Chances of Disabled
People*
professionals 26, 166-9, 170-1
Project 81 46

Q

Quilgars, D. 18

R

Rae, A. 39, 169
Reason, P. 58
Reeve, D. 128
resources 93
   funding 106-9
   location and premises 110-11
   paid staff and volunteers 111-13
Rhodes, R. 26
Riddell, S. 117, 120
rights 34, 37
Rioux, M. 35, 53
Roberts, Ed 31
Roberts, R. 11
Robson, P. 72
Rodgers, J. 59
Ross, K. 74
Roulstone, A. 187
Rowe, A. 187
Rummery, K. 42
Rust, A. 74
Ryan, J. 11, 12

S

Sainsbury, S. 20
Sample, P.L. 59, 60
Sanderson, I. 23
Sapey, B. 75, 167
Scope 31, 153-4
Scott, A. 30
Scottish Personal Assistance Employers
   Network (SPAEN) 141
Scull, A. 12
Seebohm Report 17, 41
self-assessment 117, 135
service delivery 93, 113-14
   monitoring or control 102-6
   in support of independent living 94-7
   user-led organisations 97-102
   users' views 123-30
service users *see* users
seven needs for independent living 47-8, 95
Shakespeare, T. 34, 62, 82, 90, 183
Shaping Our Lives 58, 153
Shapiro, J.P. 34

Shaw, I. 61
Shearer, A. 39
Silverman, D. 54, 66
Simkins, J. 15
Sisters Against Disability (SAD) 33
Smith, H. 73
Social Care Institute for Excellence (SCIE) 26
social exclusion 1, 4, 37, 190, 192
social inclusion 27, 37, 71, 165, 192
social model of disability 1, 3, 21-2, 29, 35-8,
   44, 49
   applying 82-6, 92
   disability research 53-9, 60, 68
   Disability/Distress Equality Training 147
   PMSU report 184
   professionals 169
Social Security Act 1986 41
Social Services Inspectorate (SSI) 27, 42
Solomos, J. 54
Spastics Society 31
   see also Scope
Speirs, J. 101
Spinal Injuries Association (SIA) 44-5, 47
Stainton, T. 124
Stalker, K. 59, 60, 84
Stone, D.A. 10
Stone, E. 62
Strategies for Living 57-8
Strauss, A. 65
Surrey Users Network (SUN) 65, 79, 87, 89
   empowerment and consciousness raising 149
   politics and campaigning 140, 142-3
   service provision 99
Survivors Speak Out 76
Swain, J. 58, 148, 167, 169

T

Taylor, M. 169
Thomas, C. 74, 82, 128, 183
Thomas, D. 3
Thomas, F. 11, 12
Thompson, N. 74
Tickner, V. 15
Topliss, E. 18, 36
Touraine, A. 30, 54
Townsend, P. 17, 20, 53
Turner, B. 19
Turner, M. 58, 74, 75

U

Union of the Physically Impaired Against
   Segregation (UPIAS) 1, 33, 35
United Nations 3
United States 3, 31-2

University of Leeds, Centre for Disability Studies 5
user-led organisations 1-2, 4-5, 49, 71, 91-2, 159, 191, 192
  accountability and user control 86-91
  campaigning issues and activities 141-6
  consultation to service provision 72-6
  dependence, independence or inclusion 159-65
  disability activism 29, 30-1
  empowerment and consciousness raising 147-52
  failings 130-5
  growth 76-82
  New Labour 26, 27
  New Right 25
  partnerships 169-72
  politics and campaigning 137-41, 152-7
  professional dominance 166-9
  promoting services 120-3
  resources 106-13
  service monitoring or control 102-6
  service patterns 97-102
  service provision 43-8, 93-7, 113-14, 120-2
  service use 123-30
  social model of disability 82-6
  users' views 115, 135-6
  see also Creating Independent Futures
users 115, 135-6
  accessing user-led services 122-3
  politics and campaigning 152-6
  and professionals 166-7, 168
  use of services 123-30
  views on mainstream services 116-20
  wants and aspirations 130-5

V

Vernon, A. 61, 183
voluntary agencies 16-17, 31, 177
  see also user-led organisations
volunteers 100-1, 113

W

Wallcraft, J. 55, 183
Walmsley, J. 59
Walton, J.K. 12
Ward, L. 58, 59
Wates, M. 75
Watson, N. 82, 90
welfare state 9-10, 13-18, 23, 28
Weller, D.J. 22
Wells, P.E. 34
West of England Centre for Inclusive Living (WECIL) 65, 78, 87, 98

  empowerment and consciousness raising 149-50
  politics and campaigning 139-41
  service provision 98, 99
West of England Coalition of Disabled People (WECODP) 78, 140-1
White, A. 18
Williams, F. 14, 176
Williams, K. 11, 12
Williams, V. 59, 67
Wilson, A. 42
Wilson, S. 147
Wistow, G. 72, 94
Witcher, S. 125
Workmen's Compensation Acts 13
World Health Organization (WHO) 20, 22
Worrell, B. 147

Y

young people 185-6
Younghusband, E. 16

Z

Zarb, G. 42, 46, 57, 58, 59, 61, 62, 95, 96, 124, 138
Zola, I.K. 33

Also available from The Policy Press

Working futures? Disabled people, policy and social inclusion
Edited by Alan Roulstone and Colin Barnes

"*Working futures? is a welcome and much needed contribution to this crucial domain of disability studies. It is an excellent resource, providing an original text that should be drawn on by a wide audience within the social sciences.*" **John Swain, School of Health, Community and Education Studies, University of Northumbria at Newcastle**

Working futures? looks at the current effectiveness and future scope for enabling policy in the field of disability and employment. The book is original in bringing together a wide range of policy insights to bear on the question of disabled peoples working futures

Paperback £27.50 US$45.00 ISBN 1 86134 626 3

Hardback £55.00 US$90.00 ISBN 1 86134 627 1

234 x 156mm 368 pages November 2005

Developments in direct payments
Edited by Janet Leece and Joanna Bornat

"*An up-to-date review of current developments in direct payments policy and practice. Essential reading for students on a range of relevant undergraduate and postgraduate courses.*" **Colin Barnes, Professor of Disability Studies, Centre for Disability Studies, University of Leeds**

From a campaigning concept in the 1970s, direct payments – the substitution of cash for services – have become a key part of UK government social care provision. This book charts the change, critically evaluating progress, take-up, inclusion and access to direct payments by different user groups.

Paperback £20.99 US$35.00 ISBN 1 86134 653 0

Hardback £55.00 US$85.00 ISBN 1 86134 654 9

234 x 156mm 320 pages January 2006

To order copies of these publications or any other Policy Press titles please visit **www.policypress.org.uk** or contact:

In the UK and Europe:
Marston Book Services,
PO Box 269, Abingdon,
Oxon, OX14 4YN, UK
Tel: +44 (0)1235 465500
Fax: +44 (0)1235 465556
Email: direct.orders@marston.co.uk

In the USA and Canada:
ISBS, 920 NE 58th Street,
Suite 300, Portland,
OR 97213-3786, USA
Tel: +1 800 944 6190 (toll free)
Fax: +1 503 280 8832
Email: info@isbs.com

In Australia and New Zealand:
DA Information Services,
648 Whitehorse Road Mitcham,
Victoria 3132, Australia
Tel: +61 (3) 9210 7777
Fax: +61 (3) 9210 7788
E-mail: service@dadirect.com.au